The Swedish Pietists: A Reader

The Swedish Pietists: A Reader

Excerpts from the Writings of
Carl Olof Rosenius and **Paul Peter Waldenström**

Edited, translated, and introduced by
MARK SAFSTROM

PICKWICK *Publications* · Eugene, Oregon

THE SWEDISH PIETISTS: A READER
Excerpts from the writings of Carl Olof Rosenius and Paul Peter Waldenström

Pickwick Publications
An Imprint of Wipf and Stock Publishers
199 W. 8th Ave., Suite 3
Eugene, OR 97401

www.wipfandstock.com

ISBN 13: 978–1–62564–738–2

Cataloging-in-Publication data:

The Swedish Pietists : a reader : excerpts from the writings of Carl Olof Rosenius and Paul Peter Waldenström / Translated and edited by Mark Daniel Safstrom.

xiv + 238 p. ; 23 cm. —Includes bibliographical references.

ISBN 13: 978–1–62564–738–2

1. Rosenius, C. O. (Carl Olof), 1816–1868. 2. Waldenström, Paul Peter, 1838–1917. I. Title.

BX8079 S95 2015

Manufactured in the U.S.A.   10/06/2015

For my great-grandparents
who were läsare
and for their children and grandchildren
who nurtured this heritage.

Contents

Illustrations

"Bethlehem Church"   Used by permission of Svenska Missionskyrkans
                        Arkiv, Stockholm.

"Immanuel Church"   Used by permission of Svenska Missionskyrkans
                        Arkiv, Stockholm.

"P.W. at Lidingö"   Used by permission of Svenska Missionskyrkans
                        Arkiv, Stockholm.

Acknowledgments

This project began earlier than I realized. While still in high school, I inherited a small library of Swedish theological books that once belonged to my great-grandfather. These books had been carefully saved by my grandparents under the stairs to their basement, crammed into three book shelves, which formed an alcove. These books caught my attention, and I often found myself drawn to the basement, to page through the cryptic language in these dusty, but beautifully-bound books, to see if I could figure out what they said. Stepping into this alcove was like walking into history, a history illustrated with engravings, grainy photographs and art nouveau embellishments. My grandparents explained to me that my great-grandfather had been a "reader" (*läsare*) in the Church of Sweden, which also proved to be the case of several generations in my family. Upon immigrating to the United States, they worshipped and found fellowship in a patchwork of immigrant congregations and schools in Illinois, Michigan, Nebraska, Kansas, and Washington, including those of the Swedish Methodists, the Augustana Lutheran Synod, and the Swedish Mission Covenant. I have since spent the last two decades exploring what it meant to be a "reader," as well as what these readers were reading. Rosenius and Waldenström were the names that loomed largest in many immigrants' private libraries, and so the current project was born. Thus, it is first to my grandparents and the rest of my family, that thanks are due for preserving and passing down this heritage of faith, as well as exploring it with me during my research.

Interest in this history led me to graduate studies at the University of Washington's Scandinavian Department, and from there, to several summers in Sweden, conducting research in Uppsala and Stockholm between 2005–2010. I seemed to always come home with a load of books gathered in antique bookshops, resources which would later prove essential in this current translation project. I could never have made these research visits without the training and support of the Scandinavian Department and its faculty, and I am likewise also immensely grateful for the generous financial support of the American-Scandinavian Foundation, the Swedish Women's Educational Association (SWEA San Francisco), and the Foreign Languages and Area Studies Fellowship (Jackson School of International Studies, University of Washington). Additional support came from the Archives at North Park University, Chicago (Steve Elde, Anne Jenner, and Anna-Kajsa Anderson), the Swenson Swedish Immigration Research Center at Augustana College, Rock Island, Illinois (Dag Blanck and Jill Seaholm), and Svenska Missionskyrkans Arkiv and Kungliga biblioteket, both in Stockholm.

Translating these primary sources came naturally, and soon after I began collaborating in the devotional journal, *Pietisten*, I started publishing short translations of the writings of Rosenius and Waldenström, among other Scandinavian Pietists (several of these translations are included in this collection). Most significantly, this took the form of the publication of my translation of Waldenström's novel, *Squire Adamsson*, in 2013/14. Thanks are due to the team at *Pietisten*, who have made all of this work possible, as well as a whole lot of fun, including Sandy Nelson, Jeffrey HansPetersen, Karl Nelson, Stephanie Johnson Blomgren, and David Nelson.

The work on this manuscript was completed during a semester in which I was funded by a grant from the European Union Center at the University of Illinois at Urbana-Champaign, for which I am grateful. This made it possible for Michelle Urberg to serve as a research assistant to me, and I am very appreciative for her valuable assistance in proofreading this manuscript. Three colleagues at North Park Theological Seminary in Chicago, Michelle Clifton-Soderstrom, Philip J. Anderson, and John E. Phelan Jr. were also kind enough to give a preliminary read of the manuscript and offer helpful comments and encouragement.

Introduction

"THE PIETIST" AND ITS PUBLISHERS

While there are many people who could have been gathered under the banner of "Swedish Pietists," this collection focuses on two preachers who bore this conspicuous title as editors of the widely read devotional journal *Pietisten* ("The Pietist"). Beginning in 1842, the popularity of the journal helped launch its editors, Carl Olof Rosenius (1816–1868) and Paul Peter Waldenström (1838–1917), to national prominence within the religious awakening. Both men emerged from the long tradition of revivalism within the Lutheran state churches of Germany and Scandinavia known as Pietism, and together mark an important turning point in which this movement began to spill out of the confines of the state church and crystallize into independent congregations, mission societies, and later denominations known as the "free churches." This historical moment was the beginning of the secularization and pluralization of civic life in Scandinavia as a whole, and bears relevance to the general cultural and social transformation of the era.

In Sweden, the most common name used for Pietists was "Readers" (*Läsare*), and it is no exaggeration to say that between the 1840s and the 1910s most of these readers spent a great amount of time reading the writings of Rosenius and Waldenström. As Pietists, they were both consciously aware of their historical predecessors and presented themselves as a continuation of this heritage. For instance, even in this sample collection, there are abundant references to Luther and to Pietists such as Spener, Arndt, and Pontoppidan. What is more, the journal's name was no accident, but had been deliberately chosen by its founder and short-lived first editor, George Scott (1804–74). The names "Pietist" and "Reader" were both pejoratives, and despite the earnest suggestions from several people to choose a better name, Scott seems to have stuck with this choice as a rhetorical strategy, precisely because it was provocative. Scott was a Methodist missionary in Stockholm backed by British and American supporters, and was thus an

1

outsider to the Lutheran cultural and historical consciousness of his mission field. His initial call had been to serve the English workers in the capital city, but he quickly attracted Swedes, as well. Choosing to identify with Pietism was a way of building on homegrown traditions in order to facilitate an expanded mission. In the strict orthodoxy of Sweden, in which citizenship was synonymous with membership in the Lutheran state church, Methodism constituted a "foreign" religion and it was technically illegal to proselytize to Swedes. Even cooperation smelled suspicious. The most prudent decision that Scott made in his ministry was his recruitment of Rosenius, on whom he came to depend heavily in his last few years in Stockholm. Prompted by a series of spiritual crises, Rosenius had sought out Scott as a spiritual mentor in 1839, quickly becoming an invaluable assistant to Scott as an occasional preacher and evangelist the following year. In 1841, he was hired as a "city missionary," and notably covered for Scott while he was away on fundraising campaigns in the United States from April to October of that year. When Scott returned to Stockholm and started *Pietisten* in January of 1842, Rosenius's responsibilities included serving as co-editor. The two also continued to share the preaching responsibilities at "The English Church" (later called Bethlehem Church), with Scott handling the English sermons, and Rosenius the Swedish. When Scott was forced to leave Stockholm because of growing criticism by the secular press, the disapproval of the clergy, and even episodes of mob violence and threats against his family, Rosenius was well prepared to seamlessly take over the leadership of both the journal and the rest of Scott's ministries.

The first two texts in this collection, "Pietism" and "A Pietist," form an explanation for the choice of the name of the journal, and serve as a sort of manifesto for a revitalized form of Pietism as an ecumenical movement. As they were unsigned, historians have often attributed them to Scott alone. However, there is no reason to exclude Rosenius from credit here, as his responsibilities at the time included serving as an assistant editor for *Pietisten*, and since the articles voice the aspirations of the editorship as a whole. It is safe to conclude that the "we" that is used throughout the essays refers to the collective editorship, as well as the intimate circle around Scott; in both cases, this included Rosenius. Scott even noted at one point that his relationship with Rosenius was quite close, likening it to "that of David and Jonathan." More importantly, these articles formed the blueprint for Rosenius's later editorship of the journal, and are fully in line with his viewpoints at the time, as articulated in his personal correspondence, such as this letter from January of 1841.

I would have it understood that even if I spend periods of my short time working together with Methodist preachers, then this will be in accordance with what I have already explained are the principles and conditions, namely that I will be working for Christ's church, might offer my life, my strength for Christ and his commands—not for Wesley or Luther, who are dead, who were servants who did not wish to be the head of the congregation— might offer my life, my service for the one holy universal church. Its members may be childish enough to want to be called after Paul, Apollos, Cephas—it makes no difference to me what name they take. So long as they are Christ's, then they are my brothers and I wish to serve them.[1]

Amy Moberg

In addition to Scott, there is another person who filled an important role during the Rosenius years of the journal, a woman named Amy Moberg (1826–1905). Moberg was Rosenius's secretary and came to be essential in his last years, as his health deteriorated. After Rosenius's death, Moberg wrote the first biography on him, in which she relates the painstaking difficulty he encountered in meeting the demands of his writing and publishing schedule. In 1867, *Pietisten* was reduced from a monthly publication to a quarterly one, but even still, no. four of that year did not come out until early 1868. As an ambitious final project, Rosenius had begun to write a series

1. Quoted in Norborg, *Den Levande Rosenius*, 19–20.

of sermons for each of the assigned texts for the church year, "Sermons on the Church of Sweden's New Texts for the High Mass" (Waldenström later continued this series where Rosenius left off, and then published his and Rosenius's collected sermons together). The sermons for the four Sundays of Advent were, in Moberg's words, "written with difficulty," while there are two sermons which she specifically notes were "dictated" (the sermons for "Christmas Day" and "The Second Sunday after Epiphany.") In actuality, these are understatements, as her role at this point was more than merely taking dictation. Waldenström later went so far as to say that Moberg had kept the journal going for Rosenius: "In the end, it was in reality she who was the one who wrote Pietisten. . . . She had so completely adopted his style that no one noticed the difference."[2] It is likely that Rosenius explained to Moberg how he wanted these texts treated, then she wrote the copy, and then read it back to him for his approval and corrections. Either way, in recognition of Moberg's contributions, I have made sure to include the sermon for the Second Sunday After Epiphany (on "Jesus and the Samaritan Woman") and added the notation that this was written "With Amy Moberg." I think these reflections on the Samaritan woman's encounter with Jesus take on added significance in light of the fact that a woman was involved in writing the sermon. For her part, Moberg pointed out that she thought it was poignant that Rosenius was meditating on how Jesus was "tired from the journey" (which he repeats seven times), at a time when he himself was utterly exhausted and was perhaps beginning to sense that his life was nearing its end.

From the vantage point of the present, it may seem natural that Waldenström would take over Pietisten in 1868. Ultimately, it was Carl Olof's widow, Agata Rosenius, assisted by another newspaperman and trusted friend, Axel Falk, who extended the invitation to him to assume the editorship. The journal was a privately owned enterprise, and thus the agreement was that Waldenström would work for a modest stipend until the sermon series on the texts for the high mass was completed, after which he would assume ownership of Pietisten. Though it was a private enterprise, the journal had come to be a central resource for many people within the Evangelical Homeland Foundation (Evangeliska Fosterlands-Stiftelsen, EFS). Rosenius had played a crucial role in founding the EFS in 1856, as a mission society and the approved venue for revival activities within the Church of Sweden. Defining the EFS as a "mission society," rather than an independent "free church" or "denomination," was an important priority for Rosenius. His philosophy was that the EFS should remain loyal to the Church of Sweden and avoid

2. Waldenström, Pietisten, 22 Dec. 1911.

separatism, while at the same time strive to be an ecumenical collaboration for all Christians in the country. Deference to official Lutheran doctrine was thus taken for granted, as the focus of the EFS was on practice. In 1868, there was a circle of people within the EFS who thought that Waldenström was the wrong choice, and might upset this balancing act, including Rosenius's brother, Martin. Carl Olof himself had initially considered other names, and for a time it even seemed to many that Waldemar Rudin (1833–1921) was the logical successor. Ultimately, the invitation came from Agata, acting on Rosenius's last wishes. Waldenström's friendship with Rosenius had begun in 1859, and the success of his novel, *Squire Adamsson,* in 1862/63 caught the attention of Rosenius and others within the leadership of the EFS. On the one hand, Rosenius supported the novel, and Waldenström seemed to think that it was due to its enormous success that he had been considered for the editorship at all. On the other hand, already within the novel, it was clear that Waldenström had taken Rosenian theology to some extremes. Where Rosenius had deferred to Lutheran doctrine, his young mentee was less careful, and the novel was both an asset as well as a liability.

Elisabet.   Rosenius.   David.   Agata.   Josef.

The Rosenius family

By 1872, Waldenström published his controversial views on the doctrine of the atonement as part of the sermon series on the texts for the high mass ("Sermon for the Twentieth Sunday after Trinity"). This prompted a firestorm of responses (about 200 publications), both affirming and denouncing Waldenström's views, with much of this criticism coming from within the EFS. For those in the EFS who were suspicious of him to begin with, this was confirmation of his having broken with Rosenius. However, there were others in the Rosenian circle who were energized by this. Interestingly, Amy Moberg, though she cautioned Waldenström to restrain himself in these debates, ultimately supported him—to the point that it eventually caused her to be asked to leave the job she was currently holding at another EFS-related newspaper, *The Stockholm City Missionary*. As never before, the national spotlight was now directly on *Pietisten,* as it glided away from the EFS and began to fuel the growing "free church" movement. Waldenström had become a folk hero, but for different reasons than Rosenius had been. He appears to have been deeply wounded by the fact that people had come to set him in opposition to his mentor, whom he had so profoundly admired and emulated. This opposition seems also to have been what prompted him to defend his Rosenian credentials for the rest of his life, and although he diverged from his mentor on the nuances of the atonement, Rosenius remained the paramount human authority for Waldenström. His first words in the issue after Rosenius's death began with simplicity and tenderness as he informed the nation: "*Rosenius, vår vän, sover*" ("Rosenius, our friend, sleeps").

In Scandinavian history, the nineteenth century is sometimes referred to as the "great century of emigration," as between the 1840s and the 1920s there was a mass exodus of Scandinavians to North America; the Swedish migration alone is estimated to have involved upwards to 1.3 million souls. Thus the religious revivals that were begun in Scandinavia, also swept through this diaspora of immigrant communities, facilitated by the wide distribution of Rosenius's and Waldenström's writings by Lutheran and free church book concerns and publishers. The legacy that these two preachers left in a number of present-day North American denominations is significant and warrants perennial re-evaluation. Among those denominations in which either one or both of these men were influential include the Evangelical Lutheran Church in America (chiefly through its Augustana and Norwegian Haugean branches), the Evangelical Covenant Church, the Evangelical Free Church, and the Baptist General Conference (Converge Worldwide). To a lesser degree, there are also interesting moments of contact with the Congregationalist and Methodist traditions. Rosenius became seen as a patriarchal figure among many within all these communities, whereas Waldenström came to be seen as an apostate Lutheran, and thus was marginalized in that tradition. As both were staunch defenders of infant baptism, they are perhaps problematic to the history of the Baptist General

Conference, though its heritage of *Läsare* Pietism was quite strong, as was the early inspiration that Baptist leaders gained from the circle around Scott and Rosenius, which included Anders Wiberg (1816–1887) and F.O. Nilsson (1809–1881). Waldenström featured most prominently within the Evangelical Covenant Church, whose adherents were initially dubbed "Waldenströmians," and which forged a deep and abiding relationship with his "Mission Covenant" back in Sweden (*Svenska Missionsförbundet*, now *Equmeniakyrkan*). However, he was also inspirational to many within the Evangelical Free Church, which to this day retains the distinction of having published the most English translations of his writings, an effort promoted in particular by J.G. Princell (1845–1915).

Nevertheless, as the significance of denominational identities now seems to be waning in our day (as well as the former tension between these traditions that once prevailed), it is perhaps especially relevant now to understand the significance of these two men who were "ecumenical" before it was commonplace. At the same time as they inspired the formation of new denominations and institutions, they simultaneously problematized the very concept of institutional, formalized Christianity. Though fully aware of and firmly rooted in the traditions and unfinished project of the Protestant Reformation and Pietism, both of these preachers were concerned first and foremost in cultivating an abiding and living faith among their readers and parishioners, regardless of denominational affiliation. Two questions that were ubiquitous in the communities that these preachers served were "How goes your walk with the Lord?" and "Are you living yet/still in Jesus?" Rosenius and Waldenström encouraged their readers to ponder such questions, as they invited them to discover the joys of congregational life and the experience of a relational faith with God.

ON THE TRANSLATION

The process of selecting texts for this reader was a challenging one in that these preachers were quite prolific, particularly Waldenström who produced a steady stream of devotional writings, letters and newspaper articles in his lifetime. Therefore, the excerpts included here have been chosen with the idea of providing a sampling of texts that present the essential concepts from both Rosenius and Waldenström, as well as their differences and similarities. Some of the texts have been chosen because from a modern perspective, they appear ahead of their time. Other passages have been chosen, not because they present particularly innovative insights, but because they reflect how these preachers understood the timeless truths of Christianity and presented them in fresh language for their readership. They both understood that their primary calling was to be preachers, and were effective leaders in the religious awakening because of their accessible style, sincerity, and evangelical warmth. Both would agree that the primary function of preaching is that the reader would be changed by encountering the text and would come to know God in new ways.

Consultation of previous Swedish anthologies and commentaries greatly aided the selection of texts and isolation of themes, including the anthology of Rosenius's texts published by the EFS (BV-förlag) in seven volumes between 2008–2010, and Erland Sundström's anthology, *Arvet från Waldenström*, first published in 1953. Most of what Rosenius wrote was published in *Pietisten*, and was then later published in stand-alone works by both the EFS and the Lutheran Augustana Book Concern, among other publishers. Waldenström also first published most of his works as series in *Pietisten*, later editing and repackaging this material into stand-alone volumes. For the primary source material from Rosenius, I have made use of the series of commemorative volumes of *Pietisten* from 1874 and *Samlade Skrifter* ("Collected Writings") from 1896–1897. For Waldenström's writings, I have used the stand-alone volumes themselves. The page numbers for the primary sources have been included in the back, for scholars looking to explore the full context of these passages. The original titles of these articles or books are included in parentheses, and sometimes differ from the themes I have chosen to emphasize in the headings.

Because of the constraints of this book, I have often skipped over certain passages, always indicating these omissions with ellipses [. . .]. In all cases this was as a means to cover more territory and eliminate redundancy, and never as a means of hopping over problematic or contradictory passages. As a merciless editor, I have insisted that Rosenius and Waldenström be concise, while still striving to include as much context as possible. That said, I encourage the thoughtful seminarian or graduate student who is inspired to dig deeper in this field *not* to be content with my translation, but to go and learn Swedish (and tangentially Norwegian and Danish) and explore the primary sources firsthand. To be frank, the field of Scandinavian-American church history is relatively wide open for research, as there is precious little of the primary sources that have been translated into English, and precious few historians and theologians who have bothered to learn to read Scandinavian. While German, Latin, Greek, and Hebrew have enjoyed the honor of being official "research languages" for seminarians, there is a mountain of Scandinavian primary sources that will sadly never be translated into English, and therefore will remain inaccessible to posterity, both in the local congregation as well as in the seminary classroom. Scandinavian Lutherans and Pietists are not exactly the same as German ones, did not always think and write about the same things, and did not come from the same contexts. Inclusive and inquisitive church historians will find treasures waiting for them by returning to the primary sources.

Translators become acutely aware of (and sometimes vexed by) the fluidity of language, and this comes to bear in particular with technical language and jargon. Theology, like all specialized fields, has settled on specific terms for articulating its concepts, which means that readers need to pay attention to nuances in local languages. One such word is "atonement," which in Swedish is indicated only as *försoning* ("reconciliation"), whereas both words could be used in English. Here I have mostly translated *försoning* as "reconciliation," because it usually fits the context better (in its adjective and verb forms), as well as the overall approachable style of both preachers. It is also less technical for modern readers; most people can personally relate to what reconciliation means, but "atonement" is lofty and seldom used for anything other than theological purposes. Furthermore, the colloquial expression "atoning for one's sins" generally has come to be synonymous with "being punished" or "paying for them," which is precisely the kind of popular misconception about atonement that Waldenström and, to a lesser degree, Rosenius often call into question. *Salighet* can mean either "blessedness" or "salvation" (*salig* as "blessed" or "saved") depending on the context, whereas *frälsning* is exclusively translated here as "salvation." *Skuld* has been translated as "debt," but can also mean "guilt." *Tro* is both a noun and a verb for "belief/ to believe," as well as "faith/to have faith," which means the context has to decide. In Sweden, Lutheran ministers were titled *präst* (priest), even though that is not done in the English-speaking world. Until the 1866 parliamentary reforms, the clergy comprised its own estate in the *Riksdag*, and the parish priest dominated local secular affairs in the village, thus the title commanded the utmost respect and deference. Even Rosenius curiously refers to Scott as "the English priest," for instance. I felt no reason to change that. The words for human being (*människa*) and soul (*själ*) both receive feminine pronouns in Swedish, which I have retained in English, partly as a matter of accuracy, partly as a means of achieving a degree of inclusivity of language. Translators in the past have often anglicized these by making them "he." In other instances where the translation may be complicated, I have signaled this by leaving the original Swedish word in brackets. The Scripture citations are composites, due to the fact that Rosenius and Waldenström sometimes paraphrase passages, at other times are translating to Swedish from Greek or Hebrew, and this results in differences between the Swedish and standard English versions of the Bible. I have first translated these Bible texts from the Swedish, and then conformed them with the NRSV and NIV for accurate vocabulary and to make the texts sound "right" in English ears.

SIMILARITIES AND DIFFERENCES IN ROSENIUS'S AND WALDENSTRÖM'S THEOLOGY

Some readers of this anthology may find the combination of Rosenius and Waldenström in the same volume to be problematic, since Rosenius remained within the Lutheran fold, while Waldenström ultimately departed strict adherence to Lutheran theology for an ecumenical variety of "free church" Christianity. Indeed, there is no reason to conflate the two, as they do demonstrate differences. However, it is a basic premise of this collection that there is more continuity between the two than there is divergence. Furthermore, the denominationally bounded understandings of them are out-dated, as well as inherently in conflict with the ecumenical messages that each of them preached day in and day out. The outline of differences and similarities below is by no means to be considered exhaustive, but merely an effort to summarize main themes.

One cannot speak about Rosenius's theology without pointing out that he was not formally a theologian. He was a layman, and decidedly so. His early interest in pursuing theological training eventually yielded to the firm belief that his status as a layman was an asset to the revival movement. He once confided to Waldenström that when there was pressure to award him an honorary ordination, he refused this on the principle that it would undermine the work of the numerous colporteurs and lay preachers in the service of the EFS. Rosenius saw his authority to preach as originating from an inner calling of the Holy Spirit, but also reinforced by an external calling from the community. He claimed to never speak without having been requested to do so, and he often urged his readers not to presume to speak or teach in conventicles or in public without such an external calling. Rosenius wrote no synthesis of his doctrinal viewpoints, focusing instead on writing devotional commentary on Scripture. Here he saw himself as following the example of Luther, who also wrote commentaries, leaving systematic doctrine to the "Melanchthons" of the world. Rosenius was not vocal in making complaints against the official doctrine of the Church of Sweden. However, it was apparent that in practice he read Scripture differently than did the average Lutheran priest, which itself was a protest of the status quo. Sermons in the early 1800s were academic,

Pietisten bore various versions of the subtitle shown here
that reads "Journal for Christian upbuilding," sometimes
also "spiritual awakening." The images of Moses pointing
to the bronze serpent and the return of the prodigal son,
shown here, were central in how Waldenström explained the
atonement. All that was required of the believer was to "look
up and live." The story of the prodigal son was a touchstone
passage for Rosenius, as well.

objective, and aesthetically refined, and thus were often inaccessible to the
average congregant; though there were many examples of priests who diverged from this norm. Notable among these "churchly" Pietists was Anders
Rosenius, Carl Olof's own father. The Pietist impulse in reading Scripture and
preaching was decidedly subjective, most intently interested in the "spiritual
upbuilding" (*andlig uppbyggelse*) of the individual and the community within
the conventicle. Rosenius, like Waldenström, saw Scripture through the Lutheran lenses of law and gospel (grace). Thus, the primary goal of reading the

Bible was to understand what the text commands/demands of the readers, and what the text claims/promises to the readers. This necessitated taking the readers through the Scripture passage, verse by verse, and sometimes word by word, to invite the readers to profoundly meditate on what these claims and promises might have to do with them personally. These thoughtful and heartfelt Scripture commentaries are what filled the pages of *Pietisten* (and it is therefore not at all accurate to refer to this publication as a "tract," as historians have sometimes done).

Waldenström held to this strategy as he continued and expanded the reach of *Pietisten* between 1868 and his death in 1917. However, unlike his predecessor, he received doctoral level training in classical languages and theology and was ordained by the Church of Sweden in 1864. (The draft of his provocative ordination sermon, as well as the subsequent apology to the archbishop, are included in the appendix.) On the one hand, he was a folksy and down-to-earth preacher, who could regularly draw large crowds at summer tent meetings and fill the great sanctuaries at Bethlehem Chapel in Gävle or Immanuel Church in Stockholm. On the other hand, he was also the formidable "Lektor" Waldenström, initially a teacher of classical languages and religion at several upper secondary schools, and later a teacher of theology at the Mission School at Lidingö, the seminary for the Swedish Mission Covenant. This final post gave him the opportunity to systematically lecture on his theology, recorded in the book *Biblisk Troslära* ("Biblical Faith Doctrine") in 1914. His extensive corpus of writings can be seen in at least three distinct categories or modes; 1) spiritually upbuilding devotional writings, featuring messages of awakening and assurance; 2) more doctrinally oriented treatises, such as those in defense of his theory of the atonement or his defense of Lutheran baptismal practices; and 3) his political speeches and journalistic writings, such as his letters to newspapers and his travelogues, which could be quite candid and opinionated and include commentary on everything from socialism to temperance. In comparing Waldenström with Rosenius, it is essential to point out that Rosenius wrote relatively little that would fall into the second and third categories, so there is not much to compare here (though Rosenius, too, could be rather blunt in his reactions to separatists and other opponents). Most of what Waldenström wrote falls into the first category, and it is also here that he most resembles Rosenius in reading strategies, as well as in thematic emphases and irenic tone. In the lead up to the atonement controversy in 1872, it was none other than Amy Moberg who reminded Waldenström that *Pietisten* was "not a theological journal," and apart from notable dogmatic exceptions, *Pietisten* was largely maintained as a place for upbuilding devotional reading in the Rosenian spirit.

Bethlehem Chapel, Gävle

Inheritance from Pietism and Moravianism

Both Rosenius and Waldenström came from the same remote region in Norrland, Sweden and thus were both influenced by the revival movement that came to be known as "new-evangelical" Pietism (*nyevangelismen*, or *nyläseriet*), which appeared in the first decades of the 1800s. In church historiography in Sweden, there has often been a demarcation between new-evangelical Pietism, and the so-called old Pietism (*gammalläseriet*). Old Pietism came to be denounced by new-evangelicals as emphasizing repentance and conversion to such a high degree that it overshadowed the gospel message of grace and the forgiveness of sins, and conflicted with Luther's own emphasis on justification by faith alone. By contrast, the new evangelicals promoted a posture of faith that emphasized the joy, peace and assurance that comes from the Christian life. While new evangelical leaders are easy to identify, exactly who is identified by "old Pietism" is unclear; historian Gunnar Westin has even speculated that there was no such coherent movement in Norrland, and that the term might simply refer to "an unproductive church orthodoxy," preached by conservative clergy and exhibited in the general sentiments of some parishioners.[3] Thus, the term may have

3. Westin, *George Scott och hans verksamhet i Sverige,* 36.

been a bit of a straw man, rhetorically useful to new evangelicals as they encountered critics on multiple fronts. Of particular inspiration to the new evangelicals was the influence from Moravianism, including prominent figures like Anders Carl Rutström (1721–1772). Moravian circles seemed to especially thrive in Northern Sweden. Since its arrival in the early 1700s, Moravianism had been tolerated to the degree that its adherents maintained a modicum of Lutheran loyalty, in keeping with the precedents set by Count von Zinzendorf (1700–1760). Zinzendorf had promoted a "religion of the heart," which emphasized the experiential and the subjective aspects of faith. The imagery in the Moravian hymns, describing intimate friendship with the Savior, as well as the close identification with his suffering and wounds, came to heavily influence the subsequent hymnody of the new evangelicals, including the hymns of Rosenius.

At the same time, there were also a number of lay evangelists who began to boldly test the limits of the regulations against "conventicles" (the most famous being the Edict of 1726). Conventicles were illegal gatherings of neighbors and friends in the home for study of the Bible without the supervision of the parish priest. These gatherings gave occasion for talented speakers to emerge as lay preachers, some of whom even began traveling to other villages to preach. Few were more influential for Rosenius than the laywoman preacher named Maja Lisa Söderlund (1794–1851). Söderlund did not challenge the church establishment directly, however, the remarkable fact that she was preaching as a layperson and as a woman was in clear conflict with the law and brought the reprimand of the clergy. Söderlund emphasized the centrality of the believer's relationship to Christ in all matters of doctrine, and though not questioning the importance of the functions of the law, she nevertheless warned against "allowing the law of Moses to frighten souls from faith in the Savior." It is easy to trace Rosenius's theology back to Söderlund, particularly in some of the anecdotes that were recorded from her sermons, like the following, preached sometime around 1844.

The one who comes to Jesus, comes to the perfect light and sees his sins much better, than if one were to see them in the less perfect light of the law. I wish to create a picture from this, which everyone will recognize. When you walk into a dark room, you see nothing of that which is in it. Then the daylight comes in, and you see all the objects in the room. But now the sun shines its light and fills up the room, and then you see these things in infinite detail. Moses casts his light, and you see many sins. John the Baptist shines his, and you see even more. But allow Jesus in—and then you will see

how sin abounds. But you will also experience how he can clean
a house.[4]

The goal of preaching like this is to invite the listener into a transformative personal relationship with the Savior. The rhetorical strategy evident here is the attempt to create urgency by presenting a picture of how wonderful this relationship will be, so that the listener will not delay in rushing to receive this grace. This is in contrast with the rhetorical strategies that were objectionable to the new evangelicals, which attempted to create urgency by emphasizing the depravity of the human condition and the judgment that awaited sinfulness. Poor "Moses" here becomes symbolic of everything that is wrong with either old Pietism or Lutheran orthodoxy, whereas Jesus becomes a superhero who overcomes human depravity by taking all the work upon himself. It is easy to understand Söderlund's popularity.

The Atonement, God's Wrath and Love

The nuances of exactly what Christ accomplished on the cross were the subject of much discussion and debate in new evangelical circles, and also constitute the primary point of divergence between Rosenius and Waldenström. Waldenström's theory of the atonement brought him international attention, first published in his famous sermon of 1872 and then expounded in subsequent writings; these included *Om försoningens betydelse* in 1873 ("On the meaning of the reconciliation"), *Herren är from* in 1875 (*The Lord is Right*), and *I ingen annan är frälsning* in 1877 ("In no one else is salvation"). As mentioned, his apparent divergence from Lutheran doctrine had brought the disapproval of the Church of Sweden and the EFS, as well as the Augustana Lutheran Synod in North America, which had been founded by immigrants in 1860. In its early days, Augustana had not initially received much support from the Church of Sweden, but instead was primarily supported through the efforts of the EFS, which provided it with preachers and resources, including the wide distribution of Rosenius's writings. The debates over Waldenström's theory thus prompted a similar controversy in the Synod as had occurred within the EFS, and ultimately resulted in the exodus of the Waldenström sympathizers, the so-called "Mission Friends," and led to the eventual formation of both the Evangelical Free Church and the Evangelical Covenant Church. This was as much a cultural debate as it

4. Quoted in Linge, *Carl Olof Rosenius; Sveriges främste lekmannapredikant,* 14.

was a theological one, and became one of the most significant identity issues for these communities during the 1870s and 1880s.

Rosenius himself had demonstrated preferences for how the atonement (the reconciliation) should and should not be explained in sermons, but this was primarily a question of emphasis. He was not apparently interested in challenging the official Lutheran explanation, as encoded in the Augsburg Confession (adopted by the Church of Sweden in 1593). In the spirit of both George Scott and Maja Lisa Söderlund's evangelistic strategies, Rosenius's explanation of the reconciliation was motivated by practical concerns of how to urge listeners and readers to rush to accept the grace available to them, here and now, as they were. There was no need to delay. Rosenius took issue with the notion that there was any prerequisite in placing faith in Christ; one did not need to overcome sin first, as this was something that Christ does in us and for us. Scholar Torsten Nilsson has explained that for Rosenius, the matter of the reconciliation can be understood as an el-lipse with two focal points. "The one focal point is the emphasis on the total depravity of humankind in sin and its inability to save itself. The other focal point is that everything that the 'law can never accomplish,' that is to say, what humankind could not do on their own strength—namely to, through the law, win righteousness and thereby salvation—this God has done in Christ."[5] Rosenius's explanation of this dichotomy mirrors that of Paul, as well as Luther, in that all of humanity has fallen into sin through Adam, yet Christ has died for all of humanity. God's wrath over sin continues to be a re-ality that afflicts us, but we may be confident that through faith in Christ we have been reconciled to God, and that God's wrath no longer rests over the person of faith. Rosenius presents sin as having been collectively dealt with in the reconciliation, in that Christ takes on all of humanity's sin, and makes salvation available to all of humanity. In becoming human, Christ not only takes our place as a sacrifice (as though we were off someplace else), but he occupies *the same place as us*. He incorporates us into himself, and as we al-low him to co-suffer what we are suffering, he makes us righteous, fulfilling the demands of the law on our behalf. Rosenius de-emphasizes the notion that Christ shields us from the wrathful punishment of an angry God, and instead emphasizes how it is that Christ *fulfills the law on our behalf, within us, in our place*. In his commentary on Romans, Rosenius stresses that what has reconciled or "satisfied" God in the crucifixion is Christ's obedience. Christ's suffering is an outcome and culmination of his perfect obedience to God. This is how God is reconciled, in that our hearts are reconciled to God,

---

5. *En har dött för alla*, 11.

through the obedience and righteousness of Christ, which is imparted to us. This is even expressed as a "gift of righteousness."[6]

Waldenström, while in agreement with most of the points above, departed from the Rosenian view of the reconciliation by attempting to clarify it, thereby taking it to an extreme. In protest of the wording of the Augsburg Confession, Waldenström would argue that it was not at all God who was "reconciled" to us, but instead that it was we who were reconciled to God, by God. He urged Christians not to speak of God being "reconciled" at all, as though God were the object of reconciliation. It is us, and only us, who needed to be reconciled. All talk of God's wrath being satisfied or "appeased" in the crucifixion was a hold-over from heathenism and was objectionable and untenable. God's righteousness demanded that we be made righteous, and this demand could never be satisfied by anything other than our righteousness. God's wrath could not be eliminated without also eliminating God's holiness and its demand for righteousness. Even now, the sinner will continue to experience God's demand for righteousness as wrath, while on the other side, the sinner who believes and is being sanctified will increasingly experience this same demand for righteousness as love. It is the sinner alone who is changed by the reconciliation. Thus Waldenström's primary adjustment to the Rosenian view was to underscore God's changeless nature, but he also objected to Rosenius's unsystematic use of payment motifs in explaining the reconciliation. Any talk of payment opened the door to the misconception that somehow God's demand for righteousness could be satisfied with anything less than our righteousness. In addition, by emphasizing how Christ has paid our debt of sin, Waldenström thought this created additional problems by failing to explain why the "sin of disbelief" was not also paid for in this transaction. In other words, our sins are paid in full, but yet we might still be damned because of lack of faith, which is a sin that is apparently not covered in the payment for the other sins. If the reconciliation is to be understood as a payment at all, it must be as a remission of debt in the form of a payment that God makes *to us*, through Christ, reasoned Waldenström.

Though Rosenius was in agreement with this in terms of emphasis, and most often speaks of humanity as being "reconciled in Christ," his vocabulary does in fact also speak of "a reconciled God" in numerous places. As Rosenius died four years before the atonement controversy, it is impossible to presume how he would have responded. How much his talk of God being "reconciled" was a conscious choice, or simply an unconscious deference to the terminology used in the Augsburg Confession, remains unresolved. But what is certain is that in every explanation of the reconciliation, Rosenius consistently

6. Rosenius, *Romans; A Devotional Commentary*, 27, 33.

presents a view of God in which God actively pursues the sinner, and in which the heart of the Father and the Son are in sync. In Rosenius's explanation of the creation of the world, he emphasizes the "council" that is held between the persons of the Trinity, in which the Father decides to create humankind only after the Son has said "I will save them." After the fall of humankind into sin, Rosenius presents an image of God as a sort of counselor to Adam, in which God pursues him and coaxes him back to himself, calling out "Adam, where are you?" Both Rosenius and Waldenström preferred to use imagery from the parables of the "prodigal son" and of the "good shepherd" when explaining the heart of God and Christ. Both also liked to remind their listeners and readers that "Christ is no half savior," but that he is a complete savior whose grace and ability to save us knows no limits. Christ is an accessible brother and friend, but also worthy of supreme devotion and reverence.

The objections to Waldenström's theory included the claim that by eliminating the tension between God and Christ, this made the crucifixion into a pointless and grim farce. What was the point of Christ's death if it was not to appease God's wrath? Waldenström countered by saying that his picture of the reconciliation, in which the heart of God and Christ are in sync, is not at all a grim farce, but in fact is more beautiful than the idea that the Christian God, like pagan gods, demands to be appeased by blood sacrifices. The crucifixion was not at all a pointless exercise, or an empty symbol of God's love, but an essential part of the process by which Christ makes sinners holy and allows them to be reconciled to God. All that is needed on the part of the believer is faith, the ability to "look up" and allow himself or herself to be healed by Christ.

For Rosenius too, the crucifixion was regarded with profound reverence. In his study he had a portrait of "the thorn-crowned Christ," which he explained to visitors as being the most beautiful thing that he owned. Yet, he chose to hang a silken curtain over the image, and only revealed it on occasions when he wished to focus his thoughts, or those of his visitors, on this image. In these moments, he would draw back the curtain, observe it in a moment of holy silence, and then close the curtain once more. This was a way of disciplining himself so that he did not take this beautiful image of Christ's sacrifice for granted.

New evangelicals like Rosenius and Waldenström were often criticized as being "hyper-evangelical," meaning that they overemphasized grace and thus presented a "cheap" faith to their listeners and readers. In reading through their explanations of the reconciliation, however, two things should be underscored. First, their historical context was one in which there was an apparent overemphasis on the law, which they both found harmful and un-Lutheran. Both were in agreement on this point, and looked to Luther's own writings to rediscover what was meant by "justification by faith alone." There was also an apparent need among Swedish Christians to hear such a message, since they flocked to hear it in droves. Second, on those points where Rosenius and Waldenström differ, this has mostly to do with vocabulary, not overall message. Waldenström is more particular and systematic in his use of terms than his mentor was. However, the message of both preachers was to convince sinners that God was so abundant in love and forgiveness that there was no reason to delay in rushing to receive the grace that was available to them. In tribute to Waldenström after his death, Nathan Söderblom (1866–1931), archbishop of the Church of Sweden, said that he had "left behind a new, more evangelical picture of God as an inheritance to the Swedish people." This inheritance is most certainly also a Rosenian one.

Doubt, Anfäktelse, and the Assurance of Salvation

Another hallmark of the new evangelical preachers was that they often emphasized the concept of assurance (*tröst*); assurance of God's love and grace, of the forgiveness of sins, of the sufficiency of faith alone, and ultimately of salvation. This emphasis was also part of the reason that their critics complained that they promoted a faith that was "cheaply bought." This critique was even thrown at the saintly and otherwise unimpeachable Lina Sandell-Berg (1832–1903), whose hymn lyrics painted a warm picture of a Savior who was always ready to embrace the sinner under "motherly wings" (*modersvingen*—hearkening to Christ's wish that he could gather Jerusalem under his wing like a "hen gathers her brood"). One sometimes gets the impression from these new evangelicals that God's job number one is to offer assurance and counseling to the sinner. In other words, their emphasis on God's friendship did not seem to require anything of the believer, as it is God who, through Christ and the Holy Spirit, is responsible for virtually everything: our conversion, our justification, our sanctification, and so on. The roles played by each member of the trinity can be confused and blurred (Rosenius's narrative emphasis at times seems to shift agency to the Holy Spirit, whereas Waldenström often shifts emphasis to the agency of God the Father). However, in response to this critique about "cheaply bought faith," one need only look to the personal testimonies of all three. In particular, Rosenius seems to have had a rather extensive and tortuous experience with doubt during his youth, and Sandell had a lifetime full of tragedies and health problems. While they presented the Christian life as sweet, this was not at all supposed to be a saccharine sweetness, but instead was often bitter sweet. Their presentation of the life of faith may seem wholly passive, but as Sven Lodin has pointed out, there is also an aspect in which the experience they describe of wrestling with doubt, of earnest prayer and supplications, contains a "hidden" activity or agency to it.[7]

Mor Enfaldiga anfäktelse (se sid. 104).

"Mother Simple's Crisis of Temptation" illustration by Jenny Nyström in Waldenström's novel Squire Adamsson, Or, Where do you Live?

There is a term often used in the nineteenth-century Lutheran world to describe the crisis of temptation, in which the believer is caught between the conflicting pulls of doubt and faith. This experience of temptation is referred to as *anfäktelse*.[8] Rosenius experienced this in heavy doses, and seems to have emerged from it by finding assurance in the Christology offered to him by George Scott and Maja Lisa Söderlund. The trauma of *anfäktelse* was precipitated by multiple factors. On the one hand, modernity seemed to threaten the security of faith, as scholars actively questioned everything from the divine

7. Lodin, *Carl Olof Rosenius; Hans liv och förkunnelse*, 64–65.

8. See Sjögren, *Anfäktelsen enligt Rosenius*. Rosenius, like Luther, emphasized this trial of temptation as having chiefly to do with one's faith in God, whereas medieval and mystical traditions had often emphasized this as a temptation of one's love for God. Spener and Zinzendorf, for different reasons, both emphasized love as the object of temptation. Waldenström follows Rosenius in emphasizing faith as the object.

inspiration of the Bible to the divinity of Christ. Also a factor was the more traditional emphasis on the functions of the law within Lutheran theology. The first function of the law was to provide the population with a general sense of morality. In this way, the instruction and discipline of the state church clergy reinforced the practical moral agenda of the secular government regarding law and order. The second function of the law was more profoundly theological. Through the demands of the law, we are made aware of our sinful depravity and inadequacy to do anything to merit salvation. This traumatic realization that we cannot fulfill the law, allows us to be awakened to God's promise to fulfill this on our behalf, through Christ. Without this anxiety-ridden experience, we would not come to know and understand the meaning of the gospel, believe in it, to repent and convert. The third function of the law is to spur the converted believer to proceed along the path of sanctification.[9] The new evangelicals seem to have thought that there was too much emphasis on the first and second functions, and not enough emphasis on the third. Rosenius's descriptions of *anfäktelse* seem to always lead to the joyful realization that it is Christ who fulfills the law on our behalf. As such, Rosenius gives greater prominence for this neglected third function. The high degree of joy that the believer experiences in stage three is due to the suffering encountered in stage two, and thus the believer will now be a properly grateful and enthusiastic participant in the sanctifying work of the Holy Spirit.

As Rosenius so candidly shares his own personal experiences with doubt, he thus creates a non-judgmental atmosphere in which his readers can confess their own doubts and fears of inadequacy. These readers are also able to make subjective comparisons between Rosenius's testimony and their own life experiences, to see where they might be in this process. Scholar Ivan Hellström notes that Rosenius saw his role as a preacher as first and foremost being an opportunity for pastoral care to his parishioners (*själavård*, literally "soul-care"). A great deal of Rosenius's weekly schedule included time for visitation and even drop-in guests who sought his counsel, and he wrote a great number of letters to answer people's spiritual questions (some of these were reprinted as booklets, such as *Bref i andliga ämnen*, "Letters on Spiritual Topics"). It is this model of pastoral care which also seems to be the main inspiration for Waldenström's character "Mother Simple" in the novel *Squire Adamsson*. Not only is Mother Simple's theology unmistakably Rosenian as she doles out spiritual advice to the other characters, but in one chapter, she herself is afflicted by a rather melodramatic experience with *anfäktelse*. In this scene, Mother Simple writhes and wriggles in despair as she contemplates the possibility of her damnation,

9. Kjellberg, *Folkväckelse i Sverige*, 276–77.

and is tempted to abandon her faith, and even end her life. Yet she is also tempted to seek out Immanuel one last time, which prompts her ultimate return to faith. Both Rosenius and Waldenström depict the Christian life as often being suspended between the poles of faith and doubt. Much like Luther and Kierkegaard, *anfäktelse* for the new evangelicals was seen as an inescapable aspect of the life of faith. Learning how to understand and deal with these experiences of temptation is a necessary step in transforming objective knowledge about theology to become a living, personal faith.

It is clear that Rosenius and Waldenström saw their essential role as preachers as being to offer assurance to their readers as an antidote to this tension between faith and doubt. Just as the Good Shepherd seeks out and calls back the stray sheep, the little shepherds, the pastors, must constantly do the same for their flocks. The individual believer is easily tempted to stray, and the role of the evangelist is thus to create a force that is greater than the temptation away from faith. Waldenström's one-sided explanation of the atonement is primarily the result of his frustrations over preachers who obscured the message of the gospel with too many qualifications. In one of his devotionals, titled "God is my assurance," he almost seems to shout at his readers when he says, "Let God's grace rain down over you!"[10] He even goes so far as to say that it is part of God's method to "assure the miserable sinner to death" (*trösta ihjäl den olycklige syndaren*), as part of killing our stubborn resistance and false impressions of our own ability.[11] Admittedly, all of this vocabulary of assurance for miserable and wretched sinners may seem like overemotional affect to contemporary audiences. But there is also a profound awareness on the part of Rosenius and Waldenström of the serious difficulties associated with the life of faith.

Sanctification and Freedom from the Law

As mentioned before, Rosenius understood Scripture in a classic Lutheran way, by viewing it through two lenses: the first being the law (the commands and demands of a holy, righteous God), and the second being the gospel (the promises and gifts of a forgiving and loving God). As Rosenius explains it, the law makes both its external demands on the actions of the believers, as well as its internal spiritual demands on the heart of the believer. Even though our reconciliation is accomplished by Christ's death and resurrection, the law retains its function as a reminder to the believer of what sin

10. Waldenström, *Gud är min tröst*, 308.
11. Ibid., 186.

is, as well as what the heights of sanctification are, which are promised to us through Christ. The law drives us to understand our incapability, while the gospel allows us to see and understand how it is that we are saved and sanctified by Christ. In Rosenius's preaching, the latter message virtually always gets the last word; he does not leave the reader hanging in suspense. He reassures his readers that sanctification is "a process of becoming," which is complete and perfect as it relates to God's accomplishment, but yet is incomplete as it relates to our own residual sinful nature. Thus there is an importance placed on sanctification, but also an overwhelming message of assurance that the believer can trust Christ to accomplish this for us.

Rosenius came to articulate his dissatisfaction with a variety of other interpretations about the law and sanctification that were current at the time. As has been mentioned already, old Pietism in Norrland was dismissed, as Rosenius identified it as being too legalistic. However, this was not simply a rejection of what might be seen as a conservative (or "fundamentalist") understanding of the law. It was also a rejection of the enlightened rationalism that prevailed in academic theological circles and came to influence prominent members of the clergy. The trend in the sermons of these clergymen was to de-emphasize the divine and miraculous aspects of the life of Jesus, instead presenting him as a supreme ethical teacher. One's happiness came from following Jesus' moral example and striving to be a good and well-behaved citizen, which meant conforming to the dominant culture. The new evangelicals fervently rejected this message, and complained that it was being promoted in several new published resources of the church, including the hymnal from 1819, the celebrated accomplishment of later archbishop Johan Olof Wallin (1779–1839). For slightly different reasons, the new evangelicals also took issue with the school of Pietism surrounding the priest Henrik Schartau (1757–1825). Schartau had come to disapprove of the emotional Christianity of the Moravians, and instead attempted to establish clear prescriptions for the life of godliness and pure doctrine. This came in the form of his systematic explanations of the *Ordo Salutis* or Order of Salvation (*nådens ordning* = "Order of Grace"). These kinds of systems appeared in a number of manifestations in late Lutheran orthodoxy as a means to describe the ordered stages whereby God allows the human being to participate in grace. Such stages included "calling," "enlightenment," "new birth" and "conversion," "justification," "the mystical union," "sanctification" or "regeneration," and "glorification." For Rosenius, this obsession with minutely defining the sequence of moments in the life of faith resulted in the over-emphasis on repentance and conversion to the detriment of the message of assurance of grace. (To a much lesser degree, Rosenius was apparently also critical of the emphasis on identifying these stages that he found in the writings of Pietist patriarch, Philipp Jakob Spener, 1635–1705). While Schartau's system was too constricting for Rosenius, he also found opponents on the other end of the spectrum. In lengthy interactions with the Finnish evangelist Fredrik Gabriel Hedberg (1811–1893), Rosenius ultimately determined that Hedberg's preaching was too "ultra-evangelical" in its over-emphasis on grace. Though they both shared a similar Christocentric message and an affinity for Moravianism, Rosenius accused Hedberg of neglecting the importance of repentance and sanctification for the Christian life. Hedberg's aggressive sermons against "works righteousness" and "legalism" might lead to hypocrisy and self-righteousness and an antinomian variety of Christianity, charged Rosenius.

With this in mind, the presentation of the law and sanctification in Waldenström's novel, *Squire Adamsson,* highly resembles Rosenius's understanding. The character "Moses" becomes a caricature of Schartau. Sanctification is taken seriously in the city "Evangelium," but only comes as a response to having received grace and is entirely the work of "Immanuel." Antinomian delusions of the Hedberg variety, seem to find their home in the city "Loose Living." On the whole, Rosenius seemed pleased with the presentation of the life of faith in Waldenström's allegory, and historian William Bredberg has noted that the novel served as a "useful compendium" in Rosenian theology. Later on, however, Waldenström came to see that he had different ideas than his mentor, regarding the degree to which sanctification should be emphasized. Waldenström concluded that Rosenius talked too much about sanctification, and even saw this as an extension of the *Ordo Salutis.* Already in *Squire Adamsson,* the character "Mother Simple" makes the claim that the law has no function for the person who is already living in the state of depravity. Such people need to only hear about grace; they are only healed by grace, not by the law. Thus Waldenström seems to be separating sanctification from the third function of the law, whereas Rosenius had retained this function of the law. Nevertheless, for both Rosenius and Waldenström, there is a common emphasis that whatever its function in our experience of conversion, ultimately "the law does not bring life." There is no reason for the sinner to delay before running to receive the grace that does bring life.

The Christian Congregation and the Life of Faith

The ultimate goal for both preachers was to foster Christian community within the congregation. All of the preceding discussion of atonement, sanctification, *anfäktelse,* etc. must be seen against the backdrop of a communally-based conception of faith. Rosenius and Waldenström had each been formed as Christians in the intimacy of Pietist conventicles and had strong mentors who facilitated their conversions and offered guidance in their spiritual trials. The Christian life they advocated was not a solitary existence. Rosenius's congregational model was rooted in his aspirations for a revitalized Lutheran state church, centered around a genuine appreciation of the sacraments and a renewed understanding of Lutheran doctrine, made possible through a close reading of Luther's own writings. The EFS was not to compete with the local parish, but instead was intended to revitalize it, by organizing opportunities for revival meetings, Sunday school resources, song books, devotional literature, and home and foreign missions activities. Though Waldenström came to be estranged from the Church of Sweden and EFS, he still retained this basic Rosenian blueprint. Whereas the EFS had been a semi-independent mission society that strove to renew the state church, Waldenström defined the Swedish Mission Covenant as a mission society that was to revitalize the whole of Christianity. This idea of the smaller church serving as a "leaven" within the larger church is the great legacy of classical Pietism, in the spirit of Spener, Francke and Zinzendorf. It is clear that Rosenius and Waldenström knew in whose wake they traveled, since they salute their predecessors regularly in their writings. Rosenius shares that his conversion experience was prompted by reading the Danish Pietist, Erik Pontoppidan (1698–1764), and Waldenström's was prompted by encountering the writings of the German, Johann Arndt (1555–1621). However, their admiration for this Lutheran heritage did not prevent them from seeking inspiration abroad, and they freely borrowed "best practices" from the Anglo-American evangelical world. The influence from George Scott and Methodist practice is abundantly clear. Waldenström, in particular, was highly interested in American Congregationalism, and seemed to think there was little difference with his conception of a "Mission Covenant" (though several Swedish-American church leaders assured him that they were incompatible, including David Nyvall, 1863–1946). The format for revival meetings, as well as theater-style sanctuary construction, used by evangelists like Dwight L. Moody (1837–1899) were clearly a source of inspiration for the Swedes. Although Waldenström would surely have found Moody's lack of theological precision to be problematic, they each shared a common message of God's abounding love for the sinner, and a similar notion that the congregation should transcend denominational lines to accommodate all believers. That said, Waldenström's knowledge of English was quite limited. When he visited Moody at his home in Northfield, Massachusetts in 1889, they apparently communicated in a mixture of broken English and Latin, and when Waldenström read the works of Charles

Spurgeon (1834–1892), it was in German translation. It was more natural for him to look south for inspiration, and he regularly attended conferences at places like Herrnhut, Halle and Basel.

The new evangelical Pietists had also reasserted an emphasis on the sacraments, baptism and communion, which they thought had been neglected by old Pietism, as well as diluted by the practices of the state church. Rosenius's career corresponded with the rise of the Baptist movement in Sweden, which called into question the validity of infant baptisms, and asserted that baptism should follow a genuine conversion experience (thus necessitating re-baptism). Distressed readers of *Pietisten* wrote to Rosenius for his advice on the matter, which came in the form of his defense of the Lutheran practices of infant baptism. But he went further, and elaborated on the meaning of baptism. This was no mere confession of faith, but a true sacrament, a historical moment which marks a time and place when grace was received. Witnessing the baptisms of infants was an opportunity for devotional reflection, in which believers are prompted to "remember" their own baptism and take assurance in it. The Holy Spirit thus "speaks" through the event of baptism, reminding the congregation of how grace is received. While Rosenius understood the cause for the criticisms of the Baptists, he rather curtly dismisses the notion that there was anything wrong with Lutheran baptism, and concludes that there was no reason to withhold baptism from infants. The issue persisted through Waldenström's career, prompting him also to write a creative defense of both kinds of baptism, which took the form of a series of conversations between two fictional characters, "Timoteus" and "Natanael." While it quickly becomes clear that Timoteus is a foil for Natanael, and that the latter represents Waldenström's case, he rather cleverly places in Timoteus' mouth the arguments of a number of prominent Baptist leaders, such as Anders Wiberg. Thus, this is his chance to walk his readers through the arguments against infant baptism, and dismiss them one by one. Interesting to note here is that Natanael is not a Mission Covenanter, but instead is a Lutheran. His defense of Lutheran baptismal practices also caught the attention of the Augustana Synod, which suddenly found an ally in Waldenström after two decades of estrangement after the atonement controversy. The Synod even reprinted a sermon that he gave on baptism in Omaha, Nebraska in 1889 (*Dop-Predikan*), with the note: "Would to God that P.W. would stand as firmly on the foundation of Scripture in all matters as he does on this one!" While Waldenström, like Rosenius, understood the reasons for the Baptists' complaints about the lack of regenerate Christian living within the state church, he asserted that infant baptism was not the cause; "One should not attempt to prevent errors by denying truths."[12] Denying the validity of infant baptisms was a worse error, in his mind, as it called into question the validity of all baptisms and sucked the sacramental function and mystery right out of it. The result was that the Mission Covenanters came to observe both forms of baptism, a practice unthinkable in many denominations.

In regard to communion, Rosenius similarly encourages his readers to embrace the event as an opportunity to receive the assurance of grace. In communion, as in baptism, the Holy Spirit "speaks" to the believer. Rosenius emphasizes the role of the Holy Spirit in speaking to us through the word, as well as both sacraments, thereby awakening us and drawing us into community around the "table of grace" (*nådenes bord*). This emphasis appears in Rosenius's most popular hymn "With God as our Friend" (*Med Gud och hans vänskap*), which was set to a vigorous tune by Oscar Ahnfelt (1813–1882) and became the virtual anthem of the new evangelical Pietists. Whereas the controversy over the interpretation of the atonement was an important theological debate, the practical concerns about communion were far more decisive and long lasting. The complaint was that in the state church, participation in communion was a social norm and even compulsory, and thus "openly ungodly" people mocked the sacrament by their participation. For decades, special communion services and even "communion societies" were arranged in the EFS for dissenters who desired that the sacrament be treated with the reverence they thought it deserved. This escalated until 1876, when a petition was presented to King Oscar II, with Waldenström among the leaders and bearing 22,300 signatures, which requested the right to freely celebrate communion outside of the Church of Sweden's tight regulations. The subsequent refusal of this request is what ultimately prompted the 1878 formation of the Swedish Mission Covenant as an independent denomination (though its members usually retained dual membership in the Church of Sweden).

Waldenström's desire to preserve the character of the Mission Covenant as a "mission society" represents a complicated effort to retain some of the priorities of the EFS and Rosenius, mentioned above. However, the basic fact that the Covenant now had its own congregations, meant that Waldenström needed to define what the congregation was, which was a task that Rosenius had simply not needed to do. The congregations of the Church of Sweden were organized as territorial parishes, in which geographical boundaries determined who was in and who was out. Scott and Rosenius's ministries had been an initial step away from this model, as Bethlehem Church served people across the parish lines of Stockholm. However, as

12. Waldenström, *Dop och Barndop*, 77.

the EFS was being established, Rosenius had urged that it *not* follow the example of the Scottish free churches and form congregations that were independent of the state church, which was the view advocated by Hans Jacob Lundborg (1825–1867). In order to affirm the Lutheran congregational model and avoid separatism, the EFS would not have its own congregations, simply its own "activities." By contrast, the Mission Covenant needed a congregational model, which was provided in large part by the leadership and vision of Erik Jakob Ekman (1842–1915), its first president, and informed heavily by Waldenström's definitions.

The purpose of these congregations was to collectively form a "mission society," which had a twofold mission: an "inner mission," to continue the revitalization of Christianity in Sweden, as well as an "outer mission," to engage in the foreign mission field. Building on the precedents set by the EFS and earlier mission societies, the Mission Covenant quickly came to be engaged in mission work in the Congo, Alaska and China, in particular. Waldenström himself made an extensive trip to China to survey the mission stations and seminary there in 1907, and increasingly used the outlet of several Christian newspapers, including *Pietisten*, to rally fundraising support. There was a large number of Mission Covenanters who also saw this mission as extending into the political arena. A remarkable number of them became members of the Swedish parliament, the *Riksdag*, and Waldenström himself served in parliament from 1884–1905. Chief among his political concerns were issues related to the temperance movement, alleviating poverty and emigration through Liberal strategies, democratizing representation, and separating the Church of Sweden from the state. In the Church Assembly, an advisory body to the *Riksdag*, Waldenström had begun urging this divorce as early as 1868, and continued with a final effort in 1908–1910 (it was not until the year 2000 that this separation finally took place). As an example of his capabilities as an orator, I have included his famous "maiden speech" in the *Riksdag*, in the appendix. Here he makes one case for the separation of the church from the state, as it related to the debates about civil marriage in 1885.

Apart from the congregation's important mission in this world, its ultimate mission was to "cultivate souls for heaven," as Waldenström phrased it. In his book, "The Kingdom of God and the Congregation," he is careful to make the case that the congregation is not synonymous with the kingdom of God, even though the congregation contains many "children of the kingdom." The believers participate in the coming kingdom to the degree to which they, like the apostles, suffer for it, as well as act as co-workers in witnessing to it.[13] He also takes issue with the way that some "sectar-ian" Christians at the time had exclusively defined the congregation. In his definition, the congregation is only for believers, but for "all believers," thus challenging both the state church model, as well as partisan attitudes among the free churches. Rosenius, for his part, also explains the difficulty of discerning who is genuinely a "believer." In this matter, as in all matters of doctrine, everything depends on the degree to which the person has faith in "Jesus alone"; this he refers to as the believer's "Shibboleth song," and is the only dependable means whereby to recognize a true Christian. Walden-ström, furthermore, took issue with the way in which some preachers erro-neously equated conversion with being "saved," saying, "It is therefore very misleading when one presents salvation as being synonymous with conver-sion, saying: 'at this or that point I was saved,' when one means converted. Conversion is the beginning, salvation is the end on the way of salvation."[14] Salvation is something that is a historical reality, accomplished by the work of Christ, but also a future reality, which is not yet completed. Membership in a certain congregation or assent to a certain doctrine is not what brings salvation. Speculation as to the minutia of Christian eschatology, such as the "thousand year kingdom" or the specific order of events connected to the re-turn of Christ, does not seem to have interested Waldenström or Rosenius. In fact, they both actively discourage their readers from becoming side-tracked by this kind of idle speculation. Their explanations of eschatology are centered on the parables of Christ, and include very little imagery from the book of Revelation. In Rosenius's explanation, while we have been told that we "know not the day, nor the hour," we can be assured that the Spirit will fulfill all things according to God's intention.

In the meantime, the function of the congregation is to seek out the lost, to draw members together in genuine community around the word and sacraments, to be engaged in the present mission of the church in this world, and to watch in anxious hope for the promised fulfillment of the kingdom. These are the hopes and priorities that have made Rosenius's and Waldenström's writings transformative and timeless for generations of their readers, and it is in this hopeful spirit that I welcome you to this book.

Champaign, Illinois
Twentieth Sunday after Trinity, 2014
Mark Safstrom

13. Waldenström, *Guds Rike och Församlingen*, 59.
14. Ibid., 22.

George Scott

1

Pietism according to Scott and Rosenius

PIETISM

By George Scott and C.O. Rosenius, 1842

("Pietism")

For anyone who has read the history of the Church of Sweden or made themselves familiar with the trends within this church, it does not need to be pointed out that pietism, both as a concept and a name, has long been known in Sweden, as well as in other countries. The name has not always been used in its original and correct sense, but when less-enlightened people have wanted to use it as a pejorative, in their intent to indicate a fanatical, hypocritical and harmful zeal for godliness, there has been no shortage of attempts to save this pregnant term from such misuse.

Indeed, even the authorities have made known their disapproval through public bans when such an important word has been misused unjustly. We will quote just one example, found in [Sven] Baelter's Ceremonies of the Church, page 283, where it says: "What efforts did not King Fredrik I make to prevent all carelessness in sermons! There are documented instances of how some clergymen used 'pietist' and 'pietistery' as though it were the name of a sect, in order to thereby identify some delusional person and heretical doctrine. The king found that 'pietist'—or the fear of God in such a form—was changed into a pejorative, which could foster contempt and disrespect among simpler minds, or at least cold-heartedness for true godliness and its practice. Therefore, in 1726 there was a regulation that 'pietist' or 'pietistery,' neither in the pulpit nor at academies and schools, should be mentioned so abusively." From this it can clearly be seen that it was not the words themselves and whether their use corresponded with an accurate, respectful definition that raised the attention of the authorities, but the "abusive" use thereof, with contempt and invective against their own holy, venerable content. It would probably also be worth mentioning, when one is aware that among the modern languages there are two that are of the most importance from a religious perspective, German and English, that in the latter, these words have never been abused as a pejorative, but the word "piety" always indicates a true and living godliness. Although the English language is certainly not lacking a variety of specific, frequently-used nicknames to indicate what people in Germany mean by "pietism," and in Sweden generally by "readery" [*läseri*].

Both friends and enemies of a living and active fear of God are, however, somewhat united on what this thing is, which is indicated by the name pietism. This is celebrated by the former as something that is altogether essential for each and every Christian, while on the other hand, the latter either judge it as completely worthy of rejection, or even if they regard it as more innocent, and indeed even useful for certain purposes (for example, as they claim, by counteracting exaggerated ungodliness on the one side with an exaggerated godliness on the other), nevertheless they explain it as being altogether superfluous for the majority of those who profess Christ. That we are uniting ourselves with the friends of pietism need not be said, for the birth of this newspaper is witness to this. We are firmly convinced that even if everything in the world changes, indeed, even as the customs of society change, all the same the word of God never changes, but what was altogether necessary to be a Christian in the time of the apostles is just as essential now. The same foundation and path for salvation; the same source of goodness in the heart, living and producing the right fruits; the same determination to deny one's self, carry the shame of Christ and flee everything that appears evil; the same mind and aspiration to work with the Master and promote his cause; the same necessity to be vigilant and pray—these things that were prescribed for Christians in the first century are also prescribed for Christians in the nineteenth. The forms change, the concepts of doctrine are bound, made clear, and fortified, the social order is overthrown and transformed even in so-called Christian countries. But piety and fear of God do not change. It is the life, the spirit, the fertility that is in all forms, institutions of learning, and societal regulations, where Christians are known and recognized.

That the majority of those who confess Christ do not believe that they need to trouble themselves with anything more than a defensible observation of the exterior form of regulations and customs, is not at all proof of the dispensable nature of a new life, awakened and sustained by the Spirit of God, an inward life as well as an outward expression, which is prescribed by the word of God. This is the case in passages of holy Scripture like these: "The kingdom of God is not food and drink, but righteousness and peace and joy in the Holy Spirit," (Rom 14:17); "In Christ Jesus there is neither circumcision nor uncircumcision, but a new creation," (Gal 6:15); "I no longer live, but Christ lives in me; and the life I now live in the flesh, I live in the belief in the Son of God, who has loved me and given himself for me," (Gal 2:20).—These and several similar passages are riddles for all too many people who bear the name "Christian." Even so the name Christian entails precisely that union with Christ, the inward transformation, and the life of holiness, about which these and similar passages speak.

However, it follows that if anyone and everyone, only because he is baptized, wants to be called a Christian, even though he, practically speaking, is lacking everything that the name entails, the result is the falsehood that the majority of Christians (more correctly: "christened," as one brilliant teacher expresses it) are not at all Christians. This they demonstrate precisely whenever they regard it as an exception and point out with mockery anytime someone else becomes eager to keep and carry out in work and deed what the name "Christian" entails. Here opinions become divided, but the Scripture cannot be annulled (Jn 10:35); it remains written in the old word, and in this case it matters more to obey God than humans. These people say one thing, but the Bible says another about the nature, direction and necessity of this new, spiritual life, which distinguishes a true Christian. And we are not among them, who want to nullify the command of God with human regulations.

This spiritual life is common to all true Christians. And from this we understand how it can be that the forms are so diverse, yet the Spirit is one, that perspectives are in abundance, yet love is in common and everything is united (see 1 Cor 12 and Eph 4). This life only exists where one knows and confesses Christ and him crucified, for this is Christ in us, the hope of glory, a life concealed with Christ in God. This life cannot exist in some form of religion, some institution of doctrine, where the doctrine of reconciliation and of justification by faith alone are not preached, but everywhere that the main teachings of the gospel exist, as, for example, the fall of humanity into sin, the ransom of Christ [tillfyllestgörelse], the work of the Spirit in the soul and similar core teachings, here too this spiritual life can spring up. However, we should not be indifferent about the purity of doctrine and its correspondence to the gospel of Christ. For to the extent that the concepts of spiritual things are vague, dark or diverge from the eternal truth of the word, then the spiritual life which depends on this doctrine will also become weak, sickly, unproductive, full of anxiety, both in the inward experience and the outward evidence.

Yet everywhere, where there is any life, often under the name pietism, there is a community. For sick children are children too and need the most tender care, so that the smoldering wick will not be quenched, the bruised reed not be broken. We openly confess our inner desire to seek to pull together all those who are graced with spiritual life, wherever they are, and through those means with which it would have pleased Christ to draw them to himself. If he has received them, then they are of course good enough to be received by us, even though we will probably still harbor one misgiving or another concerning their opinions on doctrines of lesser importance. We love to understand pietism as something, which belongs to the whole world, and not just part of it, as something common and accessible for all confessions, which hold themselves to Christ the head. And this opinion makes our own confession all the more dear to us. For we should certainly fear and tremble, if devotion for this same confession involved some necessity to be prejudiced against all other confessions, or even to suspect their capability to serve as a means to draw their adherents into the one sheep fold. We unite ourselves with the one who said: "I consider the different church confessions which rest on the foundation of the gospel as a circle of sisters, all more or less educated, beautiful, and worthy of love. I love them all, but I marry but one; to that one I will be faithful. But should I therefore decrease my affection for the rest? Certainly not. For precisely *the union with the one sister makes me also related to the rest*, and as a consequence, I stand in a nearer and dearer relationship to all of them."

It would not be probable to expect that all Christians, despite being enlightened by the same Spirit, should come to complete agreement on all spiritual matters here on earth, where we understand and prophesy in part. But when now, on the one hand, it is both natural and correct that each and every one loves and respects that church confession, that book, and even that teacher who has been the means to carry him from the darkness to the light, from death to life, so too, on the other hand, no earthly person or thing should be called "master," for our master is *one*, Christ (Mt 23:8). Therefore, if instead of saying like the one Corinthian: I hold myself to Paul, the second: I hold to Cephas, the third: I to Apollos, if we all seek to come closer to Christ, we will be raised above the earthly opinions that will lead to discord and instead truly thrive in the clean air of Christ's undivided authority. If all Christians seek to come closer to their center point—Christ—the inevitable result will be that they will also come closer to one another in mutual love, which is the true sign whereby to recognize a disciple (Jn 13:35). The present age demands the gathering of divided forces. The enemy of our soul wants in every way to divide the righteous and keep them apart from one another as strangers. May we not be ignorant of Satan's plot, but instead seek to unite everything in a blessed and healthy community, everything that is the work of the same Spirit of God, and which merits the name of pietism. Here will we find our mutual support in the bad times and warm prayers of intercession for believers everywhere.

We say with Paul: "Grace be to all, who have an undying love for our Lord Jesus Christ." We believe that in these brief words of greeting can be found that distinguishing trait, which includes and defines all true pietism. These words are not vague and irresolute, but as a product of divine wisdom stand up to the most thorough scrutiny. This greeting does not refer to any heretic, for only the rejection of the essential founding principles of the gospel merits the name heresy, and may no one carelessly play with such a terrible name or thoughtlessly condemn someone as a heretic. For a true heretic is reprehensible and under judgment. But the apostle includes in this greeting everyone, who loves Jesus as *Lord* (whereby those people are excluded who bear the name Christian, yet deny the divinity of Christ), all who love *Jesus*, the Savior (excluding thereby them, who reject the doctrine of reconciliation or do not, through faith, extend this reconciliation to the salvation of their soul), and all who love *Christ* as a prophet, priest, and king, authorized and sent by God (by this, are excluded all who deny his teachings and do not turn to his office as high priest, as well as those who, with words and deeds, explain that "we do not want this person to rule over us.") This greeting excludes all hypocrites or falsely spiritual people, for the word "love" includes a love not just professed with the mouth, but with the whole heart. Likewise are excluded all formalists or Christians only on the outside, who like Pharisees observe the outer regulations with great detail, without being driven to them by the love of Christ. Neither is there any room for the kind of people who build their hope on the fact that they were born in a Christian country, are baptized into an evangelical church and have properly confessed Christ at the communion table. All of this is well and good and should not be neglected by any Christian, but it is left out of the picture here by the apostle, and only a right-minded love for our Lord Jesus Christ is named as a distinguishing trait of those who have received grace. Finally those people are also excluded, who, despite the fact that they praise Jesus and grace and faith with their mouths, yet deny him with deeds. For it is no more possible for a right-minded love for Christ to exist without a glad and willing obedience for his will, than for a fire to exist without producing warmth.

Consider this, now: "in Christ there is neither circumcision nor uncircumcision," neither Jew nor Greek, neither a follower of Paul nor Cephas, but "a new creation," to love Christ with a right mindset, as our one and only center point and master. "And all who walk in this rule, over them be peace and mercy," (Gal 6:16). Indeed, grace be to all, who have an undying love for our Lord Jesus Christ! Amen. (Eph 6:24).

A PIETIST

By George Scott and C.O. Rosenius, 1842

("En pietist")

The limited space of this journal, as well as our desire to not cut short its essays, denies us the ability to develop our perspective to the extent that the matter deserves, on who is entitled to the name above in its proper sense, and who has been given this name undeservedly according to the world's incorrect understanding of it. As a result, our readers should not expect an exhaustive portrait of a pietist, but instead several scattered impressions and characteristic features, that, taken together, will illustrate the subjects that we hope to present here in more detail in the future.

Now if you first ask what kind of citizen a pietist is, the answer will be: *he does not belong to any country on earth.* This is in two respects. In one respect, namely, that he exists in all countries where the gospel is known and preached; and also in the respect that he is actually a guest and a stranger on earth and is seeking a fatherland, the heavenly one. Neither does he belong to any specific church denomination, but instead constitutes one of those limbs that can be found in all Christian churches which belong to the one, holy, universal church—of those who *"have come to Mount Zion, to the heavenly Jerusalem, the city of the living God, and to innumerable angels and to the assembly of the firstborn, whose names are enrolled in heaven, and to God, the judge of all, and to the spirits of the righteous made perfect, and to the mediator of the Covenant, Jesus, and to the sprinkled blood that speaks a better word than the blood of Abel."* (Heb 12:22–24) Of this we find, that all pietists in the world are each other's countrymen, the subjects of the same King, children of the same Father, though they wander in vastly separate parts of the globe, are raised under different circumstances and speak different languages. They are citizens with the holy ones and the servants of

God. And if they too, like the refugees from Madagascar and their Khoisian brethren, must make use of their Bibles in order to speak to one another; or in lacking this means, like the Scottish soldier and the Danish farmer, who by simply pointing to the word Jesus in the Postilla and then pointing to their hearts and toward heaven can communicate themselves to one another, they can so easily understand that they are fellow subjects in the same kingdom of grace, and that the unity of the Spirit forges together their diversity of external circumstances and ignites a mutual love between them.

But if now you ask the second question, *who* or *what* is a pietist, then consider this: in every place where those who confess Christ have united themselves on this one foundation and formed a visible congregation, there you will find (apart from the completely ungodly crowd, who do not even have any semblance of godliness) both *formalists*, who only enjoy the name, the semblance, the shell, and *pietists,* those who seek and own the thing itself, the reality, the kernel. These are the very living creation of God's word, as the apostle says, *"born anew, not of perishable seed, but of imperishable, through the living and enduring word of God"* (1 Pet 1:23). A pietist is the one, who not only has the name, the semblance, and the shell of godliness, but the very thing itself, the reality, the kernel, and is a living product of God's word. He desires to say that this word has become an exercise for him, and has remade his heart and life, such that he, in his heart, experiences what the word says and then practices this in work and deed. Thus he is the one who not only reads, hears, and understands what *repentance* means, but also in his heart experiences what this means. Through the word he has received the kind of heart that reveres the commandments of God, he knows his sins with remorse and fear, and he has genuinely undergone the process of laying aside these sins. In this work of repentance he has learned, though ashamed, helpless, and inconsolable as he is, to seek the grace and help of the Savior. He not only hears, reads, and understands what is meant by the reconciliation in the blood of Jesus, and about *faith* and grace, but he is also truly seeking this or even already owns this in part. He has truly begun to take refuge in the Savior and dedicate his life to serving him. And it is actually here that true *pietas* (godliness) appears, when a human being walks away from the brink of eternal ruin, from the distress of sin and the pangs of conscience, and arrives at the peace of faith and the certainty that he can claim Christ and all of his benefits. At this point the heart melts, it is transformed so that it now *truly* begins to love that which previously was more of an embarrassment to it—God and his message—and truly hates and flees that which previously was its life and desire. Finally, the pietist is the one who not only reads, hears, and understands *sanctification,* but also owns this in daily experience and evidence. A pietist does not only complain about sin, but also truly hates it, and does not only feel the suffering caused by it, but even has sincerely attempted to part from it. A pietist not only gives assent to and speaks about Christian deeds and duties, but also begins to truly practice them. And look, although this work of grace is truly being practiced, there are still flaws that remain, which demand forgiveness. He is yet a sinner, even though he is pardoned and repentant. Daily he washes his clothes and makes them white in the blood of the Lamb, daily he prays "Our Father, forgive us our debts," while he does not live as he did before, free and content in sin. This John calls *"doing what is sinful;" "the one who commits sin is of the devil;" "those who have been born of God, do not sin."* (1 Jn 3:8–9)

All of what we have said so far is the inward, godly strength, the truth and reality, that makes a genuine pietist. Although it is precisely this inward transformation of the heart that cannot be understood by those who have not themselves been born anew, nor can they believe it to be true. If then you ask a third question, what are his distinguishing characteristics, then it is not this or that church structure or doctrine, but *"mutual love,"* (Jn 13:35); and the fruit of this bears witness to the fact that he has gone over from death to life (1 Jn 3:14). Certainly pietists in all church contexts must adopt, hold fast to, and manifest the foundational truths of the gospel in both heart and life. For without Jesus *for us* and Jesus *in us* it is impossible to be godly in the meaning of the gospel. But just as, for example, the various books of the Bible are rather different in their use of language, presentation and so on, the spirit and the purpose are still similar in them all, so too the physical, outward clothing among pietists can be quite different, yet *"the Spirit is one"* and indivisible. Of this it follows that true pietists will not gladly enter into controversies with *one another.* They will remind themselves of the charge: "Welcome the one who is weak in faith, without passing judgment;" "for God has welcomed him" (Rom 14:1, 3). If God has taken such people, who are weak, sick, and imperfect into the one, true sheepfold, then the sheep of the flock should not be allowed to bite and gnash at one another. A pietist will strive and fight bravely—and ought to fight—against all true spiritual enemies, both to himself and to the church. He ought to strike down all the fortifications and bulwarks of thought, which set themselves up as a hindrance to the knowledge of God. But even though there is much at stake in the fight, he will not waste time or wear out his weapons by fighting with brothers in faith. He might observe them all as one great army, like the one that King Gustaf II Adolf so triumphantly commanded against the popish retinue in Germany. He will observe how this army is composed of a host of distinct, yet united regiments, with various weapons, various methods of war. Each regiment has its commander, its own uniform, own internal training, but all are united under their common royal banner, obeying the highest orders and rushing out with collective strength to meet the common enemy. The commander knows how to employ the regiment's various weapons and methods of war to counter the diverse assaults of the enemy. But what should the observer think, if he were to see internal division among the regiments, because one soldier had a red belt, the other a yellow one, and the third one white—internal division at precisely that moment when the united strength was so desperately needed to respond to the zealous strategies of the enemy? What else could he conclude than that these soldiers cared more and had more zeal for their own particularities than for the honor of their king and the success of his cause? What else than that the enemy would, without great difficulty, soon be able to conquer this army? The applications [of the analogy] are clear. This is also demonstrated in the words of one teacher to a colleague in another confession: "You, like we ourselves, love the faith of our childhood too much to abandon it; but for that very reason we love one another, while we love Jesus foremost."

God's word demonstrates everywhere, especially in Romans chapters 3–8, that the foundation and source for the life of grace is the same for all, and that their experiences are as similar as they are because they proceed from the same source. But since our *humanity* is also a part of this equation, how much diversity there can be, even within this unity! As one needs a real body and soul in order to be human, and all humans are alike in this regard, it is also true that in order to be a "new human," one needs the same Christ, the same Spirit of God and God's book, living and at work in the heart and in life. Though all people have physical forms and facial features that are similar enough to let us know that we all are human, nevertheless in all the population of the world there are no two faces that are so similar that no difference can be detected (this is not to mention all the endless diversity in lesser visible characteristics of the soul within the family of humanity). This is also the case with the children of God's Spirit, whose dispositions, abilities, and ways of being are all more or less different. The one who is born again will still demonstrate the same peculiarities that characterized him before, although they will have found a new direction, become accentuated or diminished. The same will be true of the person who formerly was diligent in being a sinner, but now has become diligent in serving the Lord. The weak and easily-swayed person will retain these characteristics, as will the gloomy person, the worrier, the bold person, and the combative person—they will not lose all of these characteristics. Nevertheless, the all-transforming grace of God will be at work in these people, cultivating them in the life of the spirit.

There are also certain things that are required for the *maintenance* and *cultivation* of the spiritual life: nourishment and activity, pleasure and discipline. Pietists have certain *wells of salvation* from which they joyfully draw the water of life (Isa 12:3). And around these wells a pietist can be seen not only making use of the well and thanking God for it, but also it will be evident that he has a spiritual thirst that is satisfied here, without which the wells and the journey to these wells would serve no good. Such is the Bible, for example, which previously was to him unfathomable, dry, tasteless, but now has become a meaningful, precious, holy book of God that is becoming worn with use. He can now approach the throne of grace with courage, strengthened by the blood of reconciliation which hides him from the sight of God and the books of the law, for God does not look past this blood. With gratitude he repeats the words of Jesus in Mt 6:6. The public worship service will always present him with rich opportunities for constructive reflection, for celebration and communal joy, and to enlightenment, warning and assurance. At the communion table—the table that is set for all the children of the house—he will be fed with good things; for those who wait upon the Lord will receive new strength. One can expect that pietists will begin and end their day with an acknowledgement of the Lord, calling upon his grace, peace and blessing in their devotionals at home, which are sincere and rich in blessing.

A pietist will prefer to choose for his companions those who are of like mind, the born-again and the spiritual, and though truly "confiding" only in these people, he will be "friendly" and sincere toward all. He, like everyone else, will feel the need for companionship, and will choose, as far as it is possible, relationships that will not be disturbed by the changes of time. He will seek to have friends and confidants for eternity. His social pursuits will be such that they befit him; and if they diverge from the social pursuits of the world, there will be no indication that these new pursuits are lacking in bringing him joy. For example, when the caterpillar transforms into the butterfly, one does not marvel or become annoyed over the fact that it no longer crawls in the dust or feeds on the crude cabbage leaf, but instead takes to flight up into space and enjoys the nobler nectar of the flowers. And when the pietist finds greater joy in the pages of the Bible than he ever found in a card game, more joy in the singing of spiritual songs than in carousing and drink, more joy in common prayer before the Lord than in the dizziness of the dance, do not think that he has been deceived or that what has taken place is something to be ashamed of; instead, see this as a transformation, not altogether unlike that of the caterpillar to the butterfly.

A pietist will feel the challenge, as long as there is time, to *do good to all* (Gal 6:10). As a human being, he will take part in the distresses of his neighbor. But he will not be content to merely help this person in terms of bodily and temporal needs; he also, as a Christian, will be thinking about the soul and eternity. When he remembers how he himself was recently awakened and rescued from a dangerous sleep in a house that has caught on fire, and then sees how other people are still sleeping in this same slumber, without a care for their eternal well-being, then he cannot help but attempt to wake them. This he can do by bringing them something from God's word, through his actions as well as speech. It is for this reason that he will, with passion and joy, contribute to the circulation of Bibles and Christian newspapers to spread awakening among the poor and neglectful. His duty to the Savior and to the "least of these brothers" in the heathen world, he will want to investigate and bring to completion. The commandment to "go out" (Mk 16: 15) will resound for him as though it were a command given directly to him; for he knows that this cause must be the cause of *each Christian* in order for it to become that of Christendom as a whole. For if he were to remain home, peacefully enjoying the rich bounty of God's house, then he would be neglecting his duty and passion, to use those means that are at his disposal to "seek the kingdom of God and increase it as much as he can." When he becomes aware of the harm that the use of liquor has brought upon his neighbors, he will be eager to join those who investigate the situation and attempt to rescue these people, leading them away from this practice. He regards the customs surrounding drunkenness as the stone which lay across the portal to the grave of the dead Lazarus, a hindrance which can be rolled away by human hands, and whose rolling away has been commanded them by Christ, so that he might be able to call those who are dead back to life.

We have already said that a pietist possesses a heart that has been *transformed* by grace, in such a way that he truly delights and takes joy in the things that God loves. From this follows that he can earnestly say with John: *"God's commandments are not heavy,"* that he considers them not only as duties that he *must* complete, but instead even primarily as privileges that he loves. Here lies the foundation for the remarkable difference between his general outlook on life, and that of a Christian in name only. The latter considers the Lord's commandments to be quite simply a heavy slavery, and tries to avoid and rationalize away the binding nature of these commandments. Whereas the former finds that when these commandments are put in practice, they are both to his advantage and bring a heartfelt passion, exemplified in keeping the Lord's day, in moments of devotion and the reading of God's word, and in Christian fellowship and activity, along with many other praiseworthy pursuits. But this spiritual disposition does not forbid him at all from attending to his earthly duties, for it is exactly in these duties that he has the opportunity to praise the Lord before the world. A true pietist shall always seek to attend to his worldly duties even better than ungodly people; though he, as a stranger here, cannot bind his heart to the world, but rather longs to part from it. As the Jews during the Babylonian captivity, though they longed to return home to the holy land, received the command to pray for this foreign city and engage in their activities for the betterment of this city (Jer 29:7), so these strangers should also advance the Lord's glory and their neighbor's good, each and every one as they are called here on earth. As a citizen also, the pietist will gain his sense of direction chiefly from the word of the Bible, where he will learn to "accept the authority of governors for the Lord's sake" (1 Pet 2:13); "for the authority, which is in place is instituted by God" (Rom 13:1); and he will obey the counsel of the wise man: "My son, fear the Lord and the king! Do not make common cause with rabble-rousers!" (Prov 24:21)

Now for a few words about the spiritual nourishment, activity and pursuits of the pious. Whatever is not accomplished to the cultivation of the life of grace by the means above, the Lord will accomplish through fatherly discipline, which should also be both considered as a means of grace, as well as proof of being his child. As the word of Scripture states: "If you have not experienced that discipline, which all (of God's children) receive, then you are illegitimate and not sons, *because the Lord disciplines those whom he loves*," and so on (Heb 12:6, 8). The switch will be used as it is needed, as in the case of Tobiah, Job, David, and Paul, as a thorn in the flesh, an angel of the devil, a slap in the face, illness, poverty, slander, despair, an Absalom, a child of woe, a Judas, a Pilate. It is in this furnace that faith is refined, prayer is ignited, and humility, hope, and patience are learned, whenever this cannot happen by the other proper means of grace. But O, how much happier you will be to have this bread, this discipline, and this inheritance in the Father's house, than to remain outside and have no share in it!

Our readers are probably concluding that: "this portrait of a pietist is nothing other than that of a true Christian." Well, yes, by 'pietist' and 'true Christian' we mean one and the same thing. As we have shown, the contents of the names are the same; but the world in general understands them as being completely distinct. If you investigate how things really are regarding what the world calls pietism, then you will discover that what has taken place is that the ancient tenets of Christianity have been applied to the circumstances of daily life in a genuine fear of the Lord. Open your eyes and see the bizarre hypocrisy [of the critics]: "Of course the truths of Christianity are to be preserved in the Bible, organized in the symbolical books, collected in Christian journals, employed in sermons, and celebrated as treasures of the nation and the church above all others; but—woe to the one who insists that these truths should actually come alive in the individual's heart, and be put to work in the individual's life!" His striving will be labeled "fanatical," and the one who seeks to live in accordance to the Bible, must be content to no longer be called a "Christian," but instead—"pietist."

But we, claiming the beautiful words found in one of our church's books, continually wish to pray: "Merciful and mighty God, remove all of the snares of unbelief and misconceptions, and grant that a true Christianity might become more and more present and active among us." Amen.

Carl Olof Rosenius

2

Knowing God as Father

LEARNING FROM WHAT WE SEE, TO BELIEVE WHAT WE CANNOT SEE

C.O. Rosenius, 1851

("Skapelsen och människan")

Luther once remarked that "Before a human being has truly learned to understand the first word in the Bible: 'In the beginning, God created the heavens and the earth,' she will yet remain dead; and even if she lived for a thousand years, this alone would not amount to her having become fully educated." This observation by Luther is something remarkable—in particular, that before one has learned to properly understand these words concerning *the creation*, one will remain "dead." [. . .] Paul says that even the heathens have learned to know God from creation, although they have not received the word about this creation. He says that "God's invisible characteristics, both his eternal power and his divinity, can be observed since the creation of the world, as they are understood from his works, such that they are without excuse" (Rom 1:20). How much more, then, does this apply to us, who do have God's word about this creation! The Bible's account of creation casts much more light and assurance than these visible things could ever do. Augustine has also discerned the most beautiful and secure foundations of assurance by observing God's first creations. Such is our task now, as we intend to spend a moment in paradise and, in that first beautiful morning

45

light of the dawn of time, observe our heavenly Father's love, wisdom, and power.

And the focus of our search through paradise shall be these questions: What is God's purpose for us? Where has humankind come from? *What is she*, and *to what* has she been created since the beginning of time? [. . .] When one thinks about how God created and adorned the world and filled it with such abundant riches and beauty, and that his main objective was *humankind*, her well-being and delight, and her awakening to be able to see, know and honor God—that the Lord created all of the riches of nature and the vast multitude of living creatures for humankind—and that when everything was finished, he turned to these two children of his, and said "Rule over all of this." [. . .] When one considers these things, it is appropriate to reflect upon this beautiful, lavish house, which the Lord has built for his children, humankind. From this house and its contents, one can evaluate the builder of the house, as well as the elevated rank and inheritance of the people for whom it was built. [. . .]

On the fourth day, God created the sun, moon and stars, set them in their regular courses and thus ordered the progression of time on earth, the days, months and years (Gen 1:14–19). Now the great light in the heavens was lit, the sun, which for so many centuries has sent light and warmth to our globe and even today is just as marvelous to our eyes. Then our earth was full of grass and flowers and herbs and trees—everything to the well being and sustenance of her coming master, humankind. Here we do not need to *believe*, since we can of course see all of this with our eyes today. But we shall see even more.

Amidst all of this beauty, which now blossomed and glistened joyfully on this newly-created earth, there was as of yet not one single created being, who could enjoy and take delight in all of this. This was still only a kingdom of plants. Had it remained so, then the earth with all of its riches and adornment, this paradise with its blossoming fields, its trees bounteous in fruit and its beautiful rivers, would have continued to be an empty and desolate stage, where the spirit of *life* was lacking, where no audience had yet taken its place. Our dear God did not wish to leave such a void in his creation. Besides, it was for humankind that he had built and adorned this house, and humankind was to be in his image. [. . .] Then God thought one more creative thought—a thought about *life*, about a whole world of life and movement, of innumerable living creatures—and with such power and wisdom that we rightfully should be awe-struck. At once, he produced the countless, diverse variety of living species, all with their particular forms, external and inner organs and instincts. [. . .] "And God said: *Let us make humankind.*" As marvelous and as great as both the animals and the plant life in this newly-created world had proven to be, there was as of yet no single creature with the capacity to know and love its Creator. [. . .] The heir to the house was still absent. A marvelous temple had clearly been created here, radiant in beauty and adornment, but it was still lacking a priest, who would lead the services and light the incense for this temple's great Lord and God. [. . .]

The primary thing that is remarkable in this account is that the Lord says "*Let us—let us make humankind.*" There is an indication here that *a council is being held*; "*Let us* make humankind." The Lord does not say "I want to make humankind," or "Let the earth produce humankind," but instead "*Let us make humankind.*" All of the rest of the diverse host of creatures were created without such a council being held, but merely with an omnipotent command. But when God wanted to create humankind, then a council was called. With whom was the Lord holding council? Undoubtedly, all three of the persons of the Godhead were present in this council. [. . .] Then when God had looked into eternity and foreseen the fall of humankind and all of the ruin and misery that would follow as a consequence, then he did not wish to release this important creature from his creator-hand, without first holding council about this, and not until the Son, the eternal word, had taken upon himself the salvation of humankind. But as soon as the Son said "I want to save the race of humankind," the Father said "Then I want to create them. Let us make humankind." This counsel of salvation [*frälsningsråd*] had certainly already been decided by God. For the apostle Paul says, that "God had chosen us in Christ before the foundation of the world" (Eph 1:4). And Peter says that Christ, God in the flesh, revealed for the salvation of humankind, "was chosen before the foundation of the world" (1 Pet 1:20). [. . .] Immediately after the Fall, the Father sought out our first parents in their terror and shame and announced to them this foreordained salvation, which would come about through the "woman's offspring." He would later reveal himself often to the patriarchs and renew this promise. The Holy Spirit would speak so clearly through the prophets about the coming "Deliverer," "the shoot from the stump of Jesse," the "great Prophet," "the Lord's Anointed," as being "pierced for our transgressions and stricken for our iniquities," such that an apostle in the New Testament could not have spoken more clearly on these matters. But in particular, the "only begotten Son, who is in the care of the Father, has revealed these things" (Jn 1:18), which is why he is called the "faithful and true witness, the beginning of God's creation" (Rev 3:14). [. . .] Without him, God would have no point of union with humankind. And this foundation has been laid so deeply that it can never be removed. Let us praise God's everlasting counsel of love [*kärleksråd*] for all eternity! [. . .] For those inexperienced, happy-go-lucky people, who do not suffer from any distresses, and also for vibrant and believing Christians, for whom this word is everything, this reflection is not necessary. But whenever a Christian comes into darkness and crises of temptation [*anfäktning*], such that he doubts all of God's word, then the Lord will refer him to the work of creation, which he does not need to believe, but can see with his eyes. For example, when faced with concerns for sustenance, the Lord will say "Look to the birds of the sky—your heavenly Father feeds them; are you not worth much more than they?" [. . .] Perhaps it seems to you that you are abandoned by God; perhaps there is some specific situation, in which you feel utterly helpless, and neither you nor anyone else in the whole world seem to be able to do anything about it; and perhaps you have called out to God, until you are hoarse and exhausted, yet everything appears in vain. [. . .] Is it possible that things really are as they seem? Do you not understand that hidden in the very midst of all this, might be your mysterious, yet faithful God? As long as you do not fight against his well-ordered plans [. . .], it is altogether impossible that God would not give you everything that is best and to your benefit. [. . .] Ponder deeply this question of Christ: "Are you not worth much more than they?" The Savior explains that: "You are worth more than many sparrows!" Think about that! The Lord himself has said that this is so. Indeed, Christ must have understood our worth, he who so dearly bought us. [. . .] Now besides, we are at every moment surrounded by an infinite number of God's good works. So we ought to be able to learn from what we see, to even believe that which we cannot see.

"ADAM, WHERE ARE YOU?"

C.O. Rosenius, 1851

(*"Syndafallet och dess följder"*)

God's love is so entirely free, undeserved and independent of the sinner, for it is based on someone else's service and intercession, the "woman's offspring," the "Lord's man," the "Lamb of God, who bears the sins of the world." The one who does not believe in him, who does not pause before the voice of the Lord and allow himself to be reconciled to God, but instead remains off at a distance, he will remain at a distance for all time. But the one who believes in him, who hears God's voice, allows himself to face punishment for sin and take assurance in the "woman's offspring," he "shall not perish, but have eternal life," even though he knew every evil in his heart, as we see here with Adam, indeed, even as all of the serpent's venom seethed within him.

And the Lord God called to the man and said to him: "Where are you?"

God *called* to Adam. He did not leave him in his wrath, but sought him out and called him to himself. Such is the mind of God. But about this, we have spoken much already.

God enters into the garden, in the cool of the day, and calls out for Adam: "*Where are you?* Why are you hiding? What has happened now? You used to come out to meet me with joy—now you are hiding! For what reason?" This is how the Lord speaks with him, in order to awaken him to confession. That the Lord's question is designed for this purpose, we can see from Adam's answer, which in response to the question, "*Where are you?,*" begins to explain *why* he has hidden himself (Gen 3:10). This now is the first example on earth of God *calling* to a sinner; this is the first time that a sinner is awakened to repentance. The Lord begins by bringing him to contrition. For in these words, "*Where are you?,*" there lies, as Luther says, the *voice of the law to our conscience*, the purpose and object of the law, which is to convince the sinner of his fallen and wretched state. For while nothing created is invisible to the Lord, but instead everything is laid bare and revealed to his eyes (Heb 4:13), all the same the Lord calls out, "Adam, where are you?" With this he means to say: "Now I am coming to question you. Come forth into my presence and answer me; what now has become of you? Where have you gone? Where is the marvelous image of God, to whom I gave dominion over the earth? Where is he now, lying hidden behind the trees? And do you imagine that I cannot see you? You are keeping yourself hidden from my face. Where do you think you are going?"—Such is the nature of the Lord's questioning. Therefore, Adam must immediately come forth and begin to explain himself.

Consider this—this calling voice, this shout, "Where are you?," is something each and every sinner must perceive from God. This first example applies to every age in history, and for all the children of Adam. First, this is a *fatherly shout* to the believers, when they have gone astray. Already as small children we often perceive this, that when we have sinned, a voice within us says, "what have you done?!"—provided that the good voice of the Spirit is not drowned out, and the ears deafened to the commotion of vanity and desire. But in particular, there is something which all believing Christians feel daily—this unceasing call, "Where are you?"—when they, for example, have done something rash, sinned or gone astray, immediately there is the anxious cry, "Where are you? What have you done?"—Or when they have landed among the children of vanity, when they, out of weakness, fear of others, or the desire to please other people, have participated in vain speech and in some way, through words or deeds, denied their Lord, they, like Peter, immediately fall under the searching gaze of the Savior, who speaks within them, "Where are you? O, what have you done?" This sting is the Friend's way of exhorting us to repentance—an experience, which is worth more than all the world's gold! Woe, woe to the Christian who no longer perceives these insights, these cries from within!

Second, this is the cry of awakening to those who are spiritually dead, who live in the world without God. In the midst of the garden of worldly delights, vanity, and sin, there will often come a cry from within their inner being, "Where are you? It is not well with you, you are in need of repentance, of conversion." Once they have been converted to the Lord, they confess that they had perceived this cry for a long time and were sought out by the Lord, and also that this had often interrupted their enjoyment of sin. In particular, "in the cool of the day," when enjoyment has passed and they enter into solitude or the night's rest, then there comes the cry from within, "Where are you?" Or when they hear the word, in a sermon or Scripture, and they come to the communion table before the face of God, there comes this accusation concerning their sins, or their unfulfilled repentance, or of the necessity of their conversion, "Where are you? Time is flying, when will you repent?" And the one, who does not completely convert and return to God, all the same must understand that someday, whether he wants to or not, he will have to come before the presence of God. Indeed, someday—sooner or later, now or in eternity—every human being will hear this cry, which they will feel in the marrow of their bones, "Where are you?—What have you done?" For it is impossible that any sinner will be able to escape the almighty, holy God. [. . .]

As we have just said, this applies to every age in history, and for all the children of Adam. Each and every person must come before the Lord to give an accounting of his sins, now or in eternity. The matter is like this: we are all sinners—in this there is no distinction; if we were judged on this account, then no one would be saved. The difference is only this, that some try to keep at a distance from God—try to constantly escape him—and do not come while the time of grace is at hand, in order to seek and receive grace. Christ says: "This is the verdict" (the reason for judgment), "that the light has come into the world, but human beings loved the darkness more than the light, for their deeds were wicked" (Jn 3:19). If we return to the light, and reckon our sins with God, then all will be well, even if we were the most terrible sinner. As the Lord says—and, O, that we could take these words to heart—"Come and let us reason together; Though your sins were blood red, they shall yet be white as snow; and though they were crimson, so shall they be like wool" (Isa 1:18). [. . .]

Here we see in Adam, how all human beings are and behave when they have sinned and perceive the voice of the law calling to their conscience, but before any bit of the gospel or faith has taken root in them and transformed their hearts. If God had immediately called out: "Adam, you have been forgiven. I know how you have sinned, but I have forgiven this." Then Adam would have, with deepest humility and regret, confessed and cursed his sin and said: "I have sinned, I have sinned! Merciful Father, forgive me!" But as long as there was no hope for forgiveness in him, but instead only fear and trembling before God's judgment, then his heart would have remained closed, hard and bitter toward God. "The law cannot bring to life," it does not make the human being good and pious, but instead only increases sin in the heart; "the law only brings God's wrath." [. . .]

But the most destructive evil that the serpent planted in our nature, was the misconception "that we could be our own savior and helper." The word, "You shall be like God or gods," took deep root, left deep marks in our nature, namely all manner of pride, and in particular this most damaging misconception, "that we ourselves have the power to resist what is evil and to do what is good." "Free will" in this meaning, is the dream from which all [false] confidence and all despair originate. If the awakened soul could only be convinced that she is capable of nothing, that free will is lost, that she is sold under sin, then she would soon come to have assurance in Christ, abandon her project of self-salvation and "cast herself as though dead at the feet of Jesus," resting on his sheer grace. [. . .] No, free will is a dream from the days of paradise; it has not existed in the human being, ever since Adam abused it. Since this time, the human being has been like a beggar of grace, who has been forced to beg from God every crumb of strength; and because she must beg, she is not able to take this before it is given. If the Lord were to let go of us, then we would hurl into the abyss. This is the true condition of humankind after Adam's fall.

KNOWING GOD AS OUR TRUE FATHER

P. P. Waldenström, 1891

(Guds eviga frälsningsråd)

O, that we could one day truly learn to know God! In reality there is no one, in whom we have so little confidence as God. We are plenty capable of believing in human beings, plenty capable of believing in angels, plenty capable of believing in Christ, but when it comes to God—of him, one expects only judgment, death, and damnation. "For the sake of the Virgin Mary, he will show us grace," the Catholic thinks, "but if we didn't have her help, then we would not fare well with God." "For the sake of Christ," others think, "God will be able to show us grace, but were it not for Christ being our protection and our shield, then we would not fare well with God." That God for his own sake is merciful, graceful, and full of goodness, as well as forgives wickedness, rebellion, and sin (Ex 34:7)—who believes that? No, we more or less fear and tremble before God, as though before something dreadful. If a terrible storm breaks out with rain and gale and thunder and so on, then we have the expression: "This is *the Lord's* weather [*ett Herrens väder*]." *The Lord's* weather is synonymous with *terrible* weather. Just think, what an expression! [. . .] Where does this come from? Answer: Only from that heathendom, which is rooted in our nature, and that heathendom, which has been preached into us since our childhood. O, how far we are from being able to know God as our true Father.

Therefore, let us study—diligently study and practice this truth—that no creature can look upon us with eyes as tenderly as God can; no father can search for his wayward son more mercifully than God searches for sinners; no mother can feel greater joy when she sees her wayward son return back home, than God feels when he sees a sinner return to him again. There does not exist a father's or mother's heart that is more willing to blot out, forgive, or forget a lost son's or daughter's sin, as God's heart is willing to forgive the sins of everyone, who, like the prodigal son, will turn around and come home again. A prodigal son is the sorrow of his father and mother, a source of many tears, many sighs, and much anguish, a cause of many anxious conversations and deliberations, many sleepless nights. But what is it that prompts all this? *It is a sorrowing love*—a mere spark of that fire, which dwells in the heart of God. If the son will return again, *then love could not be greater, and sorrow shall be turned into gladness.* And this is how God, too, rejoices when he sees sinners off in the distance making their way home.

THE LORD IS GOOD AND RIGHTEOUS

P. P. Waldenström, 1875

(Herren är from)

If we want to truly see, how true it is that the Lord is the God of our salvation, then we should compare his words with his deeds. Who is it who has so loved the world that he gave his only begotten Son? It is the God of your salvation. Who was it, who in the fullness of time cast your sins on the only Son, as well as allowed him to taste death for you, in order that, through his blood, you would have an open spring to cleanse you from all your sin? It was the God of your salvation. Who is it, who during your time of disbelief over the years has had patience with you, who despite your ungodliness waited for you to change your mind, indeed even seduced you in order to capture you back to life? It is the God of your salvation. Who was that man, who felt his fatherly heart overwhelmed by rejoicing, when you in that foreign country decided to go home and confess your sins? Who was it, who then raced toward you, fell upon your neck and kissed you and did not deal with you according to your sins but instead forgave you your misdeeds and clothed you in new garments? It was the God of your salvation. Who is it who ever since has had patience with you, provided you with clothing, sustenance, house and home, wife, child, health and all? Who is it, who daily has comforted you in distress, chastised you when you needed it? Who bore you on faithful father's arms, preserved you in all your ways, so that you would yet live despite all your unbelief, all your negligence and all your sins? It is the God of your salvation. Who is it, who promised to bear you into your old age and until you have turned grey, indeed, through death and into the new Jerusalem? It is the God of your salvation. And the one, who in everything plans to keep his word—it is the God of your salvation. [. . .]

This verse to which we now turn (Ps 25:8) is one of those verses that is among the most beautiful and full of assurance in all of Scripture. For it is with words like this that the Lord frequently helps "wretched people." God, grant us the grace to be able to simply see what it is that is truly written here. All spiritual upbuilding depends upon him opening our minds so that we are able to understand the Scriptures. O, Lord Jesus, do open our eyes, ears, and hearts!

David continues here, not to pray, but to interrupt his prayer in order to ponder that goodness and grace of God, about which he had just been praying. And then he says *"The Lord is good and righteous, therefore he instructs sinners in the way."* Thank you, dear Lord God, for such words! This is not something that we ever knew from nature. Our theology was always thus: If *we* are good and righteous, then the Lord would instruct us in the way. This is something that we believed was the nature of the matter, but God's word does not say this. Instead we find: Not that *you* are good and righteous, but that *he* is good and righteous, that is the reason why he instructs sinners in the way. [. . .] Therefore, we may certainly hide these words in our hearts, as well as diligently use them as both shield and helmet, spear, and sword. And they shall certainly be needed when the devil comes and terrifies my conscience, saying: "Look, if you were good [*from*], then you could be certain that the Lord would preserve and lead even you, as he does with others. But now you must be able to see that in you is no goodness [fromhet], but instead only a hard and ungodly heart. Therefore it is a false and self-assuming belief that you take assurance in the Lord Jesus." See, when the devil shoots such fiery arrows into my conscience, then I would be helplessly lost and would have to despair, if I did not have anything better to hold fast to than my own goodness. [. . .] Therefore, in this case I must look around for something other and higher than my goodness, as well as begin in another way, namely that I grasp hold of this spear: "The Lord is good and righteous," I charge back at the devil, saying further: "To the degree to which I am or am not good, that is for God to judge, here it is a matter of something else, something higher than my goodness, namely God's goodness and righteousness; and even in that moment, when I feel as though I am at my most ungodly, I must yet hold forth this truth, that God is good and righteous. Thus, depart from me, Satan! That I am not good, this is something that I knew already; but that God is good and righteous, this is written in God's word, and one should hold on to God's word as holy, delight in hearing it and learn from it."

Regarding the word "righteous," Luther in an Advent Sunday sermon makes the following remarks, worth pondering: *"That word, 'righteous' and 'righteousness' actually means pious and piety [from, fromhet]. And when we in our mother tongue say: 'this or that man is pious,' then the Scripture says: 'this or that man is righteous or upright.'—Therefore, Paul also says (Rom 1:17), that God's righteousness is revealed in the gospel; that is, in our mother tongue: God's piety, namely his grace and mercy, is preached in the gospel.— Take careful note of this little fact, that wherever in Scripture you find this little word: 'God's righteousness,' you know that according to the language used in Scripture, this indicates the grace and mercy of God, poured out over us through Christ."* [. . .]

But, you say, doesn't Scripture teach us this: "According to his love of course God *wanted* to make fallen people blessed, but on account of his righteousness he *could* not. Righteousness was namely offended by sin and could not make concessions on its demand for punishment. Therefore love found a means and a way out, giving the only begotten Son, so that righteousness might find satisfaction for its demands in his blood, and our debt of sin would thereby be paid in full, and so on." To this we respond that this is written nowhere in God's word. And if it is not written in God's word, then you should regard it as a human doctrine. Indeed, even if you find it among many pious teachers, then let go of it all the same, reverencing God's word more than all human esteem. But if people accuse you of pride, then know that it is more humble to bow before God's word, than to slave away under human doctrine. Those pious teachers have never intended that their word would matter more than God's word, in case they in some regard should be found to have spoken against Scripture. As Luther says: *"The holy fathers were human beings. Who wishes to be held accountable for assuring me that they are teaching correctly? Who would be willing to lay their trust in and die for something that they teach beyond Scripture and God's word?"* [. . .]

Take care, therefore, that you do not create a false picture of God's righteousness, but instead know, that the highest righteousness that is in God is that he loves sinners, has mercy, and does not withhold anything when it comes to their salvation. This is what you see in the only begotten Son, about which the prophet sings, "See, your king comes to you, *righteous* and a helper." Know also, that in the Father is no other righteousness than that which you see in the Son, as the Lord says: "The one who sees me has seen the Father." But in the Son you see the kind of righteousness that goes around doing good and helping all people, seeking out the lost, and bringing back those who have gone astray, forgiving sins, preaching the gospel and, finally, offering its life for sinners. When someone therefore wishes to teach you to set love and righteousness in opposition to one another, then know that this is a human doctrine. For as we have said, to love enemies, this is the highest righteousness, which can be found in heaven and on earth. Indeed, to see how completely united righteousness and love are, look to the law, which is an expression of God's righteousness and see that the law demands that one be righteous as God is righteous. The law demands precisely this: You shall love, love your enemies, love them as yourself.

GOD'S WRATH

C.O. Rosenius, 1844

("Om den oföränderliga rättfärdighet, som de trogna hafwa i Kristus")

But isn't God eternally irreconcilable with all sin, instead loving righteousness? How can he then look upon me as being righteous, equally in those moments when I manage to make mistakes and sin, as well as in those moments when I do his will? Answer: Truly, God has a holy and eternal wrath toward all sin, but is this ever a reason for us to not acknowledge and praise the wondrous wisdom of the *reconciliation*? All of this wrath was borne by the only Son and poured out on him. *The Lord cast all of our sins upon him. . .* [Isa 53]. If I were not clothed in his righteousness, then the least of my sins would be sufficient to condemn me; but it is in considering the righteousness of Christ that the apostle says *that there is no condemnation for those who are in Christ Jesus* (Rom 8:1). And when God chastises the sins of his children, with whom he is most scrupulous, then this does not occur out of wrath or to demand the *debt* of any sin, but instead is out of love—in order to weaken and kill the *root* and *desire* of sin. Therefore, he said about the children of his Son: "But if they violate my laws and fail to keep my commands, *I will punish their transgressions with the rod, their iniquity with torment, but I will not take my grace from him. . ."* (Ps 89:30–33). About this Luther speaks in his explanation of the 51st psalm, that sin must be considered in two ways: first as being *forgiven* on account of Christ's righteousness, with which we are clothed through faith, and for which our remaining sins are not counted against us; second, as being *inherent* to us and providing the occasion for the daily purification, through which the Holy Spirit weakens and kills the sin that remains in us. [. . .] "Thus, there is no difference between us human beings (in God's eyes); all of us are sinners and are made holy in Christ alone (as soon as, and as long as, we have faith in him). The repentant robber on the cross is, in Christ, equal in holiness to Peter, and nothing is contingent on the fact that Peter and Paul have done greater deeds than the robber, you or I have. For we are all, by our nature, sinners and in need of God's grace and mercy." [. . .]

But truly grasping and comprehending this mystery of the gospel is a rather difficult art. Indeed, it is only possible to the extent that God himself sends us the light of the Spirit to open our eyes and minds. [. . .] Our blind, rebellious reason, our sluggish, narrow hearts and our inclinations will resist this and battle against this mystery with all our strength—in particular, when it comes to applying this to our own lives.

A RECONCILED GOD, AND A HEART THAT IS RECONCILED TO GOD

C.O. Rosenius, 1847

(*"Kristi rike ett förlåtelserike"*)

We might be able to believe that God so loved the world, that he gave his only begotten Son for her. We might be able to believe, that God's Son, out of this same burning love, became a child of mankind, was born in a manger, wandered on earth for more than thirty years in poverty and contempt, and finally suffered, sweated blood, was flogged, crucified, and died in order to provide us with grace—and that he did all of this for the world, for a terribly sinful and antagonistic mob, for his enemies. But we do not seem to be able to believe that when we have finally comprehended the gravity of our sins and begin to seek his grace, that he then will actually forgive our sins. Instead, we work and struggle in prayer, in order to persuade him—persuade *him*, who has demonstrated his burning love for us, when we were yet unreconciled sinners, who had no atoning sacrifice [*skuldoffer*, guilt offering] to give, when we were yet enemies! O, this terrible disbelief and darkness in our hearts, which prevents us from being able to see the glory of the Lord! We ought to easily be able to see that since God has given us his only begotten Son as an "atoning sacrifice" (Isa 53), that this was not intended merely for good and pious children, but instead for real sinners, for the world; that he must have truly intended to forgive sins; that he must not have intended to look upon our merits and deal with us according to our sins, but instead that it was certainly his full intention to forgive them! As Jesus himself says, "God did not send his Son into the world in order to condemn the world" (for she was already condemned), "but instead so that the world would be saved through him" (Jn 3:17). Otherwise it will be the case that whoever does not want to have mercy, must then have wrath; that the one who does not want to be rid of sin, but wishes to remain in his sins and the service of the world and the devil (or, even if he is awakened and anxious, that he yet does not want to believe in God's Son), that such a person will remain under condemnation. "For the one who does not believe in the Son, he shall not see life, but instead God's wrath will remain over him" (Jn 3:36). But "let the one who thirsts, come; and let whoever wants to, come and take the water of life for free" (Rev 22:17).

If now someone asks, "Since not all people will be saved [*saliga*], then how shall I know that I have forgiveness and grace with God?," then we can answer that you must begin by believing in God and his word, by hearing, believing, and embracing this grace, which is for all people, even the unfaithful. Then you will have received a grace, which not all people have. "What is this grace, which is for all people, even the unfaithful?" Answer: a reconciled God, the obtainment of the forgiveness of sins, which is waiting for whomever will come and receive it. "What is it then, which not all people have?" Answer: A heart that is reconciled to God, a faith, which accepts the forgiveness of sin and lives in God. "Where is this written?" In 2 Cor 5:19–20 it is written: "God reconciled the world to himself in Christ, not holding their transgressions against them, and imparted to us this word of reconciliation. . . . We implore you on Christ's behalf: Be reconciled to God!"

In Rom 5:10 it is written: "We became reconciled with God, through the death of his Son, while we were yet enemies." In Col 1:14 it is written: "In him we have redemption, the forgiveness of sins." [. . .] Here it is written expressly that God has in Christ reconciled to himself not just the faithful, but the world, and that this reconciliation was effective without him holding their sins against them. This took place in Christ, not in our conversion. But now he exhorts human beings: "Be reconciled to God." This is all that now remains to be done. Here it is written that we were reconciled with God, through his Son's death, not through our own remorse, repentance, seriousness, prayer or faith—all of which are not a requirement for this—but instead only that we would receive this grace that already exists for us. No, it is written here, "while we were yet enemies." Here it is written that the redemption, which took place through Christ's blood, was the same as the forgiveness of sins. Indeed, our sins were blotted out on one single day, when the inscription was made on the precious stone, "the cornerstone" [Zech 3:9]. Here it is written that we were ransomed by Christ from the curse of the law, on that day, in that instant when he became a curse in our place, which occurred when he was hanging on a tree [Gal 3:13]. Alas! Woe, that the world is not aware that this has taken place! That she does not know the history of our race; does not know, that in one instant, the race of humanity was ransomed, delivered, rescued, and won from all sins, from the power of death and the devil, just as in one instant, we long ago fell into sin!

Now then, see here: *this* forgiveness of sins, *this* deliverance, which has just been mentioned, this belongs to every human being, pious and impious, faithful and unfaithful. No matter what your current state may be, at the very least your sins have been removed, blotted out, forgiven, cast into the depths of the sea—this took place in the hour of the Lord's death. If you hereafter will be condemned, it will not be because of your sins, but because of your unbelief and that you remain distant. [. . .]

We now come to the full significance of what Luther means when he says "*the kingdom of Christ is a kingdom of forgiveness,*" when we apply this to *the mutual forgiveness between people,* which is the precondition for all Christian life together on earth. We know that the sum of the law is *love.* The one who loves his neighbor, he has fulfilled the law. . . [Rom 13:8–10]. All of Christian life is realized in love. But what are the conditions for a constant love between people? The same thing, which is a condition for a constant friendship between God and human beings, namely a constant *forgiveness.* [. . .] Indeed, it is *forgiveness* alone, which in this fallen state of ours is the only foundation for all good relationships, first between God and human beings, and then between human beings mutually. This is the sum of the word of God; just as when John wanted to summarize all of it, he said, "This is his commandment, that we shall *believe in the name of his Son, Jesus Christ, and love one another,* according to the commandments he has given us" (1 Jn 3:23). This is how we can have peace, both with God and with our brethren; this is the kingdom of heaven on earth, paradise in the vale of tears!

GOD'S WRATH

P. P. Waldenström, 1877

(I ingen annan är frälsning)

We come now to the chapter on *God's wrath.* Doesn't Scripture often describe how God becomes angry, and doesn't it appear frequently in our songs, that "God's holy wrath in blood is quenched" and so on? To this we respond: Completely correct, but where is it written in Scripture, that God's holy wrath is quenched in blood? We see quite the opposite, that in Scripture it speaks about God's wrath with just as much seriousness *after* as *before* the shedding of Christ's blood. For *God's wrath is nothing other than the character or form that God's righteousness takes on in relationship to sin.* It is in its essence the same as God's righteousness. To "quench God's wrath" would therefore be the same thing as quenching God's righteousness. And that is certainly not what Christ accomplished. No, God's righteousness can never in all eternity take on any other form in relation to evil than disgust and wrath. This much is clear: God's wrath over sin could not be removed through the death of Christ.

But what about God's wrath over the sinner? Isn't that quenched? We ask here the same question as before: Where is that written? No, because we see that these statements still apply: the wages of sin is death; God does not allow himself to be mocked; what a man sows, that he will also reap, and so on. Now suppose one says, "God's wrath continues to afflict human beings after Christ's death, not because of sins against the law, but only on account of lack of faith." And we ask once again: *Where is that written?* If that indeed has happened in Christ's death, that God was appeased by the fact that Christ had been punished for the sins against the law, so that now the punishment for sin no longer can afflict the human being, then it can be asked whether or not the sin of *unbelief* wasn't also among those sins for which Christ was punished. If one answers "yes" here, then it can be asked: how can the punishment for unbelief still afflict the human being? Hasn't God been appeased toward human beings in regard to the sin of *unbelief* just as much as in regard to the sins against the law? But then, of course, no one would be able to be condemned. If one still maintains that only sins against the law, but not the sin of unbelief, has been punished through Christ, then it can be asked: Can it be that the sin of *unbelief* was not included in that sacrifice, which Christ performed in regard to sin? What other means would we have to ever be able to win forgiveness for that sin? Or is there forgiveness for *some* sins from a different source, other than being included in the sacrifice of Christ? Just think, that would certainly be a peculiar characteristic of the sin of unbelief, if it could only be healed through something other than the sacrifice of Christ. Whichever way we turn here, we end up with sheer improbabilities. And what else should we expect, when we derive our conclusions by starting with things that are not taught in God's word? [. . .]

This matter concerns the following differentiation: In the one case we get a God, whose heart was engulfed in wrath because of our fall, but who through the bloody sacrifice of the Son allowed himself to be appeased. In the second case, we get a human race that is so lost, that it can only be saved through the sacrifice of God's only begotten Son, and a God who so loved that human race, that he gave this sacrifice.—In the former, we get a Savior, upon whom God quenches his wrath in order to not "need to be angry with us, despite the fact that we are sinners." In the latter case, we get a Savior upon whom God places our sins in order to thereby make us righteous and thus save us from the death, into which we by our sins have come. In the former case, conversion would be a conversion to Christ in order to *escape* the Father, and the art of faith would be learning to use the Son and his accomplishment as a shield and defense against the Father. In the latter case, conversion would be conversion to the Father through Christ, and the art of faith would be learning to see the Father in Christ *and* in the accomplishment of Christ see the Father's own accomplishment of our salvation. Which portrait of God most resembles the father of the prodigal son, or the God whose name is love—this we will leave to our readers to determine. We will merely say: Thank God that this concept is not the same in those dear Christians' hearts and experience as it is in their heads!

GOD'S LOVE

P. P. Waldenström, 1891

(Guds eviga frälsningsråd)

God is love—that is where we need to stop, therefore, when we are searching for the ultimate foundation of his works. God's love does not have its origin or source in anything else, for then there would be something that was higher and greater than God. Therefore this love cannot likewise be diminished by anything. If it had its origin in something other than God himself, then it would naturally be changed whenever this changed, but since it has its origin solely in God himself, it can therefore never be changed. If love were to be changed, then God would be changed and then he would no longer be God. The springs of water in a country may be dried up during the dry summer, thereby diminishing the water in the rivers as they run dry, but the sea is always just as full of water. Similarly, a human being's heart might burn out like charred embers, but God is love, and love can never be anything other than love. Everything with God is eternal and perfect. [. . .]

To our hearts it might seem natural, that because of our sin, God's love would have diminished, if not to say that it had completely become transformed into hate and wrath. But that this seems natural to us is a result of the fact that *this lies in our own nature* to be transformed in this way, when someone has sinned greatly against us. But this transformation from love to wrath that takes place within us *is not a remnant of God's image*, but instead *a drop of that poison*, which the serpent injected into the hearts of our first parents. That the heathens think in this way about God is natural, *for they have nothing to judge by apart from their own natures*, and this will never be able to teach them anything else about God than what they experience in themselves. But we have God's word, which burns eternally, and it is not for us to judge as the heathens do. [. . .]

When someone comes to you, therefore, and tells you something different about God, do not let yourself be led astray into thinking that this sounds clear and natural, for that is of course how everything sounds to our nature, which has been corrupted by sin. Instead, hold yourself close to God's word. This is to say, that even when we had sinned, God yet remained the same, as he had been for all eternity, and furthermore continued to love the fallen world. This love was not at all weakened, but instead such a burning love that he did not regard any sacrifice too precious, but for her salvation even gave his only begotten Son. About this Paul writes, "God demonstrates his love in that Christ has died for us, while we were yet enemies" (Rom 5:8).

There is no greater love than when one sacrifices the most precious thing he owns for the salvation of his enemies. [. . .] The one who has seen someone become poor for the sake of his friends, he has seen a great measure of love; the one who has seen someone joyfully go to his death for a friend, he has seen an even greater measure of love; but the one who has seen someone joyfully go to his death for an enemy, he has seen *love itself*. God is love. [. . .]

"Yes, but," you say, "God is of course also holy and righteous." In this you speak the truth, but if you believe that to be holy and righteous is the opposite of what it means to be love, then you will find yourself in a very common, but very great error. Nothing is as holy and righteous as it is to love. [. . .] When someone comes to you therefore and wishes to frighten you by saying, "Of course God is love, but he is not simply love, but also righteousness," then let this be a word of *assurance* to you, so that you think, "God be praised for this! If my God were not righteous, then I would never be able to be certain of his love, for the unrighteous person's love is always fickle; but since God is righteous, then I do not need to doubt that he loves me." But if someone says to you again, "Yes, but you have sinned greatly against God," then do not let this confuse you either, but instead answer, "All the more I need to know that God is righteous, for only the one who is righteous can love the one who has sinned against him."

GOD'S GRACE IS BETTER THAN LIFE

P.P. Waldenström, 1887

(Samlade Predikningar I)

Translator's note: this sermon was given for the second day of Christmas in the Uppsala Mission House.

Text: Ps 63:1–9. In this psalm we hear first and foremost that David was in *distress*, but on the other hand as well, how he during this time of distress found his *help* and his support in the living God, who was with him in all of his ways.

David's life was a life full of tumultuous circumstances. Sometimes he was exalted and sometimes he was brought down into the deepest degradation, sometimes he experienced the most terrible sorrows and sometimes the greatest joys. [. . .] Here we read now, that David was in the desert of

Judah. It was without a doubt during that time when he had to flee from Saul. He had already been anointed king over Israel. But despite this, he was forced to live like a fugitive, who is on the run and must take refuge wherever he can in order to escape the enemies who are trying to take his life. [. . .]

In *every* age the saints have had to live through such tumultuous experiences. And it is the *strength of faith* to be able to hold fast to the Lord and his promises not only when one is dancing in the sunlight over blossoming meadows, but also and especially when one is wandering through the valley of the shadow of death, and cannot see or perceive anything, when it seems as if God has surrounded himself with a wall of bronze and forgotten to be gracious. [. . .]

Today—the second day of Christmas—is called the day of St. Stephen, and on this day since ancient times, it has been the tradition to preach about the stoning of Stephen. It is of course lamentable to see how the fury of his enemies was not able to be pacified by anything, but instead that they violently took him out of the city and, without a verdict or investigation, had him stoned, not because he had done any crime, but merely because he had preached about the salvation and resurrection from the dead that is in Christ Jesus. However, Stephen was not at all mournful about this. Quite the opposite, Stephen was *very euphoric.* When he was about to be carried off, even in his last moments he was able to pray both for himself and for his enemies. He could cry out: "Lord Jesus, receive my spirit!" and he could even cry out and say: "Lord Jesus, do not count this sin against them!" We do not say that Stephen is to be pitied, and neither do we have pity for him either, but instead we praise saints like this, who have suffered and died for the sake of the Lord Jesus' name. [. . .]

Therefore let us always hold onto God and our Lord Jesus Christ, and not misunderstand those times when the paths he leads us on are confusing to us. We still own the promise of eternal glory, as long as we belong to him—altogether as David still owned the promise of one day being able to sit on the throne of Israel, although he now had to meander his way through the desert, pursued by the mighty king Saul. [. . .] "I will seek you early," it goes on to say, "and my soul thirsts for you." David was not thirsting for the royal power, which had been promised to him, but rather for the *living God.* For it was more important for him to belong to God and to have him, than to own anything else in this world. [. . .] "I have looked for you in the sanctuary," he continues, "to behold your power and your glory. For your grace is better than life. My lips praise you."

"Your grace is better than life." David would rather die than lose God's grace. This is the true spirit of reverence for God, that one would rather let go of one's own life than to abandon God. The savior says also to his disciples: "The one who comes to me and does not *hate* his father and his mother and wife and child and even *his own life*"—that is to say, to be prepared to leave all of these things—"he cannot be my disciple." And in another place he says, that the one who loves *his life* and seeks it, he shall lose it. "But the one who hates his life, he shall find it." This is as though to say: "The one who is so concerned for his bodily life, that he, in *the choice* between *keeping it* and *keeping me* decides to keep his life and lets go of me—this person cannot be my disciple." A disciple of Jesus must be of that mindset, that he, in the choice between his life and Christ, lets go of life. [. . .]

O, my friend: God's grace is better than life. Let go of the world, let go of its friendship and favor and, starting right now, find the courage and resolve to belong to the Lord Jesus and no one else. David says in the preceding psalm: "In God alone my soul finds its peace, my help comes from him." He is the only one, who can grant me true security and true rest and make a human being truly happy. [. . .]

When David says now: "God is *my help*," that is to say, God is my helper. It is very common that such expressions are used in the Bible. This is what David says, "You are my *peace*," that is to say, the one who gives me peace. "You are my *assurance*," that is to say, the one who assures me. "You are my *light*," that is to say, the one who enlightens me. And in the same way the savior says, "I am the resurrection," that is to say, the one who awakens the dead. "I am the life," that is to say, the one who makes the dead to live. And this is what John says: He is reconciliation, that is to say, the one who reconciles our sins, and who reconciles us with God. [. . .]

"God is my help," says David here. And this is the best situation one can possibly have here in this world. For if God is my help, I will always have counsel, counsel for life, counsel for death, counsel for eternity! "His name is Wonderful, Counselor, God, Hero, Everlasting Father, Prince of Peace."

"Under the shadow of your wings I will rejoice." Just as the little chick feels secure under the wings of the hen, this is how David feels under the shadow of God's wings. He says in Psalm 91: "The one who sits under the shelter of the most high and rests under the shadow of the almighty, he says to the Lord: You are my refuge and my fortress, my God, in whom I find my assurance. With his feathers he will cover you, and *under his wings* you shall find protection." He is not simply saying here, that he feels secure under the shadow of God's wings, but even that he is *rejoicing* under the shadow of God's wings, and feels as though God is completely enfolding him in these wings. Just think, what an excellent picture is painted here! Just imagine being able to sit under the shadow of God's wings, and rejoicing and knowing that whatever may happen, it can *never* be that God's faithfulness might fail you! It can never be that God might abandon or reject his own. It can never be that God's grace will ever have an end.

Paul Peter Waldenström

3

Knowing Jesus as Christ

CHRIST FULFILLS THE LAW IN OUR PLACE

C.O. Rosenius, 1851 & 1852

("Upprättelsen och det första evangelium" / "Guds eviga nådeval")

When then, through our God's intensive mercy, the blessed "offspring of woman" came to help his poor kinfolk, this took place as he was born under the law. It pleased our merciful Father to allow the blessed offspring of woman, the man Jesus Christ (1 Tim 2:5), to stand as a mediator in the place of all humankind. He made it a founding law of his kingdom of grace: "As everyone who is in Adam will die, so shall everyone who is in Christ be made alive" (1 Cor 15:22). "As through the one man's disobedience the many have become sinners, so too through the one man's obedience shall the many be made righteous" (Rom 5:19). Christ was that "second man of grace," the second Adam, and just as all of us who are in Adam had to endure that test, whereby we all became sinners, so too would we all be taken up in the man Jesus Christ and in him endure our second test. He would stand "one for all and all in him," before the law of God. The Scripture says, "He appeared before God on our behalf" (Heb 9:24). "If one has died for all, then all have died; for the one who did not know sin, God made him to be sin for us" (2 Cor 5:14, 21). For us. Take note: *For us.* Here is now the reason why he had to fulfill the law in our place—he was "born under the law, in order to redeem those who were under the law" (Gal 4:4–5); and again, "What the law was not able to accomplish, weakened as it was in the flesh, this God has done when he sent his Son" etc. (Rom 8:3). In our place, "born under the law," he loved God with all his heart, with all his soul, with all his strength and all his mind, and his neighbor as himself; for "on this hangs all the law and the prophets" (Mt 22:37–40). First he loved God above all. In everything that he did and spoke, he looked to the will of the Father. He said, "My food is to do the will of the one who has sent me" (Jn 4:34). He was obedient to the Father until death, indeed, until death on the cross, taking on the form of a servant, etc. (Phil 2:7–8). Even then he loved his neighbor as himself; everything that he did in the world, he did for us. In short, everything that the law demands, but is not able to obtain from us, this is what was lavishly done by him, who was born under the law for our sake. [. . .]

While our mediator was thus carrying our sins, all of the *curse of the law* came upon him, that is to say, all of God's wrath, disfavor, and torment, which all the sins of the world had earned. This battle began in the garden and was so intense, that it even forced from the brow of our strong hero that awful sweat of blood, in the midst of his prayers and tears, as though he were a weak, powerless sinner. Keeping the statutes of God is no trifle, but instead is the most serious business. When God had cast our sin on him, he was not able to even complain before God that he was innocent, but instead had to stand in the presence of the Father as a great sinner and taste all the curse of the law. This was accomplished in his death on the cross, which encompassed all the curse of the law (Deut 21:23; Gal 3:13). [. . .]

The law is so sufficiently fulfilled, that it need never again condemn those who believe in Christ. It certainly continues to force its way into our conscience; it hunts us, threatens us, and causes us to worry; but in truth we "are not under the law, but under grace." If a Christian were still able to be condemned under the law, then Christ's death would be in vain, then there would have been no accomplishment in it, even if he had died one hundred times for us. O, what marvelous freedom! Sin will never again be reckoned to us, and the law will never again condemn us, as long as we keep to Christ.—*Death* has been so defeated, that even though he continues to terrify us, he is yet in reality for the Christian merely a light sleep and a secret, underground road to our long awaited homeland of eternal life.—*The devil* is so defeated, that as long as we keep to Christ, he cannot do us the slightest harm, other than what God, to the benefit of our discipline, might allow him to do. [. . .]

And so now, through Christ's marvelous victory, the whole world is just as truly and completely delivered in Christ, as she previously had been fallen and lost in Adam, and may receive eternal life just as undeservedly through Christ, as she once received through Adam sin and death as an inheritance. The inheritance from Adam we still see and feel every moment, both in us and in the world; but the inheritance in Christ we are only able to see and feel as it is proclaimed to us and believed by us.

*   *   *

Not one letter or dot of the old divine law of righteousness could be yielded. It was equally impossible for the old man to fulfill the law; he could not give something that he no longer possessed, namely true righteousness and holiness. Now, either God's purpose in the creation of humankind would have come to nothing, and his pride and joy, the children of his image, would have been eternally lost, or God himself would need to conceive some counsel to the salvation of humankind. Then he had mercy on us, in his own free love, "to the satisfaction of his will, to the praise of his marvelous grace," and he dedicated to our salvation his own beloved Son. This eternal and original Word—who also, out of the same mercy and love, willingly took it upon himself to become the brother of humankind and the chieftain of her salvation—became human and in his manhood, through his fulfilling of the law and enduring death, restored what was lost, and in his goodness reintroduced in us once more the image of God, which he himself makes possible. [. . .] The apostle says, "He has elected us in Christ."—"God is love," but not such a love that could look at sin through its fingers, or concede any of the demands of God's holy righteousness. It was for this reason that he conceived of this counsel, whereby his righteousness and his mercy could be satisfied, namely through one man, through whom we could be found holy and unpunishable before the law (Rom 8:3; 2 Cor 5:21; Gal 3:13). [. . .] God now sees the whole of the human race enveloped in Christ, and therefore reconciled in Christ, righteous in Christ, holy in Christ, unpunishable and good. But the Lamb has been slain since the establishment of the world (Rev 13:8), namely before God's sight. This is the foundation of everything that God has provided for the children of humankind from the very beginning, as a reconciled God, a gracious and benevolent Father, who with intensive mercy sought out his prodigal sons and embraced them with love, as soon as they willed to return. This is something that the Lord God already had revealed to Moses, when he sat on the mountain in the cleft of the rock and glimpsed God's glory: "The Lord, the Lord!—a God, merciful and gracious, slow to anger, abounding in tenderness and faithfulness, who maintains grace to thousands, who forgives misdeeds and sin," (Ex 34:6–7).

CHRIST BECAME A CURSE FOR OUR SAKE

C.O. Rosenius, 1858

("De trognas frihet från lagen")

But it was not enough for us that the entire life of the Son of God on earth for over thirty years was a constant fulfillment of the law. In the end he had to also endure the punishment that we had already deserved, namely all the curse of the law, in order to thereby ransom us from this. [. . .] "Christ has ransomed us from the curse of the law, when he became a curse for our sake; for it is written: cursed is everyone who hangs on a tree" (Gal 3:13). Consider now this ultimate foundation for our freedom from the law! Here we see both terrifying and marvelous things. [. . .] Christ, a curse! What a lofty mystery! The one blessed by God—a curse! What a strange medicine! From curse comes a blessing; from poison, a drink of health; from wrath, grace; from death, life.

The apostle's words here are very profound and require a thorough reflection. First he uses the name Christ (the anointed one). From this we are prompted to think of this person's entire office and the holy anointing, whereby he became ordained to the high office, to be the reconciler and defender of humankind, their high priest and king. To such an office, one would be anointed with a good-smelling oil. This gives us two indications of our abundant assurance! First, the entire errand of God's Son on earth, his *office*, to which he was anointed and ordained by the Father, was precisely to be *the reconciler* and *defender of humankind*. We therefore have great things to expect from him. And second, this good-smelling oil gives us the indication that, since all human beings after the fall into sin were under the curse and had become like the stench of decay to the holy God; that because of this, Christ as the anointed one had to step in between, so that the good smell of his anointing would drive away the stench and make us pleasing to the Father. Note: this shall always be another person who does this—not we, sinners—always another. This is indicated everywhere in Scripture.

But the apostle now says, that this blessed one of the Lord, his delight and his "beloved," has become a *curse*. This is a terrible word. First, the very word "curse" itself indicates something terrible, and every bad thing, with which the Lord threatens sinners in the law. Just as the word "blessing" indicates all of God's grace and everything good, which God in his love can pour out over his friends in time and eternity, so its opposite, the curse, indicates his divine wrath and disgust, and all of the bad things which God in his holy wrath in time and eternity is capable of bringing over his enemies. [. . .]

The most remarkable relationship, which explains these terrible words—that Christ was a sinner before the eyes of God and became a curse—is that all of this took place for us, as the words of the apostle expressly tell us. He does not say that Christ has become a curse for his own person, but instead for us—for us. All the power lies in these words: for us. Christ, as far as his person is concerned, is certainly innocent, holy, and blessed, and could therefore not on account of his own sake become "a curse before God." However, as according to the law, all grave sinners (for example murderers) had to be hanged and be cursed before God, so too according to the same law, Christ had to be hanged on a tree as a curse. For he has taken upon himself the person of a great sinner and murderer, indeed, not merely one, but all sinners and murderers together. For before God, we are, all of us, great sinners and murderers, and for that reason deserve eternal death and condemnation. Once Christ had taken upon himself our persons, our case before God, our sins and their deserved punishment, he then had to stand before God and be held accountable for it, since we are sinners, murderers, and evildoers, and as such are to be punished. This is what all the prophets in the spirit have clearly foreseen, that Christ would become the greatest of all sinners on earth. As the prophet Isaiah says, "The Lord cast all of our sins upon him; he was counted among evildoers" (Isa 53). [. . .]

As strange as all this sounds to the great darkness of disbelief in our hearts, we should yet ponder this, that as truly as the Scripture does not lie in this great main teaching, that God "cast all of our sins upon his Son," and that he is "the Lamb of God, who takes away the sins of the world," so it was also true that all of our sins had to become completely his sins, as if he himself had committed them. [. . .] In short, he is the person who now before God represents all sinners and has had cast upon him all the sins of human beings in the entire world, *who have ever existed, who now are,* or *who will be.* For our merciful heavenly Father saw that we, through the power of sin and the curse of the law, became so miserably oppressed and were so hard imprisoned, that never in all eternity would it be possible for us through any of our own strength to liberate ourselves. So he gave his one and only beloved Son as a mediator and a savior, laid all of the sins of humankind on him and said, "You shall be the sinner, who took the forbidden fruit in paradise; you shall be David, who committed adultery and murder; you shall be Saul, who persecuted and killed my saints; in short, you shall be what *all human beings* are, as though you alone committed all of these people's sins." [. . .]

We will now see what it is that the apostle says Christ accomplished by becoming a curse for us. The apostle says that Christ thereby *ransomed us from the curse of the law.* And he uses a word, which was properly used in regard to the ransom of slaves. In such a market there was always a seat of judgment arranged. When someone made a payment of the required sum for a slave, in order to release him into freedom, then this purchase had to be reviewed, witnessed, and confirmed. The situation of the ransom of slaves gives us indications as to the qualities of our redemption in Christ. Namely, first that it was a purchase, which always presupposes that there is a value or ransom, which will correspond to what is bought. Here the costly sum was not silver or gold, but instead Christ's precious blood, or both the action and suffering of his obedience. Second, this ransom of ours took place through Christ according to the law and justice, and it was reviewed by the judgment of the heavenly Father, approved, and confirmed, so that it would be valid for all eternity. [. . .] And if we just had the eyes of faith to see this, then we would be altogether in paradise, however unworthy we might be—such a marvelous thing has God given us in his Son. May God increase our faith!

If we were now to make a short summary of the above paragraphs about this blessed freedom—the sum of everything that Christ has given to us, when he became our brother and the fulfiller of the law, "born of woman, born under the law," and finally became a "curse for us," when he was hanged on the tree—we find that the Lord God himself has already made such a summary in one place in the holy Scriptures. This is when he proclaims his gracious design [råd] in the establishment of a new covenant with human beings, a new and better way of salvation than the covenant of the law was. May God open our minds as we now reflect upon this! The precious bible passage is Jer 31:31–34. [. . .] First, this ought to already awaken everyone's attention, that the Lord God says, "I shall make a new covenant"—"*I shall make a new covenant*"—and expressly says, "not like the covenant that I made with their fathers on that day, when I brought them out of the land of Egypt," subsequently leading them to the mountain, Sinai. Note here that the Lord says, that he would make a covenant, which would not be like the covenant of the law. [. . .] But the Lord God also expressly describes what the difference between the two covenants would be. It was in particular in three ways: first, that in the previous covenant, the law was written on stone and the hearts of humankind were unwilling, so that the Lord "had to force them;" but now the law would be written on the heart itself and the mind, that is to say that he will give us the holy Spirit's inner desire and love for what is good, which will become in us *an inner, living law*. The second is that, whereas the previous covenant's laws and rights could be communicated from one human being to another, while the moral law, however obscured, lay in human nature itself, even among the heathen (Rom 2:14), by contrast, the new covenant would be such that a person could not enter into it through any amount of education from other people, but instead, as

Jesus outlines it, "they will all be taught by God" (Jn 6:45). This is what Jesus often said, "No one comes to me, without the Father drawing him"; "No one will know the Father apart from the Son, and the one, for whom the Son will reveal it." And the apostle says, "No one can say: Jesus is Lord, except through the holy Spirit." The third distinction was that, whereas according to the previous covenant, sins would always be avenged, always bring punishment to the sinner, now, according to the new covenant, they would be forgiven, remitted, not be reckoned, "never more be remembered." But this point is introduced with a meaningful "for"—"for I will forgive. . ."—which shows, that this forgiveness is the foundation and reason for the two previous points. Indeed, so it is that the whole of Scripture gives witness, as well as all of experience, that the human being first learns to know God, when the law becomes written on her heart, through an inner desire for the way of the Lord's commandments, when he forgives her all of her sins and offers assurance for her heart (Ps 119:32). [. . .]

But now that sin has been thus reconciled and the law satisfied, then the believer has no more cause to fear God's wrath. Rather it is exactly the opposite; now all divine love and fatherly tenderness is over him; now no human understanding can grasp or believe the love, with which God embraces and cares for such a child. For God is truly in his essence an endless love—"God is love" (1 Jn 4:8). And this love is now no longer hindered by sin and the law. [. . .] Note this mystery: the saved and believing human being is God's own work; he alone created her, he alone redeemed her, he alone converted and sanctified her; and it is to be expected that one will love one's own creation. Our great insanity is that we constantly look to ourselves and our own merits. If God were to look upon these things, then no one would be saved. As true as it is that God cannot lie, so it is that he never looks to the human being's own merits, when she worships the Son and believes in him. God sees her only as being in him—and then she is abundantly attractive and precious in his eyes. [. . .]

How shall I be able to believe that I am in a constant state of grace and friendship with God?—My temptation to despair and unbelief is particularly severe when the devil presents *God's own words*, which seem to condemn me. First the whole Bible contains a great many terrible threats for self-confident, ungodly hypocrites. Since the world is full of such people, there must be something in God's word that speaks to them. But a spiritually-poor soul, who is being chastised by the Spirit, will of course be made aware of everything that is wrong with her, and will say: "Indeed, I am so self-confident, I am ungodly, hypocritical and so on. All of this is rooted in my old heart, of course." This is what the devil will use to thereby kill and bring down my poor faith. [. . .]

Here it is certainly necessary to deeply and profoundly reflect upon what God's *covenant of grace* involves; namely that all of these judgments and threats will only afflict *those who are without Christ*—or will only afflict *the sin* itself and the *outward human being*—but not at all disturb the *state of grace* [*nådeståndet*], as long as they are under Christ. God will certainly use the law to discipline and correct whatever is wrong in my life, indeed, even with outward punishments and torments, persecute and kill my sins. However, at the same time, I am in an eternal grace. He only avenges himself upon my enemy, sin, which according to the spirit I also hate, but he is not avenging himself on *me*, who in Christ am completely free from all wrath, all the judgments and threats of the law, have a constant forgiveness and am already recorded in heaven as his child and heir. Christ clearly demonstrated this, when he chastised his disciples for quarrelling about who among them was the greatest—such an abominable sin!—but then, directly afterward as if nothing had happened, speaks about their places of honor in heaven (Lk 22:24–30). [. . .] Isn't it necessary to *deeply and profoundly reflect upon this distinction*, to allow the commands and threats of the law to only afflict *sin*, but not our *assurance of being God's children*, but instead retain our certainly about the eternal grace through Christ! This is the true freedom from the law.

About this, the pious [Philipp Jakob] Spener, with much consideration and caution, has said: *"The believers are in this way free from the law, that they have a* complete *and* constant *forgiveness for their sins. [. . .] First, if she again becomes converted and comes to Christ, both the sins which the human being had committed before her conversion, when she did not stand in grace, and for those sins through which she happened to lose her state of grace, these will be so completely forgiven, however great they might have been, that they will never need to be considered again. Second, this forgiveness is comprised of this, that as long as the human being stands in faith and thus does not willingly serve sin, all of her inherent depravity and her sins of weakness, which are still attached to her and which will bring her to ruin, whether through failure and imperfect practice of what is good, or through sinful desires, thoughts, words and deeds (which, if she were not in Christ, would be condemnable)—that all of these sins through divine grace will not be reckoned to her, but instead, because of Christ, these will be overlooked, as if she had not committed them. This is the foundational thought in Paul's words: 'So now there is no condemnation, for those who are in Christ Jesus, those who do not walk according to the flesh, but instead according to the Spirit.'"*

THE ROCK OF OFFENSE, THE GREAT MYSTERY

C.O. Rosenius, 1846

("'Stötestenen,' den stora hemligheten")

Did not the prophet (in Isa 8:14–15) once prophesy that Christ would be a *stumbling stone* and a *rock of offense*? We understand that humankind is fallen, sinful, and depraved; that she must feel her sins, have contrition, and become righteous; that she needs to wake up, pray, struggle, and so forth. About all of this, we are in agreement. But one thing that divides us is that some people believe (as the Scriptures give witness) that even before all of the above takes place within the human being, that God is already gracious, reconciled, appeased; namely, that this has happened in the reconciling death of Christ, and that the sinner merely needs to receive this grace, which already exists waiting for him; that all repentance, experience of sin, contrition, and the like, merely have the purpose of preparing room within the sinner for grace, and not to prepare room for the sinner within the heart of God; indeed, that neither righteousness nor sanctification are possible before a sinner takes part in this already existing grace. Others think, that God first becomes gracious and appeased toward the sinner, only once the sinner has become and done all of these things that were just listed above, truly feels his sins and has contrition over them, repents, believes, is sanctified, and renewed; that the sinner must become better and then believe on Jesus, and so on.

Truly, this is the problem, here is the mystery, here is the question under debate, the solution to which depends on the Spirit's light through the gospel of Christ's life and salvation [*salighet*]. Therefore, this is worth us taking a closer look. The question is, namely, if God is reconciled and gracious toward *all* sinners, the whole world, or if he is reconciled and gracious only toward the *righteous* [*fromma*], but un-reconciled and wrathful toward the ungodly and unfaithful; if God became reconciled and gracious through the *reconciling death of Christ*, or if he only *becomes* such through our *repentance and belief*; if the grace in God's heart is based on *Christ's death*, or on our *belief*. In other words, the question is what *Christ's reconciliation actually involved and accomplished, what was carried out in and through Christ's death*—namely, if God through this reconciliation truly was reconciled. Also, does God being "reconciled" mean that God's holy demands in the law were satisfied and that God has now adopted a gracious, tender, fatherly mindset? [. . .] Thank you, holy Father, who not only sent us your Son and reconciled the world with yourself, but also in your holy word have spoken so clearly on these matters, that we do not need to ask about what this or that person or this or that book might say, indeed even about what our own reason and opinion about these things might be, but instead can look to what you yourself have written in your holy Scripture! Your word here is our secure assurance and strong fortress, against reason and opinion, against the objections of the devil and all of his apostles! Scripture says clearly, that *all* the sins of humankind have been cast onto the Son by God himself, and on that one day were carried away by this Lamb; that Christ was the second *Adam*, who cured the injury caused by the first, satisfied God's righteous demands according to the law, paid the debt, took away the record, and nailed it to the cross, and so on. And one might ask: "Wouldn't God be gracious toward a person in whom he finds no sin?!" Here it is clear, that no human being will be condemned on account of sin, but only on account of her having strayed from God, only on account of lack of faith. [. . .]

See, if God has cast all of our sins on Christ, then truly they no longer remain on our backs! And "*all* of our sins" surely cannot be the same as "some people's," or only "the sins of believers"? The Lamb of God took away the "sins of *the world*"—"God reconciled *the world* to himself"—"*the world*"! Can this merely be the righteous and good children? The believers? "And we were reconciled to God through his Son's death, *while we were yet enemies.*"—Was it in the moment when we became converted, believers and were sanctified? [. . .] Was it through our contrition and tears? Through our prayers, our healing and repentance? Was it through our belief and sanctification?

So we ought to learn once and for all, what Christ's reconciliation involved, as well as to understand *what is and is not* the function of repentance, contrition and belief, and how these things are necessary for us. Namely, they do not serve to prepare room in the heart of Christ for us, but instead to prepare room for Christ within us. This is not so that God might be made capable of receiving us, but instead that we might be made capable of receiving him and his grace. For God is already reconciled, grace has already been won for us, before our repentance and faith, through Christ alone, God's beloved Son. [. . .] These are the conditions of *the new covenant*, about which the Lord speaks in Jer 31:31–34. When God's Son paid the debt from the previous covenant, *took away the sins of the world*, reconciled all human beings, *broke down the dividing walls and enmity, when he through his flesh abolished the commands of the law* (Eph 2:14–15). So, now God has placed before humankind a new test, namely to believe in Christ, to honor the Son or to trample on him, to receive grace or to despise it, to come to the wedding or not.

THE GOOD SHEPHERD

C.O. Rosenius, 1856

("Den gode herden")

What an assurance it is when Christ explains: "I am the good shepherd!" Just think, what an assurance this is for a poor sinner, who feels his wretched powerlessness in everything, that Christ observes the sinner as being like a *sheep*. We are nothing more, we are simply *sheep*, for whom *he* is the good shepherd, who would rather lay down his life than see his sheep be lost. Just think, what assurance, when one also, in his worrying, understands the rest of the dangers faced by "the little flock," sees how easily the sheep can be led astray. What an assurance, that he who has "all *power* in heaven and on earth," he is the shepherd for the sheep, he shall care for them! And just think, what an assurance and guiding principle it is for all under-shepherds, the "little lads," as Isaiah calls them (Isa 11:6), who both inwardly and outwardly are faced with this question: "Are you showing the sheep the true way, are you treating them right?"

What assurance to own this guiding principle, this definitive pattern set by the Lord himself, who says: "I am the good shepherd!" Truly, we all have to bow before this over-shepherd and conform to his example, otherwise we are not truly good shepherds. "If someone does not have the Spirit of Christ, then he is not of Christ." [. . .]

We see here how God observes human beings as being like *sheep*, lost and powerless *sheep*, for whom it is impossible to care for themselves and defend themselves against the wolf, but instead are completely dependent upon a shepherd. This is how the Lord everywhere has described humankind, and he constantly works to disabuse us of this misconception, which lies deep in our nature, namely, that we ourselves have the light and strength to be able to help ourselves. [. . .] Sheep are, of all animals, the most vulnerable, defenseless, and simple. They lack the teeth necessary to fend off the wolf, they lack the claws to slash him, they lack the horns to impale him. Besides, they are known for their lack of wisdom, such that it has become a proverb that a very dense person can be called a "sheep." See this is, spiritually speaking, what we all are, merely fools. [. . .]

But furthermore, take heed of this, that the Lord does not say: "I am *a* good shepherd," but instead, "*the* good shepherd." What can this mean? The first and proper meaning is certainly that he is the good shepherd that has been promised by Scripture. [. . .] But the second thing indicated here is that Christ is also the only shepherd of his kind. He is the good shepherd in such a meaning that there are no others like him. This is an important truth, both to our warning and to our assurance! Christians should be on guard against idolizing any of the under-shepherds. It is an idolatrous and harmful relationship when you become dependent upon a person, and for example, this person dies or moves away, and then all of your assurance and guidance will be lost at once. On the other hand, if this teacher were to depart from the way of truth, then you also would stray from the truth. Just think, what a danger! No, a Christian must have the Lord alone as his stronghold and his heart's desire. [. . .]

But now let us consider the signs of the good shepherd's undeniable love and benevolence for the sheep—namely those that he himself and the prophets presented. Listen to what the Lord Christ first says: "The good shepherd *lays down his life for the sheep.*" Here is the great sign. But isn't this old news that we have heard so often before! Who wants to listen to this again? Many people truly feel inclined to fall asleep at this observation. And all the same, it is precisely this concept, before all others, which can set an ice-cold heart on fire and bring a dead person to life, if only God's Spirit might open our minds. [. . .] "I lay down my life for the sheep"—do you still doubt his love and benevolence for the sheep? Would you rather believe your dark, deceitful heart and the devil, who says, "He is indifferent to you, he does not care for your distresses, he expects you to conquer your evil on your own, he expects that the sheep shall defend themselves against the wolf" and so on? O, be on your guard against such dark ideas and allow your Savior, once and for all, to be who he is. [. . .] "No one has greater love than this, that he lays down his life for his friends"; in this I have just cause to come to the conclusion that of all the things I might experience, see, feel, and think, nothing is as certain as what Christ has given witness to in the laying down of his life. He may come to test me in confusing and troubling ways, he may leave me to the devil and all evil, for as long as it is his will. Yet I will nevertheless be able to believe that within him there remains hidden a heart that bleeds with intensive love. And as long as I stand in his grace, though I may still judge myself, I may also flee to his mercy, and he will not ever be able to truly leave me. No, indeed, our faithful Lord cannot lie, since there is already in his heart "joy over the one sheep that was found" (Lk 15:7). [. . .] However often he might hide himself from his children, or however hard he might test them, this I cannot tell. But I know that nothing is as certain, as what he has proven with the laying down of his life. Since he has come to be a child of humankind for our sake and then a sacrificial lamb, then I can truthfully conclude that he is not indifferent to his sheep. [. . .]

See here is another passage, which also talks about the sheep, but with even clearer words can speak to us of the shepherd's death. In Isaiah 53:6 it sounds like this: "We all have gone astray like sheep, each and every one to his own way; and the Lord cast the sins of us all upon him." Here it is said, firstly, that all of us have gone astray, like sheep—lost sheep, of course, who wander errantly in the desert. [. . .] Now, consider what the Spirit of the Lord here indicates as our great error in this question, namely: "Each and every one to his own way." Each and every one looks to his own actions. The one thinks: "If I just could be truly serious in my godliness, could truly love and fear God, etc., then I would be able to hope for grace." But the prophet explains here that this would be to go astray. This is not sufficient; you are too depraved and you are altogether too lost, no matter what you do. The other person thinks: "If only I could truly and bitterly feel remorse for my sin, truly and intently be vigilant and battle against it, etc., then I would be able to hope for grace." But this, too, would be to go "astray," says the prophet. Everything is in vain, whatever you do. This task requires a completely different kind of man. [. . .] Christ himself says that he shall care for and preserve his sheep, that "no one shall be able to pluck them from his hand," and that he "shall give them eternal life" (Jn 10:28). [. . .]

With this, the Lord touches on the subject of those cold-hearted and easy-going shepherds, who satisfy themselves with only caring for the good sheep, who already are gathered into the flock, but do not take any trouble to seek out the lost. This is not what the good shepherd does, says Christ. Even if he had one hundred sheep and one of them was lost from the flock, then he would leave the ninety-nine in the desert and go after the one that was away, until he found it. Here we have, first of all, a great assurance that even if we are really lost, really have strayed from the true flock, if we in our minds and in our life have fallen into a lost state, even then Christ will not leave us there. [. . .] Indeed, he says that it is precisely when the lost sheep returns that this brings him a greater joy than he has over the ninety-nine who were not lost. He says that he will take the lost sheep on his shoulders with joy—that he will not strike it or drive it before him, but that he himself will carry it. And this is not as though it were a heavy burden, but instead he does this "with joy." Listen to this! These are Christ's own words "with joy!" Whom can I believe, if not Christ himself? O, what an incomparable Lord, full of grace! [. . .] In addition to the great assurance that this news brings us, we should also take this lesson, that if we would like to be good shepherds, then we must be "shepherds after his heart" and do as he does, in that we will not abandon any lost sheep as though unrecoverable, but instead will do everything necessary to seek it out. [. . .]

It ought to be to the benefit, awakening, and blessing of any soul who has gone astray to receive, through the Spirit's grace, the remarkable words about these things from the highly enlightened bishop Erik Pontoppidan in his book, "The Marvelous Mirror of Faith." After he had given account of the many different meanings of the word "faith" in the holy Scriptures and demonstrated that there are no fewer than eight different meanings, and concludes by presenting the one kind of faith that has the power to save us, which is this one: *"the contrite heart that takes refuge in Christ, to receive and embrace the service he offers"*—then he adds: *"Now take good note of this eighth and final kind of faith well; for none of the others can be taken as an indication of the human being's state of grace. A human being might practice great faithfulness in her words and deeds, great diligence in her duties, she might know the entire Bible, adhere to and acknowledge all that it contains, and with bravery and perseverance confess true doctrine, indeed, even pay for it in her blood and—if the situation of the congregation requires it and God so wills it—perform signs and miracles in the name of Jesus; but despite all these things, this person might still end up in hell—and not have the true mark of being a child of God. For it is this final kind of faith alone, which makes us righteous and can save us."* Think seriously for a moment about this puzzling relationship. And all of this is precisely what we have been saying with the passages of Scripture and seen in Christ's own words. May God show us the grace to be able to once and for all pause to hear his word!

But here we understand what it is that Christ says about his sheep: "They hear my voice, and they follow me." This comprises the first and distinctive fruits of truly knowing Christ. O, when a poor, lost sheep, properly knows his good, faithful shepherd, the one who will lay down his life for their lives and now knows and loves them and cares for whatever they need, then it becomes his desire and his vital need to be able to follow such a good shepherd. It is impossible that a person can know him and not love him. And it is impossible that one can love him and not want to follow him. If he has not begun to occupy your heart, such that you would gladly be willing to leave everything in order to be his friend and follower, then you have not truly come to know him. Yet, let us explain this more. It is true that "faith and the knowledge of Christ comes in many degrees," that it can grow infinitely, and that a weak faith cannot bring with it the same love and sanctifying power, which a stronger one could. Therefore we might be easily led astray, if we constantly attempt to identify ourselves and others based on the merits of the lives we lead. It is for this reason that the wise words of Pontoppidan above are very much worth your consideration, namely that the kind of faith he mentions is the only dependable indication of a human being's state of grace. [. . .]

The sheep need only to hear his voice, and through his voice everything will be made right, they will be cured and receive his help. And, by the power of the Father, no one shall be able to pluck them from his hand. For

Christ says: "For the Father, who has given these to me is greater than all." Listen, for it is through God's power and not through our own that we will be preserved until our salvation. O, that we now could persevere in holding onto this true image of our good shepherd!

CHRIST'S OFFICE AND WORK ON EARTH

P. P. Waldenström, 1891

(Guds eviga frälsningsråd)

In these words [1 Cor 1:30] the apostle Paul expresses the entire meaning of Christ's office and work on earth. Nothing, furthermore, can be more important for us to hear than this. Especially in a time such as the present, when people everywhere are questioning, debating, indeed quarreling about this question in many cases, it is of importance that we return to God's own word and there lift up our hearts to God and ask: "Have you spoken on this, and *how* have you yourself explained the meaning of this deed, that you sent your only begotten son into the world?" [. . .]

Each and every person, who reads the Bible with open eyes, will see immediately, that the Lord Christ is the very center point of this entire book. The Old Testament with all of its prophecies and illustrations points toward him. Hardly had humankind fallen before the preaching about Christ began. *The woman's seed shall trample the head of the serpent*, that was God's first witnessing to Christ. [. . .] Indeed, one can freely say that all the books of the Old Testament, as well as the old covenant and the people of this covenant, existed solely for the sake of this person, Christ. Therefore, these Scriptures can never be understood if they are taken out of their context with him. [. . .] But even more, the New Testament revolves around Christ as its center point. At the introduction of the New Testament, John the Baptist stands crying out about him, "After me there will come one, who has been before me, whose shoe string I am not worthy to untie; change your mind-sets, for the kingdom of God is at hand." [. . .] As we continue observing the general history of the world, we see how there has never been anything else since the beginning of the world that has so scandalized the nations as the question of Christ. Not merely the most intense spiritual and academic battles, but also the bloodiest wars have been tangled up in this question. Even the greatest upheavals in the secular and civil arenas have been closely engaged with the question of this extraordinary person, Jesus Christ. [. . .] That he was something out of the ordinary, this everyone can see from the signs that he performed. Similarly, everyone must now admit that Jesus was not an ordinary person. But there continue to be battles about *who he is*, and these battles shall surely continue until he comes again. The natural human being shall never learn to know him. The darkness, which lives in her heart, so darkens her understanding that she cannot see who he is.

Yet, that human beings arrive at many conclusions about him, this is not itself of any significance. The main thing is whether we have some word of *God* that can tell us who he is. And this we have. When Christ was baptized, the heavens opened over him, and a voice was heard, which said: "This is my beloved son, in whom I am well pleased." When he was later transfigured on a mountain in Galilee before his disciples Peter, James and John, the same voice was heard. About himself, he indicated over and over that he was the Son of God; and this in such a way that everyone should understand that he did not call himself God's Son in the same way in which others might call themselves the sons or children of God—he called himself God's *only begotten* Son. [. . .] Such a thing is never said about any angel or human being. No, Christ alone is God's Son in the absolute highest and proper meaning. It is for this reason that Paul emphasizes that all divine fullness was manifested in Christ's person. Note: all divine fullness, not just *some* of God's fullness, for example God's Spirit or the mind of God or something similar, which also can dwell among the faithful; no, instead *all divine fullness*. Christ is, in a word, all of what God is, with the one exception, which distinguishes them, namely that God is the Father, who bore him, and he is the Son, who was borne of God before all things created (Col 1:15). In this regard Christ also says: "The Father is greater than I" (Jn 14:28). Otherwise it obtains, what the apostles say, that he is equal with God. Everywhere in his letters Paul also juxtaposes Christ with the Father. Christ as well juxtaposes himself with the Father, when he commands his disciples to go out and baptize in the name of the Father, Son, and Holy Spirit. [. . .]

But at the same time as Christ is God's only begotten Son, borne of the Father, he is also the Son of Man, a true and actual human being, altogether like one of us. Without a doubt, the mystery of this divinity is great, God is revealed in the flesh, as the apostle Paul exclaims. This only begotten Son of God—who was in the form of God and possessed eternal glory, through whom and to whom all things are created—he did not take equality with God for granted, but instead degraded himself and become human. He allowed himself to be borne of a poor woman, altogether like any other poor human child. His mother wrapped him in bands of cloth and needed to care for and tend to him, altogether as any other child. He grew up, learned to sit, learned to walk, learned to read, altogether as any other human child. Then he worked in his foster father's workshop in Nazareth, built houses, perhaps also chairs, tables and everything else, altogether as any other woodworker. His foster father taught him how to use the tools, and he gradually improved in his occupation, became stronger and more talented. He grew in wisdom, age, and grace before God and other people. When he was fifteen years old, he knew more than when he was twelve, and when he was twenty years, he knew more than when he was fifteen. This is how he grew and became all the more pleasing before God and human beings. O, wonderful mystery! God's only begotten Son is altogether like a son of man, altogether like one of us! It is no wonder that the limited human understanding has struggled with this mystery, century after century. It is understandable that people would be awestruck upon pondering these things. But this is the extent to which he has humbled himself, our wonderful Lord. [. . .]

God—*God*—our great, beloved heavenly Father, from whom we have fallen away, he is the one, whom we have to thank for this, that the only begotten Son has come into the world. When we had good reason to expect an *angel of death* from heaven, so we received instead the only begotten Son, full of grace and truth. This is the kind of thing our God does. Therefore David says: "Taste and see how *sweet* [*ljuvligt*] the Lord is," and again, "His name is *sweet*." In our heart, which is a false bible, it says: "His name is *dreadful* [*gruvligt*]!" But in the true Bible, which is God's word, it says "His name is sweet"—and that is the distinction.

PUNISHED BY GOD?

P. P. Waldenström, 1881

(*Smärtornas Man*)

"And," says the prophet further [in Isa 53:4], "*we regarded him as punished, stricken by God and tormented.*" It is as though he wished to say: "He came to save us, he took upon himself our distresses, as though they were his own, with the intent to save us from them. But instead of receiving him with joy, we raised ourselves up against him and struck him down. And when we did this, we regarded him as punished, stricken and tormented by God. We thought, that when we tortured him and mutilated him, that we were doing nothing more than carrying out God's righteous judgment. Indeed, we even congratulated ourselves and thought that we were doing God a service by tormenting and striking him. And when he finally was hanging on the cross, then we did not see anything other than clear evidence that God had entirely rejected and damned him." How it all went in reality, this we can read in the account of Christ's passion. Most terrible of all is how this manifested itself in the mindset of the Jews, when those who were at the Lord's cross mockingly said, "He has placed his trust in God; may He help him, if he is the son of God!" Think, how entirely accurately the prophet has written all of this.

Sometimes people have interpreted the prophet's words as though he wished to say: "We regarded him as punished by God on account *of his own sins*, and that this was our error: not that we regarded him as punished *by God*, but in that we regarded him punished *for the sake of his own sins;* for he was indeed punished by God, but for *our* sins, not for *his own*." But this is not what the prophet is saying. What *he* indicates as error is that we have regarded him as *punished by God*. If the prophet were to have meant the former, then he would [not] have left out exactly *those* words, *upon which that interpretation would have depended*, namely the words, "for the sake of his own sins." But the prophet has surely expressed this concept as he meant it, and for us it is safest to read it according to how he wrote it, and to depend on this, without imagining things here which he did not write.

By our nature we imagine that God is such that he cannot be appeased unless he is able to strike back. If he is going to spare the guilty person, then he must have someone else to strike in his place. And people call this righteousness. This perspective on God is the logical outcome of the above mentioned interpretation. But God is not like this. This image of God we can leave to the heathens, who are lacking God's word. Our God is a God who out of his great mercy has sent his only begotten son Jesus into the world, not in order to strike him in our place, but in order to deliver us from our sins, make us pure and holy and transport us home to God again, away from whom we had fallen. Any teaching that in one way or another makes the Son into a helper, a protector, a shield for sinners *against* the Father—all such teachings are foreign to the Bible and altogether in conflict with the word of the Lord: "The one who sees me, he sees the Father" (Jn 14:9). God does not want to be regarded in a different way than how you see the Son.

THE DEBT OF SIN

P. P. Waldenström, 1881

(Smärtornas man)

In the law regarding debt offerings [*skuldoffret*] there is a small condition that is of particular importance in order to sort out this question. Namely, it is written in Num 5:7–8 that if someone has transgressed against the Lord in such a way that he has dispossessed his neighbor of something, then he is to make restitution to the proper owner or his next of kin (if the owner is dead). But if the owner is dead and does not have a next of kin to whom the payment can be made, "then restitution of the wrong must be made to the Lord, that is to say the priest, in addition to the ram of atonement, with which the priest shall atone him (the guilty person)." In this I see three remarkable conditions, namely 1.) that the priest is presented as God's substitute, and not as the substitute for the sinful person. This is altogether the same way that the Bible presents Christ's work as Savior, in that he is God's substitute, and never presented as the substitute for people. Going further, I see 2.) that the ram of atonement is *expressly not counted* as part of the restitution, such that he himself is not presented as any kind of restitution. Finally, 3.) I see, that the priest does not reconcile God by acting as the substitute for the sinner, but instead the priest acts as God's substitute and reconciles the sinner by means of the debt offering. All of these conditions necessarily exclude any thought that the debt offering is a payment to God as a compensation for sin.

All talk of a payment of the debt of sin is in complete conflict with God's word. Monetary debt can be paid, but not debt of sin. If the debt of sin could be paid, then that would mean that a person through some payment could make it so that the sin was no longer a debt. But that would be to completely turn God's word on its head and to destroy all morality. All sin is debt and crime and cannot be transformed into anything else, even through payment. The debt of sin can be forgiven, but never paid. When therefore in the Bible the debt of sin *is likened* to monetary debt, there is never a word spoken about payment as a condition for forgiveness. The man in Mt 18:23 who was in debt to his master by ten thousand pounds, received the whole of his debt cancelled, without there being any mention of someone making payment in his place. "Everything that you owed, I gave to you, for you asked me," said his master. If he had *meant*: "Everything that you owed, I gave to you, because another person had paid the debt in full"—*then why didn't he say that*? And how should those who listened to this parable of the Lord, be able to understand that he secretly was thinking of a kind of payment, although he did not mention anything about this? It is possible that there was some Pharisee, who heard the Lord's speech and thought: "O, if someone cancels a debt of ten thousand pounds, then he must have received payment for this from someone else. No one is so good that he would cancel such a large debt for absolutely nothing. If someone were that good, then he would be more righteous than all of us Pharisees put together, and that is not possible." But if the Lord was thinking of some payment, why did he speak of something completely different? One cannot think, of course, that

he shared this parable in order to confuse, but quite the opposite, in order
to enlighten those people with whom he was speaking, such that they might
know how it is that God forgives sins, and how therefore even they ought
to forgive—completely and for nothing—what each and every brother of
theirs has broken.

THE MEANING OF RECONCILIATION

P. P. Waldenström, 1877

(I ingen annan är frälsning)

*Translator's note: most of this passage is lifted verbatim from the "Sermon for
the Twentieth Sunday After Trinity" from 1872, which I have here marked in
italics. The text added in the 1877 version is left unitalicized, and represents a
clarification of Waldenström's initial thesis. The original emphases have been
indicated with underlining.*

*If we consider the heathens, who only have the light of nature in spiritual
matters, then we find that they chiefly have the following things in common
with what is taught in Scripture: first that they sense, that a God exists, on
whom they are dependent; second, that they sense that the proper relationship
between them and this God has been broken by sin; third, that they sense
that their happiness and salvation [salighet] depends on the restoration of this
proper relationship. But beyond these points their ideas lead them astray. They
reason that, in the same way that they themselves become bitter in their hearts
if someone transgresses against them, and become so full of hatred toward that
person that they must be appeased through good deeds if a good relationship
between them and the criminal is to be restored, they similarly transfer these
feelings to God, thinking that the hindrance for their own salvation is based
in a certain cruelty, which has filled the heart of God on account of their sin,
and which must therefore be appeased, if they are to be saved [saliga]. For this
reason the heathens also understand the concept of reconciliation, but this is
the kind of reconciliation which originates with the human being and seeks to
reconcile and appease a cruel god. It is to this end that they offer all of their
sacrifices and divine services.*

*It is onto this scene that God's kingdom enters and confounds all of this
hairsplitting, by preaching a different sermon in the gospels, which exposes the*

wisdom of the wise as insanity, teaching 1.) that through our fall into sin no change entered into the heart of God, 2.) that there was therefore no cruelty or wrath on the part of God toward humankind, which through the fall into sin came to obstruct the salvation of humankind, 3.) that the change, which occurred at the fall into sin was a change in the human being alone, in that she became sinful as well as fell away from God and the life that is in him, 4.) that as a consequence of this, a reconciliation was needed for her salvation, but not a reconciliation that would appease God and present him once again as gracious, but instead which took away the human being's sin and presented her once again as righteous, 5.) that this reconciliation is accomplished in Jesus Christ.

That now through our fall into sin no change from love to wrath has entered into the heart of God toward humankind, this we could certainly already know from the fact that throughout Scripture it is indicated that God is unchanging. He remains who he is, regardless of whether humankind stands or falls. But what is more, Scripture witnesses to this with definitive words. So says John: "God is love," not simply, "God loves," no, but instead that in his very essence, eternal and unchanging, that he is love, and can never cease to be love, without at the same time ceasing to be God. Likewise, the Lord himself says about the basis of our reconciliation: "God so loved the world, that he gave his only Son." But if he loved the world, the fallen world, such that he offered his only begotten Son for its salvation, then that would of course mean that he loved the world despite its fall, and in that case no change would have taken place in his heart on account of the fall.

Here one might object, "certainly God loved the world after its fall, but he was able to do that because he was able to foresee the sacrifice of the Son, whom he had decided to give when he foresaw the fall of humankind." But on this point it is appropriate to do what one must in spiritual matters and questions, to make the main focus: Where is this written? And further: When God foresaw the fall of humankind and for that reason decided to give his Son, what was it, which moved him to that decision? Was it anything other than his love for this human being, whom he foresaw lying in her fall? Truly, here we even see behind this eternal decision once again to the only foundation: "God so loved the world." And here we must stop, for to ask what the foundation is for God's love, this is to ask, why God is God. "God loved, because he loved, and therefore he gave his Son," says Rosenius, quite to the point.

From all this it is now clear that the hindrance for the salvation of the world never was any wrath toward it in God's heart. Certainly the Scriptures give witness that through the fall of the world, a hindrance was laid for its salvation, in that a wall of division was raised between the world and God. But this hindrance and this wall of division was never comprised of that God's heart was overcome by any wrath toward the world. No, here this love remained so unchanged, that even after the fall of humankind in the fullness of time, this love found its highest expression, namely in the giving of the only begotten Son. From this it also follows that the reconciliation, which occurred in the giving of the Son, never in any proper sense had the aim of reconciling or appeasing <u>God</u>. For how should he be reconciled, who <u>loved</u>, and loved to the point that his heart burst with mercy toward the sinner?

"But," someone might say, "what becomes of all of Scripture's talk concerning God's wrath?" Answer: God's wrath is spoken about in two ways, namely partly as a wrath over <u>sin</u> partly as a wrath over the <u>sinner</u>. Regarding God's wrath over <u>sin</u>, we understand that this <u>cannot</u> through Christ be taken away. God <u>must</u> hate sin, as long as he is the holy God. Wrath over sin is, in other words, the backside of love for righteousness. Where the latter is, there must the former also be. Regarding God's wrath over the <u>sinner</u>, this can only be spoken about in this meaning, that the one who enters into sin, <u>is afflicted by</u> this wrath of God over <u>sin</u>. And this relationship has not been changed by Christ's death. The wages of sin for the sinner, who through unbelief remains in sin, are still today the wrath of God and death; the apostle's words still apply: *"the mind of the flesh is death; if you live according to the flesh, you will die; what a human sows, she will also reap,"* and so on. Where <u>sin</u> is, there God's wrath remains unchanged, as certainly as God is a righteous God. And to be saved from this wrath, this can take place only <u>by being justified from sin</u> (Rom 5:9). Indeed, even when the only begotten Son gave himself and descended into our sin, then he too was afflicted by this curse and God's wrath, which is over sin. *But as has been said, this is properly speaking God's wrath over sin and not over the sinner. Entirely as a father's wrath over his child is not a wrath over the child but rather over its sin, even though it might be referred to as a wrath over the child, and even though it yet <u>afflicts</u> the child who is sinning. But regarding the child's <u>person</u>, in his heart there is nothing but burning love and mercy.* [. . .]

Nevertheless, <u>humankind</u> needed to be reconciled in order to be saved, including that her sins needed to be taken away, so that she might not need to be eternally and helplessly <u>afflicted</u> by God's wrath, which is over <u>sin</u>. And Christ was given to serve this purpose, as John says, "He is reconciliation for our sins and not only for our sins but for the entire world's." Therefore we must, on the other hand, watch out for making the error that the giving of the Son was <u>merely a demonstration of love</u> from God's side. Scripture teaches with clear and definitive words, that it was a <u>sacrifice of reconciliation</u>. *But observe this, that it was not <u>God</u>, who through this sacrifice would be appeased, but instead it was <u>humankind</u>, who through this should <u>be made righteous</u>, which was necessary if she was to be saved at all. For it was on her side that the* *hindrance lay, namely it was her sin. It was humankind alone and not God who, on the day of the fall, fell out of goodness. It was <u>she</u>, who became God's enemy and went away from him, but not <u>he</u>, who became her enemy and went away from her. No, when <u>she</u> went away as his enemy, even then he so <u>loved</u> her, that through Christ, he <u>pursued</u> her in order to take away, not <u>his wrath</u>, but instead <u>her sins</u>. For when he gave his Son, it was not a matter of finding a person, on whom he could <u>quench his wrath</u>, if he was to again be able to love the world, but instead to find a person, through whom he could <u>save humankind</u>, the fallen child, whom he loved unchangingly, because he is love.*

Otherwise, Christ would not be <u>our</u> savior, but instead <u>God's</u> savior. Therefore, in his suffering our Lord Jesus is not our substitute to take away God's wrath, but instead <u>God's</u> substitute to take away our sins, and <u>in so far as</u> he is our substitute, then it is <u>our</u> sins that he bears, for us that he suffers and becomes cursed. In his being raised up, however, he is <u>our</u> substitute with the Father, and this is as <u>our righteousness</u>.[*] [. . .] *For when he came in human form, he came on God's behalf as his only begotten Son, sent by him to take away our sins, but when he will return in divinity, he will return, so to say, on our behalf as our brother,* to be our eternally valid righteousness before the father.

[. . .] But if someone asks, is it entirely incorrect to say, that it is God who became reconciled in Christ? No, certainly. Here what Luther says can apply, "Everything depends upon a good interpreter." If it is understood this way, that God's demand for righteousness has been satisfied through the worthy work of Christ, then certainly this expression <u>can</u> properly be used. In this meaning we know also how many evangelical preachers, in particular Rosenius, have made use of this to the upbuilding of countless souls. *Scripture teaches namely, that salvation [saligheten] is based in the living union of the soul with God. But because God is <u>righteous</u>, no such blessed [salig] union can be given to the <u>sinful</u> human being, because for <u>the sinner</u> God's righteousness is no blessedness, but instead an all-consuming fire. If the sinner therefore is to come into blessed union with God, then precisely because <u>God is righteous</u>, the sinner's sin must be taken away and he be presented as righteous, as God is.* And this has been accomplished through the fact that God laid the <u>sin</u> on his only begotten Son and allowed him also thereby to <u>be afflicted</u> by the wrath of God, which unchangeably rests over sin (2 Cor 5:21; Gal 3:13). *In this way it was precisely a result of God's righteousness that the removal of sin became a necessary condition for the salvation [salighet] of humankind. <u>In this meaning</u>, it becomes accurate to say that through Christ's reconciliation, God's demand for righteousness became satisfied, not out of some demand by God for <u>revenge on the sinner</u>—after all God loved him—but instead out of the demand of God's righteousness that <u>the sinner be justified as</u>*

a condition for his salvation. *Out of his unchanging fatherly love, God willed the salvation of humankind, but since* he *was* righteous, *she* could not *become saved as long as she was sinful. Now, however,* since the sin has been taken away, the transgression covered over, and the misdeed reconciled, *it is not in* conflict *with God's righteousness. Indeed, neither is it merely in* agreement *with God's righteousness, but purely and simply is a* necessary result *of God's righteousness, that the one who is of the faith of Jesus will be saved, no matter how wretched he is in himself. For in this faith, he is no longer a sinner but righteous, for he is in Christ and Christ's righteousness. But where righteousness is, there God's righteousness is sheer delight, life, and blessedness, just as surely as the same righteousness of God is sheer wrath, death, and condemnation wherever unrighteousness is.* We do not need to sing, as our hymnal does, that "grace goes in place of justice." *No, as true as it is that God is* righteousness, *shall the one who believes in Jesus be saved. The deliverance we have is so complete,* such that John says, "If we confess our sins, he is faithful and just, such that he will forgive our sins" (1 Jn 1:9). *And Paul shows in Rom 3:25–26, that God presented Christ as the seat of grace* [nådastol] *in demonstration of his* righteousness, *both in that he had overlooked the sins committed during the days of the Old Testament, and in that he now will make righteous the one who is of the faith of Jesus.* [. . .]

But if someone says: "how will you explain what it means that Christ has taken away sin?" To this I will reply that this is the very mystery itself, which I cannot explain—but it is enough for me that it is written so. Those people who speak of the appeasement of God's wrath are equally unable to fathom or explain that concept, however much they think they are able to do so. And even if they could, I would yet live much more securely upon that which God has said than upon that which they have been able to explain. [. . .]

It is in this context that people have also remarked, saying: "What then is to be made of Christ's bloody struggle in Gethsemane, indeed all of his suffering, other than a cruel farce, if his work was not to reconcile God?" This question is truly upsetting. When humankind is so fallen, that it can only be through the blood and death of the only begotten Son that she can be saved and restored, and that God would love her so much, that he would even sacrifice his Son, then it sounds horrible when she asks, if this death is nothing more than a cruel farce, because it merely accomplished the blotting out of her sins.

Then people have also asked: "Have you considered the consequences that the teaching you are promoting will have on the doctrine of righteousness by faith?" In answer to that question, I would pose this question in return: On what foundation does that doctrine stand most securely—on the foundation that in Christ's death, <u>God was appeased</u>, or on the foundation that in Christ's death the <u>race of Adam was made righteous</u>? On the former foundation, there can be no higher doctrine built than <u>exemption-from-punishment</u> by faith [*straffrihet genom tron*]; the latter foundation alone is sufficient to support the doctrine: <u>justification</u> by faith—and that is more, infinitely much more.

*Translator's note: In the original 1872 sermon, this sentence reads: "In his being raised up, however, he is the Father's substitute <u>for the sake of our justification</u>."

THE FRUIT OF SANCTIFICATION IS NEW LIFE

C.O. Rosenius, 1844

("Något om helgelsen")

The next great main point in Christian doctrine concerns *Christ's reconciliation* and our reception of this by *faith*, which is the most important and urgent matter for sustaining our spiritual life; or more properly said: our spiritual, indeed, our eternal life is to be found in these main points: The righteousness of Christ for us and the sanctification of the Spirit within us. These relate to one another in the kingdom of grace, as *creation* and *sustenance* relate to one another in the kingdom of nature. Thousands of souls, who have "begun in the Spirit have ended in the flesh," simply because they did not take this point to heart early enough or seriously enough, did not sufficiently heed the Lord's word and the Spirit, when he wanted to work sanctification within them.

Consider this story: A human being is awakened and begins to anxiously seek her salvation. As usual, she first comes under the slavery to the law and its miserable attempts to work out its own righteousness; she seeks to improve herself, casts off her sins, keeps watch, prays and struggles against them, in order to, once this has finally succeeded, only then accept grace and assurance in Christ; but this constantly fails; sin becomes overwhelming for her and she falls; she may well stand up again, but falls anew; she does the very things that she had previously shunned, she becomes so certain, stubborn, and rash that she is terrified and despairs.—In short: "sin abounds." In this miserable condition she happens to hear the gospel of how Christ "has come to save *sinners*," in order to *"make the ungodly righteous,"* how we may become righteous without any service of our own, without deeds, without the assistance of the law (Rom 3), by grace, by faith alone. Here she receives life and is saved. In these words of grace she finds her deliverance, her assurance, her kingdom of heaven on earth and now truly begins to live in that marvelous freedom of being God's child; for "he who the Son has made free, he is free indeed." Now this life of faith will be immediately followed by a new, holy mindset that is willing and prepared for all good deeds. She now finds a new strength and ability to walk in the imitation of Christ. Now sanctification has truly begun. She has now been planted in the right place, and like the willow tree by the stream of water, she is planted in Christ and lives in his reconciliation.

Who would be able to believe that just here, in the midst of this season of springtime blossoms, in the midst of the growth brought by the rain and sunny warmth of the word of the gospel, that worms or rot might emerge, which might soon bring this beautiful planting to ruin? Nevertheless, such things regrettably happen. [. . .] The justified human being is certainly free from the guilt of sin, judgment and condemnation, but she has yet another enemy, which quickly is able to bring all of this newly-won treasure to naught. Namely this is our evil flesh, our inherent depravity, which incessantly wishes to keep covenant with the devil and the world. And although this inherent sin is not counted against you and does not condemn you as long as you remain in Christ, it can all the same cause other evils, if it is not attacked in time and, in daily repentance, is crucified and killed—indeed, this is a terrible evil, which is referred to as *"choking" and "killing" the spiritual life*, which Jesus expressly said about *the thorns*, which grew up alongside the good seed and choked them—and then the whole treasure will be lost, as though you had never won it. [. . .]

From this we can first observe, that not everyone needs to worry themselves about sanctification (in the usual meaning, as a result of faith). The one, who has not been freed from sin—and thus cannot say "God be praised! I am free, I am justified, I am saved in the death and blood of the Lamb, holy, pure and good," but instead is still anxious about her pardon and righteousness before God—such a soul does not need to, indeed, *ought* not trouble herself with sanctification. Instead she ought to first understand how it is that she has been freed from her sin, before she can receive the *fruit* of becoming holy. If she thinks that it is first through sanctification that she becomes free from sin, then she is still wandering about in the darkness. Here the apostle says expressly that you must already have been freed from sin, before you have the fruit of sanctification. Also in the next chapter (Rom 7:4) he says, that we must first have *"died to the law* through the body of Christ," before we can "bear fruit to God." And Jesus says that just as the branch cannot bear fruit without having (previously) been united with the vine, neither can we be in him without this coming by faith (Jn 15:4).

The second thing we should learn here is that our freedom from sin before God is something that is complete, at the same time as the holiness within us remains incomplete. Regarding our freedom from sin it is written: "You *have been freed* from sin," but regarding sanctification: "*to* sanctification," that is to say, *in order to become* holy. Righteousness before God, with all of its aspects (freedom from sin, the law, wrath, eternal death, and so on), is something that has already *come into being*, or something that has already taken place, already is complete; but sanctification, the Spirit's work in us, with all of its aspects (faith, love, godliness), is a *process of becoming*, or something which is not yet complete, but is a work in progress. This we ought to take into consideration and beware of changing the Spirit's word; we may not change "becoming" to "come into being." [. . .] When Jesus says to his frail disciples Peter and Thomas: "You are *completely clean*" (Jn 13:10), I ought not say, "I am only partially clean, but also unclean, or in some moments clean and in other moments unclean." Instead I ought to know enough to say: "I am in myself at every moment unclean, but before God at all moments clean in Christ, indeed, 'completely clean.'" When Paul here says to those people who had not become holy, but instead merely had begun to become holy, that they nevertheless before God were "*freed* from sin," I ought to also allow this to be so and say: "In myself it is merely a *process of becoming*, but before God it has completely *come into being*." See, this is an essential trait of sanctification, for according to our faith, so will the fruits be sanctification.

But here we also find an answer to the question about the *height of sanctification*. As not everyone arrives at the same opinion in this question, it must be viewed from many sides. If someone asks how much holiness he ought to have in order to receive grace, then he has already been given the answer: *none*; for you must first receive grace, be "freed from sin," before the true sanctification can begin at all. But if you ask someone, how great this holiness must be, which as the fruit of faith confirms the veracity of a person's faith and Christianity, then we find from these words, "the fruit you reap leads to sanctification" [Rom 6:22], that where faith is true and alive, where a person is truly "freed from sin," there will always follow, as a fruit, a new *spirit* that is holy, or what the Scriptures call "a clean *heart*," a new mindset and delight in God's law, as well as a new *life*; for this is what is meant by *becoming holy*. As this new spiritual mindset is not the work or enterprise of a human being, but instead is a participation in God's nature, or God's Spirit dwelling in the faithful, it thus follows that it is so beautiful and clean that it cannot tolerate the conscious practice of any single sin, but instead suffers from this and struggles against everything that it knows to be sinful and displeasing to God. So too, a true Christian can never perform any sin, which he definitely *knows* to be a sin, without suffering from it, and struggling against it and wishing himself free of it, indeed if possible, free from all desire to it. But this does not only apply to the external and more egregious sins, but also to the interior, finer and invisible sins, such as indifference, sluggishness, self-assurance, pride, self-love, evil thoughts and so on, all of which will become a torment for any conscientious soul. A false Christian, by contrast, can certainly perform many sins; but since he is lacking the Holy Spirit—this beautiful, clean Spirit—then he will never be able to properly evaluate or perceive these inner and more hidden sins, and furthermore, will remain in the sinful practices that he loves the most and is able to hide or excuse. [. . .] But if a Christian, who is in a constant struggle against all sin, is overcome by a desire and falls into sin, after which he once again with repentance and faith stands up, then this is not called *doing* a sin, but instead of *having* sin. "If we say that we do not have sin, then we deceive ourselves, and the truth is not in us." "And if someone sins (falls into sin), then we have a defender with the Father" (1 Jn 1:8; 2:1).

Thus we also understand from the words "to sanctification," that where faith is alive, there out of necessity sanctification has begun, but is not complete; there will certainly be new light, but not full light; certainly a good will, but not a purely good will, instead also an evil one; certainly a new speech and a new life, but one that is lacking the diligence, strength and constancy that it ought to have; this will entail a process of struggling, working, battling, and this is what is called sanctification. For sanctification does not mean having become holy, but instead becoming holy. Sanctification is not the same as purity. When one is cleaning, there is much impurity in motion, and so it is also with sanctification that there is much unholiness in motion. About this, Luther says in one sermon for the Sunday after Christmas: "The kingdom of Christ is so constituted, that his Christians are not perfect saints, but instead they are merely beginners in the midst of growing." [. . .]

To trouble oneself with this question—how far in sanctification a human being *can* come—is rather pointless. The true motivation to pursue sanctification is not the height, which some saints have reached, but instead the height toward which they have all strived, and toward which God has commanded us to fix our eyes. The height is beautiful to behold, and while beholding it, we come closer to it. If our eyes are fixed on this goal, we will not be led astray. At the same time, we should never forget that since we are in Christ "freed from sin," we are already saved and at each moment, just like the robber on the cross, are prepared to enter into paradise. [. . .] Praise be to God! He has given us a human being, who was the perfect image of God, to behold and to follow, "the man Jesus Christ," who was "the radiance of God's glory and *the image of his being*" (Heb 1:3). If we wish to see the image of God, to see how we should be and what we should become, then we should simply look to Jesus, not to how he was as God's Son or the Lamb of God, our reconciler, but instead to how he was as a human being. In this way, God has given us, not simply the most perfect and most beautiful model to behold and to follow, but also what is most precious for us, in that he at the same time is our hope of salvation, our savior and defender with the Father. [. . .] God's image in Christ is comprised and exemplified in the following ways: He had an intimate fellowship with his Father, and the Holy Spirit dwelled within him; he had the law of God in his heart, that is to say, he was full of love for God and human beings; he was full of wisdom and light, of grace and truth; he was so eager to do the will of his Father, that it was his *food*, that is to say, he truly hungered after being able to do the Father's will; it was his life, so that he could not live without doing the Father's will; he took no delight in himself and did not seek after his own praise, for he was humble in his heart; his heart was meek, he did not curse when he was cursed, did not make threats, when he suffered, but instead abandoned himself to the Father; but he worked for the Father's glory with a holy zeal for the hardhearted; what is more, he was mild and compassionate and was moved by an intimate participation when he saw the misery of human beings; the one, who needed his help, he was glad to help, without investigating if this person was worthy of it or not; in temptations [*frestelser*] of the devil, he was firm and immovable, keeping himself to God's word and commandments; he looked to his Father for everything and often spent entire nights in prayer; he did not seek what human beings call 'good days,' neither did he aspire for the treasures of this world; he was always perfectly content with the situation, in which he found himself according to his Father's will; whatever was difficult, he bore with patience and submission to please his Father; his conduct was holy, and he could candidly ask his enemies, "Which of you can convict me of sin?"; he professed the truth, even when he was certain that it would cost him his life.—These things are the signs, which the Scriptures have given us of this altogether most perfect image of God, the model and goal of our sanctification.

CHRIST SANCTIFIES AND RENEWS THE SINNER

P. P. Waldenström, 1891

(Guds eviga frälsningsråd)

The sanctification of the sinner is also part of the work that God has given Christ—Let us remember that! This is part of his function as high priest. As completely and perfectly as the work of justification belongs to him, just as completely and perfectly does the work of sanctification belong to him. And as surely as we are made righteous before God through faith, just as surely it is that only through faith are we sanctified in him. The one work has just as little to do with our own strength and worthiness and efforts as the other. In Christ, God has given us everything that has to do with life and godliness—in Christ alone. He is the man; it is he who will do this. [. . .]

Then what is the nature of sanctification? Answer: *Sanctification takes place as the new life and righteous spirit, which has been born in the human being who has been justified by faith, ever more begins to pervade her entire being and all of her strength, so that she becomes ever more like God.* Sanctification is the renewal or restoration of the human, who was corrupted to sin, back to what she was intended to be by God. And the pattern for this renewal is the human Jesus, the perfect human, the true manifestation of God's essence, as we in the following discourse shall see. This is why the apostle Paul says that his inward self is "renewed day by day" (2 Cor 4:16), and again, that this new self is "renewed into the image of its creator" (Col 3:10). In Rom 12:2, he exhorts the believers to be "transformed by the renewing of their minds." In and through this, that they are in Christ, then they are new creations (2 Cor 5:17), created in Christ Jesus to do good works (Eph 2:10), new people, created to be like God in true righteousness and holiness (Eph 4:24). And this news concerning sanctification is what now applies to the *whole* person's comprehensive transformation according to the image of Christ. This perfect sanctification is the perfect salvation, the utmost and highest aim for all of God's counsel of salvation [*frälsningsråd*] and work in Christ Jesus. As Paul says: "May the God of peace himself sanctify you completely, that all of your spirit, soul and body might be preserved blameless at the return of our Lord Jesus Christ"(1 Thess 5:23).

The importance that is placed on sanctification in the holy Scriptures can be seen overall in the earnest and intensive exhortations to sanctification, particularly when it is directly explained that without sanctification, no one may see the Lord. The apostle's words sound like this: "*Seek after peace with everyone and after sanctification* [*helgelse*], *without which no one may see the Lord"* (Heb 12:14). There have been and continue to be preached many sermons, which regard it as "evangelical" in numerous ways to weaken the meaning and gravity of Scripture's teaching about sanctification, as though it belonged to the law and not to the gospel. Indeed it is often regarded as a "free evangelical sermon" *[fri evangelisk]*, when the words of Scripture concerning sanctification are presented in such a way, as though they were not intended to accomplish a real sanctification, but merely to convince us that we are lost sinners, who do not need to be saved through our sanctification or any good thing accomplished in us, but instead merely and solely by undeserved grace through faith. One cannot begin to express in words how much damage sermons like this have caused. And yet—doesn't it sound enticing! But the words of the apostle are clear: "Without sanctification no one may see the Lord." [. . .]

The New Testament never counts the teaching concerning sanctification as belonging to the law. Christ never said to the apostles: "Go out and preach the *law and gospel* for all of creation," but instead: "Go out and preach the *gospel* for all of creation." But in this word "gospel" he also included the teachings about sanctification. Neither do the apostles say that they have received the ministry of both the *law and gospel*, but instead always only that of the *gospel* (2 Cor 3); however, that they assign the teachings of sanctification to the ministry of the gospel, this is shown in all of their letters. For this reason, the apostles never conflate *the sanctification and good works of a Christian* with *the works of the law*, never speak with ill regard or even contempt about the piety *[fromhet]* and sanctification of the Christian, as though it only belonged to this world as a sign of belief and had nothing to do with his salvation *[salighet]*. No, they treat this matter so seriously that they flat out explain that without sanctification no one may see the Lord. The *works of the law* are those works, which a person does as a result of the threat of the law and force of their own strength in order to be righteous before God; *good works* are those works which proceed from and are the fruits of the new, holy spirit, which the believer through new birth has received. The attributes of the one are not the attributes of the other. When Saul, the Pharisee, worked in his own strength in order that, by living according to the law, he could be righteous before God, then he was doing the "works of the *law*." He counted these works as his boast and his joy. But then he had to count them as a detriment or loss, indeed even as excrement and impurity, because he had *worked against Christ* (Phil 3:7). But when this same Saul had become a Christian and now was found in Christ Jesus, righteous through faith (Phil 3:9), then his life overflowed with "*good*" works, the fruits of the spirit: love, joy, peace, longsuffering and so on (Gal 5:22), and concerning these works, he never said that he counted them as a detriment or impurity, or that they (as with the works of the law) were a hindrance to him in winning Christ or being found in him. In contrast, he says in one place: "Our boast is the testimony of our conscience, that we have conducted ourselves in the world with the simplicity [enfald] and purity of God" (2 Cor 1:12). *He was forced to surrender the works of the law in order to win Christ*, but *good works were the fruit of him having won Christ.* The works of the *law* are a *hindrance* to life in Christ, *good* works are *inseparable* from life in Christ. This is how great the difference is between them.

In light of this, we see that neither Christ nor the apostles present the teaching about sanctification as though it were designed merely with the aim of striking down and crushing Christians or making them sinful and at fault. Instead we find everywhere that their earnest intent, is *that this godliness to which they exhort us, shall come to fruition in the believers.* [. . .]

But what then is meant by the words, salvation is by grace through faith? "Now if this is by grace, then it is not by works, otherwise grace is not grace," of course, as Paul says clearly in Rom 11:6. [Suppose someone asked,] "but if it is through our sanctification, then it can't be through faith, right?" This is a serious misunderstanding, and one that has brought an inestimable amount of harm. The salvation of humankind is, from the beginning to the end, a work of God's pure, undeserved grace without any of our own service or merit. Any and all meddling of our own merit or righteousness will be confounded. *"But in what way or by what means* does it come about that divine grace can make the human blessed [salig]?" This is the question to which the whole of God's word responds: *By the means that grace makes her holy.* Take note, and note it again: Here it is not a question of *merit,* but about the *means* and *way.* A grace, which makes humans blessed [saliga] in any other way than by making them holy—Scripture knows nothing of such a grace. Nothing enters into heaven, which is unholy, which makes abomination or falsehood (Rev 21:27). These are clear and indisputable words of God. Only that which is pure and holy can be in heaven; and this is not an accomplishment of the law—no, it is *the great accomplishment of divine grace*, that it *truly* makes the unclean clean, the unholy holy and *by this means* carries them into heaven. A grace which would transport unholy and unclean human beings into heaven would not be a saving grace, but *instead merely a grace, which would transform heaven into a home for sin and wretchedness,* as is the case here on this earth. And God has surely given his Son a better work to accomplish than this. [. . .]

"Yes, but," you say, "if I, in my heart, sense a terrible ungodliness, what then shall I do? In this case, shall I say farewell to God's grace?" Answer: If you, in searching your soul, find that you truly are not asking after God, that grace has neither brought about a new, holy mindset, nor transformed your outward life, then you are not a Christian, and in this case you should acknowledge this and change your mindset and believe in Jesus, that you might *be* a Christian. Though, you shouldn't believe that you are helping your cause simply by convincing yourself that no matter what you shall come into heaven through God's free grace. Neither should you say farewell to God's grace, but *quite the opposite,* as an *ungodly* and unconverted person *now in all sincerity* take your refuge in the grace that God has revealed in Christ, in order that you might be saved. And if you are someone who has long been regarded as a Christian, then thank God that he has now revealed your self-deception to you. [. . .]

Once I had approximately the following conversation with a man, an upright disciple of Christ, who now has passed away several years ago, believing in Jesus. He had just heard a sermon on good works, which had not pleased him. "I do not have any good works," he said. "Then neither are you a Christian," I answered. "Yes, indeed," he said, "A Christian I am, without any good works, by free grace alone through faith in Jesus."—"But faith without works is dead," I added, "and a dead faith certainly makes no one into a Christian; in Christ Jesus nothing amounts to much without faith, which is at work through love, as Paul says, and if you do not have any of this love, then this can be taken as a sign that you are not in Christ Jesus. If you had the faith to move mountains and did not have love, then you are merely a resounding gong and a clinging little bell, but no Christian."—"Yes," he said, "I would never claim that I am anything other than an ungodly sinner, and that my salvation [*salighet*] rests solely on the foundation of God's free and pure grace."—"Now then," I added, "but if you are an ungodly sinner, then you have no salvation to expect at all, but instead are headed for condemnation, however much you might appeal to the pure foundation of God's free grace." The man was a pious and loving Christian, whom everyone could clearly see was a disciple of Christ, but this kind of exaggerated speech he regarded to be part of true evangelicalism. And he spoke this way out of a fear of self-righteousness. O, how easily in our thoughts we can fall from the one delusion into the other. [. . .]

Christ is neither a deficient savior nor a half savior, but he is truly able to carry out his office as high priest, which is to make his people holy. When we hear such a message, then even the heart of the most wretched of sinners must surely be able to grasp hold of hope.

Bethlehem Church, Stockholm, "The English Church"

4

Invitation to the Christian Congregation

RECOGNIZING THE TRUE CHURCH

C.O. Rosenius, 1854

("Den sanna kyrkan")

First we should understand that with the "city of God," the true church, this does not mean any external congregation, which might include all of a country's inhabitants, as though to indicate everyone who is baptized to Christ. Neither does this indicate any smaller church denominations, which are held together by the elements of grace, such congregations as those the apostles speak of in Jerusalem, in Rome, in Corinth, etc., which yet include hypocrites and false brothers. But instead, what is meant here is the holy, universal congregation, which for example is spoken about in Eph 5:23–32 and in Heb 12:22–23 and several other passages. Namely, this is the "communion of saints" and is comprised of Christ's limbs within all churches and denominations, which have the word of Christ, the one essential seed of God's kingdom, and therefore are spread out across the whole world. This is "the bride and the wife of the Lamb," who for a time will live in a hostile foreign country, far from her rightful home, her bridegroom's palace. This is the body of Christ, who yet here on earth has much to suffer and awaits her deliverance. This is the congregation of the Lord, the Good Shepherd's flock, and his "foster sheep" [fosterfår]. This is "the holy temple of living stones, built on the foundation of the apostles and prophets," where the "cornerstone" is Jesus Christ himself. This is the "citizenship of the saints and the household of God," among whom the Lord lives and presides as a father in his house. This is the planting of the Lord and "his garden, where he walks in the fields among the lilies." In short, this is the "living city of God, the heavenly Jerusalem, the congregation of the firstborn, whose names are inscribed in heaven." [. . .]

Could there exist something so marvelous here on earth, which could correspond to the Scriptures' word about this city of God, the people of God and the bride of the Lamb? We confess in the third article of faith: "I believe in a holy, universal church, the communion of saints." Where can this be found? Have you ever seen this? Here we heed the words of Luther: "[. . .] Our holiness is in heaven, where Christ is, and not here before our eyes, as though it were a good for sale in the market" (Luther's preface to Revelation). [. . .]

O, what then is the distinguishing mark, by which the people of God can be recognized, those whom the Lord himself knows as his own? This question is one that is the most piercing for all honest souls. May we then in such an important question take the answer only from the mouth of the Lord! What does the Scripture say about "those inscribed on the mountain of Zion," the most beautiful portrait of God's church on earth? Indeed, it was by a shibboleth that they were distinguished—"a song, which none of them could learn, except for those who were inscribed." This is the only distinguishing mark!—"Christ, Christ," the eternally new song of the heart, the heart's only all in all. "You have been slain and have purchased us unto God by your blood, the Lamb who was slain"—See, this is the shibboleth song [Rev 14:1–3]. In other words, to clarify, everyone who belongs to this living body of Christ are those who, in their sufferings with sin and their seeking after salvation, gradually have come to discover that their only source of assurance, life and blessedness [salighet] is in the Savior, and the Savior alone, such that *he, he* is the whole object of their heart's desire and their heart's peace—their heart's great sorrow, when he is absent, and its greatest joy, when he is present. [. . .]

Isn't it remarkable, that in all countries and in every age, in every nation and race and language, there one can find Christians. Despite all of the different national characteristics and customs, they are all in this regard so similar to one another! They might be rather different in certain other regards, in gifts and callings, as well as in certain specific opinions. But in one regard, they are all the same—*Christ, Christ* is their life and their song. [. . .] See, these are the ones, who comprise the people of God, which is indicated in our text as God's city [Ps 46:4–6]. In truth, this is a peculiar city! Seemingly small and plain, and yet so great and marvelous—vast in its expanse, as with the world, stretching from pole to pole, and immensely grand in its inner essence and its ultimate destination. [. . .]

Indeed, God's planting resembles a palm tree, which thrives and grows all the more vivaciously, the more that it is pressed down by adversity. So too will the fiercest storms that the church faces only allow her to increase in freedom, courage and strength. And it will never be beyond her ability to handle—certainly beyond our own, but never beyond his, who is the one who bears the brunt of them. May we never forget, that Zion is the "city of God," that "God dwells within her," and that our cause is *the Lord's* and shall be carried out by *him* to victory.

THE CHRISTIAN CONGREGATION HAS ROOM FOR ALL WHO BELIEVE

P.P. Waldenström, 1899

(Den kristna församlingen)

"What is the Christian congregation?" The word "congregation" [*församling*] corresponds to the Greek word *ecclesia*, which properly speaking means a "calling out" and indicates a gathering of people in general. The crowd of people who made a riot against Paul in Ephesus (Acts 19:23–41) was called a "congregation," as was the legal assembly (verse 39). In Acts 7:38, the people of Israel who were gathered in the Sinai desert were called the "congregation in the desert." But then the word "congregation" (*ecclesia*) is used to indicate specifically *the Christian congregation*. And in this case, she is called the congregation *of God* (1 Cor 1:2 and other places), sometimes the congregation *of Christ* (Rom 16:16 and other places), sometimes *the congregation in Christ* (Gal 1:22), sometimes the congregation *of the saints* (1 Cor 14:33), sometimes, and most often, merely *the congregation*.

The congregation of Christ is thus *the communion of saints*, as it is written in the apostles' creed: "I believe in a holy, universal church: *the communion of saints* [*de heligas samfund*]." But these saints are all of those people, who in truth, by faith, belong to God and Christ. When it is said, therefore, that the congregation is the body of Christ (Eph 1:23, 4:12 and other places), the bride of Christ (Rev 19:7), God's temple and dwelling place (Eph 2:21), God's and Christ's flock of sheep (Jn 10:16, 1 Pet 5:2, Acts 20:28), or that Christ is the head of the congregation (Eph 1:22), or that Christ loved the congregation and gave himself for her (Eph 5:25) and so on, it is clear that with the congregation is meant the *whole communion of saints on earth*.

One might also place emphasis on the words: the *whole communion* or *congregation* of the saints [*samfundet/församling*]. This is not the same as *the total number*. The apostles have never envisioned the believers as being amalgamated as a communion, as a congregation. They have never envisioned, never imagined, never spoken about Christians as being so many stones, scattered here and there in the field, or as limbs, separated from one another, but always as stones *constituting a house*, as limbs *constituting a body*.

This communion was and is scattered here and there on earth, and in this case one can speak of the congregation in this or that city (for example, Rome, Corinth, Ephesus and so on), or in this or that house (Rom 16:5), or the congregations in this or that province (for example, Galatia). This is what we usually call the local congregation. A *local congregation* is thus *the congregation of Christ in a certain place*. To her can be attributed the same characteristics and names, which can be applied to the communion of saints as a great whole.

"Can the state church be a Christian congregation?" From the basic principle outlined above, there are several important additional conclusions that follow. First and foremost, it is clear that *the state church is not nor can it be* a Christian congregation. She envelopes the citizens of the state without regard to belief or unbelief, without regard to whether they are in Christ or not. Within it, the most brazen denier and mocker is just as much a member as the most pious saint. The state church is, as the name suggests, an *institution of the state*. She has come into existence through a decision of the state, she is sustained by the state, her laws are established by state authority, and she can be abolished by the decision of the state (decision of the king and the Riksdag) altogether as any other state institution. But the *church of Christ* has not come into existence and is not sustained, nor can it be abolished through the authority or decisions of the state. [. . .] This situation is naturally not affected by the fact that within her there can be found many true Christians, indeed, many believing priests. [. . .] Indeed, if all of the believers—both priests and lay people—were to exit the church, then she would still stand there all the same as a state church. She is not in any way dependent on whether she contains a thousand true Christians or not a single one. [. . .]

"Has the state church in our country not brought any blessing?" To this question can be answered both "yes" and "no." It has brought a blessing in that the state has shown interest for the Christian religion and defended it. But it also has brought great harm, in that it has enslaved the church beneath it. This intermingling has brought the consequence that the resulting state church has done much damage to the Christian congregation. [. . .] Religion has always provided stability for more than just the individual person, but also provided *stability to nations and states*. Even a heathen religion is better than no religion. For the heathen religion gives assent to the existence of a divine power, upon whom humanity is dependent, and before whom humanity is accountable, and this is a moment of truth, which positions her, despite all errors, high above the nakedness of a lack of religion. Thus, the state not only can, but also must take interest in religion, if it is to properly understand its own charge and wellbeing. Religion is in actuality foundational to states. Legislation and morality among a people—whether it be a heathen or Christian people—have always had their basis in its religion.

But from this it does not follow at all that the state shall function as a church. The state shall do what it can to support and promote religious enterprise and also to secure its freedom. In this regard it can do much. Among us the development has been moving in this direction for some time, even if it has been moving slowly. The greatest remaining step is namely that *the Lutheran church would cease to be a state church, and as a free church be positioned alongside the other church denominations with the same rights and obligations as these.* Then there would be truth in this arrangement, and the state would stand as an external protecting force for the one as well as the other against encroachment from all sides. [. . .] Such a reorganization of the current state church would lead to truth and freedom. And when the time is ripe, this will surely take place. But to try and topple the state church with one fell swoop, this is something that believers should not participate in. [. . .] Nothing would be won by this. One should instead work within her to build up a true Christian congregation. If someone were living in an old, dilapidated house, then it would be appropriate for him to wish to build a new one. But in that case, he should not begin by tearing down the old one. [. . .] Let us calmly and in all meekness continue on this path, so that when it is time for the dissolution of the state church, the Christian congregations might have attained the level of stability, which is necessary for them to be able to rise to the task and responsibility that will be required of them. [. . .] It is when the butterfly is ready, that the chrysalis bursts. If one breaks it apart too early, then the butterfly will die.

"Are the free church denominations then Christian congregations in the biblical meaning?" No single church denomination can be the congregation of God. *The New Testament never speaks about any church denominations*, but instead only about congregations. The word church and congregation are therefore in the original language one and the same word, and also indicate the same thing. *All church denominations are without an exception merely sects.* The word *sect* means a part that is cut off from the rest, and all church denominations are merely cut off limbs of Christianity, pitted against one another. This is in conflict with all of the New Testament's teachings about the congregation.

There is a very common objection that I have received when I have spoken on this matter. People have asked: "Do you mean that all of the congregations in Sweden should annex themselves to the Swedish Mission Covenant or be absorbed up into it?" To this I answer "no." The Swedish Mission Covenant [*Svenska Missionsförbundet*] is not a *church denomination* [*samfund*] but instead merely a *mission league* [*förbund*], that is to say, an association [*förening*] of Christian congregations for common mission enterprises. The Mission Covenant has no churchly authority over the individual congregations, their preachers, prayer houses, congregational governance, or any of their internal affairs. Through its board [*styrelse*] it receives and stewards the financial resources gathered in the interest of mission, sent in from the congregations, as well as takes care of the affairs related to the common missions—all in accordance with the decisions that the congregations themselves make through the delegates [*ombud*] they send to the annual general conferences. And these general conferences are not synods [*kyrkomöten*] but instead mission meetings [*missionsmöten*]. The board which is appointed to this is not a church board, but instead a missions board. Let us therefore not let objections like the one mentioned above cloud our view of this important distinction we've just outlined.

"But are the individual congregations of a denomination Christian in the biblical meaning?" [. . .] If an association of believing Christians is established, comprised of people from only one social class—for example an association of believing members of the military to the exclusion of other believers, or an association of wealthy believers to the exclusion of the poor, or an association of believing employers to the exclusion of believing workers and so on—then anyone ought to be able to understand that such an association *cannot* be a Christian congregation in the biblical meaning. [. . .T]he foundational precondition for a congregation to be Christian in the biblical meaning [. . .] is that the Christian congregation in a given place *shall be an expression of the communion of saints*, that is to say an association of Christians *solely on the grounds that they are Christians*, such that there is no difference between free and slave, rich and poor, educated and uneducated, military and civilians, workers and employers and so on, but that all are, as Paul says, *one* in Christ Jesus (Gal 3:28).

But the matter does not stop there. This also applies to cases when an association or congregation of Christians is formed in a given place, based on a certain perspective on doctrine, which forces them to exclude people, whom they acknowledge as belonging to Christ, yet who have another perspective on doctrine. They themselves might certainly be Christians, but *their association* is not a congregation of Christ or God in the New Testament meaning. [. . .] To call themselves a *congregation of Christ,* yet exclude *members of the body of Christ,* is just as absurd as calling themselves a congregation of Christ and incorporating within themselves the openly ungodly. The *biblical Christian* congregation asks the person who is seeking to join them, "Are you a *Christian?*" The sect-congregation asks, "Are you Lutheran?"—"Are you Baptist?"—"Are you Methodist?" and so on. If he is not, then there will not be room for him in that congregation, despite the fact that he might otherwise be the most pious and serious of Christians. [. . .] In the congregation in Corinth there were parties that formed, of which the one claimed to belong to Paul, the second to Peter, the third to Apollos, the fourth to Christ (1 Cor 1:11–12). Paul seriously chastised this fleshly "quarrel" as being in conflict with the concept of Christ's congregation. [. . .]

"But," someone may respond, "it would still be impossible to unite *all* believers in one area; there would always be some people who were standing on their own; and then the congregation would not be a Christian congregation, since it would not be encompassing all Christians in the area." No, that is not accurate. When a congregation *has room for all who believe in Christ,* such that it does not exclude any of the members of the body of Christ, but merely the unbelievers, then it would in fact be in its essence entirely a Christian congregation, and its nature as such would not be nullified by the fact that there were some believers who positioned themselves outside of her and formed their own party. [. . .]

"But it would be impossible," one might say, "in the long run to manage to keep the congregation together merely on the grounds that her members were believers in Christ, since among them there would be any number of different opinions in sway." Answer: first and foremost, there is no congregation which does not contain *a number of different opinions in sway.* But these different opinions need not prevent them from staying together. [. . .] In the second place, there have existed and do exist congregations, which are built solely on the grounds that their members are believers in Christ. *All of the apostolic congregations were such.* And they demonstrated themselves capable of staying together, despite many different opinions. "Well then, how long?" you say. Answer: as long as love prevails within them. "But what about after that?" Well, when the love has grown cold, then the congregation is dead and what help would it be to attempt, with the aid of confessional documents, to try to hold the corpse together? [. . .] So, the congregation, in which there is not room for everyone who is in Christ, that congregation is a *sect* and not a Christian congregation, even if *all* of its members are living Christians, and even if it in *all other aspects* is organized as a Christian congregation.

This naturally does not apply in the cases where a congregation in one area is divided in half, due to the fact that its membership has grown to such an extent, or because the local conditions reached a point where true congregational life and fruitful congregational care was increasingly hindered. Instead, such divisions are advisable as soon as one notices that this would be to the benefit of congregational life, and that economic obstacles do not stand in the way. The main prerogative would be to make sure that each of the new smaller congregations would retain the character of the Christian congregation. [...]

THE PEOPLE OF GOD IS ONE BODY

P.P. Waldenström, 1904

(Davids Psalmer med utläggning)

Of Zion it will be said: "This one and that one were born therein." Ps 87:5.

The people of God is a people in its own right. When someone becomes born in Zion, that is to say, when someone through faith in Jesus becomes born from above, then he is a member of this people, without regard for which nation he belongs to in the worldly sense. Here there is no Jew or Greek, here there is no slave or free, here there is no man and woman; for each and every one of them is one in Christ Jesus, says Paul (Gal 3:28). This is the only way through which one can conceivably unite all nations into one. Mighty kingdoms have been built in this world. The one people group has subjugated the other. There are also nations that consist of a multitude of different peoples. This is managed for a time. The whole thing is held together by force of weapon. But sooner or later it falls apart.

In the Christian congregation, on the other hand, a melting together is supposed to happen, in which all the differences of class and nation are supposed to disappear. Even if it goes slowly, it happens nonetheless—and it is surely happening. This is not only a matter of a superficial unification, but a true melting together, and even now one can already start to see the faint beginnings of this. For wherever on earth believers meet together, they feel themselves drawn together as brothers and sisters. This is God's love in Christ Jesus, which makes them soft and melts away that which previously held them at a distance from one another.

Moreover, this may now come as a challenge to all believers, who have in this world assumed superior attitudes, not to be superior and exclude those believers who are lower, but instead think: "This person is born in Zion, he is in Christ Jesus just as I am, a child of God just as I am; yes, it can even be so that in God's eyes he is superior to me, and that he will eventually assume a place far ahead of me in the kingdom of God." May this also be a challenge for those who are insignificant in this world, so that they are not jealous of those who are exalted but instead think: "Now, I am born in Zion, just the same as they are; we both belong to God's own people, to the same royal priesthood. Our lot down here is different, but up there we will both radiate in the same eternal glory. It will all come to be so in a short little while." The believers are all one single body, whose head is Christ, says Paul. O Lord, our God, give us your Spirit, so that we may understand this glory!

SPIRITUAL PRIESTHOOD

C.O. Rosenius, 1843

("Om andligt presterskap")

The apostle Peter says: "You are a chosen people, a royal priesthood, the holy nation belonging to God, that you may proclaim his deeds, who has called you out of the darkness into his wondrous light" (1 Pet 2:9). And the Lord Christ himself says: "the one who does not gather with me, he scatters" (Lk 11:23). Now as it is not the charge of *one single* child of God to "scatter," therefore it is the charge of them *all* to gather with him, "to do good toward all, and indefatigably to seek to increase God's kingdom, as far as one possibly can" (*Swenska Psalmboken*). This is the will of Christ. But since our earthly duties often hinder this heavenly and spiritual work, he has thus designated some wise people, who will have this as their sole profession, their cause, for which they will wholly offer themselves. The rest of the spiritual people are to do these things alongside the work of their earthly calling, and proclaim God's deeds with all their being, in their prayers, words, and deeds, as they are called. Already here one should be able to understand the difference between spiritual priesthood and priesthood in the general sense. Similar to the Levite priesthood, their charges include these three spiritual things: 1) *to teach*, discipline, assure, admonish; 2) *to pray for the people*; 3) *to sacrifice*, namely their own flesh, their whole life, and thereby serve as an example for others. [. . .]

But their gifts and their calling and situations are different, just as the limbs in a body do not all have the same function. [. . .] Here we can see that this should not be understood as though each person is to work exclusively in one way, and have no part in the gifts of the others. But instead, what is indicated here is that each and every person has a particular gift. For example, the one who generally lacks the gift of speaking and teaching, but instead has a slow tongue, can all the same still do *some* speaking, can, as the shepherds of Bethlehem "spread the word" in their simple shepherd speech, tell about what they have seen at the manger of Jesus; or like the woman at Jesus' grave, run to bring the greeting from the risen Savior and pronounce this glad tiding to those sorrowing souls: He is risen! It does not matter whether this is spoken in feminine or simple language. *Everyone* must preach with their *lives*, and *everyone* must *pray* for the people, and so on. This belongs to the charge of *all* Christians. [. . .]

But there is *one* particular instance, which Christians ought to exercise particular wisdom and caution, not only to avoid provocation, but also for the sake of their own conscience. This is when several people are *gathered in Jesus' name*, for their mutual upbuilding in holy faith, where they are all equally entitled to lead the devotions. In this case, sufficient caution is called for that no one steps forth, without having been called to do so by the others present. For without this calling, then this could easily devolve into disorder, quarrels over rank, and secret or open dissatisfaction. Also, the one who had the most self-confidence or who presumed to be the most talented, would always be the one to step forward, even though this would be precisely an indication of not being the most talented. Neither should you, as well, step forward without having been called to do so, otherwise you may need to prepare yourself later for bitter pangs of conscience as you will have given the devil occasion to test [*anfäkta*] you with the question of "who called you to this," and then you would be defenseless. Here too the words of James apply: "Not every one of you should strive to be teachers, knowing that those of us who are teachers will receive greater judgment" (Jas 3:1), as well as what Luther in such strong words speaks about those who push their way into the teaching profession without calling. It is to be pointed out here that the apostle and Luther are speaking about *the teaching profession*, as an outward and actual *profession*, which does not include the mutual teaching, admonishing, and upbuilding which goes on between believers, all of whom belong to the *spiritual* priesthood, which is to say, every Christian. It is also to be pointed out that the apostle Paul (1 Cor 14:29–31) and Luther himself urge that in such gatherings as those indicated above, not merely *one* person shall speak, but whoever has "something revealed to them," and in that case "the first one should be silent" (What Luther urges here cannot appropriately be applied in the temples, and thus is not meant by Luther as such. He speaks here of those instances, in which each Christian in every region, after the example of Stephen, ought to preach). But here we are speaking of those instances when the people who have gathered do not want, or are not sufficiently able, to have several people speak, but instead desire to have one leader for their devotions. Then it is the case that no one, without having been called, may step forward, or even offer oneself, but simply wait until requested to do so. Neither is it the case that simply because one has been requested previously, that one should always feel entitled to step forward to lead devotions, which would be the same as assuming the role of teacher. This is something that Spener, who had much experience with religious gatherings, particularly disliked. But instead, one should always be certain that those present have requested this service. This is in particular necessary for his *conscience*, when it may later on ask him with bitter reproach: "who has *called* you to do this? How do you know, that this is God's will?" Then it will be a great assurance to be able to say: "it was necessary because I was compelled by the request of the people; I have not merely been moved by the Spirit, but also always by the outward calling of people. I have known from the law, that God requires that each and every person shall serve his neighbor, whenever he can, and do for others what God would have him do. Indeed, I did not have the right to deny this service, when it was requested of me." [. . .]

The *spiritual* priesthood does not abolish any outward and human order, but instead works most powerfully and beautifully *in the midst of* and *alongside* the faithful carrying out of the work of our earthly calling, in the way that the Lord invites us to do in Deut 6:7: "You shall impress these (my) words on your children, speak about them *as you sit at home, or walk the road, when you lie down and when you get up*." But perhaps the difference between the spiritual priesthood and the common meaning of the term would be most clear through the following simple analogy: In a city, *all* the citizens are accountable to take precautions in using fire, first for themselves, but also when they see someone else doing something that could cause a fire to break out, they must warn against this, and especially if the fire does spread, they must not hide this fact, but immediately cry out about this. But this does not mean that everyone is a tower watchman or fireman; neither does it mean that they are to abandon their own profession and go out to watch for fires. There are people who are appointed to stand in the tower or to walk around the town at night. But take note, that somebody who is not a fireman may occasionally also notice a fire and need to run around to notify others about this. What foolishness it would be if someone said: "You are not a fireman, you should be silent about the fire, you are making yourself out to be a tower watchman!"—The application is easy.

LAY PREACHING

P.P. Waldenström, 1917

(Tänkvärda ord)

[Anonymous excerpt from *Minneapolis Veckobladet*:] "On a recent Sunday evening, the one writing these lines had occasion to be a member of the audience at an evangelical meeting which in our day is rather unusual. In a community several miles outside of Minneapolis, there was to be a series of revival meetings. But the preacher, who was not able to come, instead sent in his place a group . . . of congregation members.

The hall was packed full of people, but on the platform there were seated about a dozen businessmen instead of a preacher. Probably more than one of the audience members wondered what kind of a gathering this was supposed to be, but when it was over, certainly everyone wished they could attend more like this. [. . .] Most of them were businessmen, who from Monday morning until Saturday evening, were occupied with earthly affairs, but who also had the desire to deliver the testimony of their faith, which had become priceless to them. It was a meeting that would not soon be forgotten. [. . .]

This hour gave rise to a question among the audience members: "Haven't we become too dependent on the clergy?" [. . .] We forget that all believers in the Lord are priests, who are to proclaim the merits of Christ, and that we can do this both in our lives and in our testimony, as God gives us the gift. [. . .] Why not a little more lay preaching nowadays?"

*   *   *

Thus far, the cited newspaper. The undersigned would also like to chime in on this question. Why not? Without a doubt, our congregations possess many gifts, which could be put to use in a much wider extent than now to the great blessing of the preaching of the word in the general worship services. It has to be admitted, and that with joy, that there are gifted men who are engaged everywhere proclaiming the gospel. But this happens most of the time in places that lack a preacher, or in more remote prayer houses, where the congregation's regular preacher is not able to preach. In the prayer houses of the larger congregations—which nowadays are being made more and more to be churchlike—it seldom happens that "laymen" publically stand up in the general worship services. People expect studied preachers— or as they are increasingly being called, pastors—or some evangelist, who happens to be on tour and comes to visit.

Now it is clear, that one should thank God that we have a rather large and growing host of preachers of the gospel, who have gone through the Mission School [at Lidingö] and thus have had considerable studies. They may, of course, when they are in the role as the leader of the congregation [*församlingsföreståndare* = senior pastor], be called "pastors," *for that is what they are*, as well as "preachers." But there is a risk that people should be on guard against, namely that *these preachers and pastors might become a new estate of the clergy*, a hierarchy, which is separated off from the laity. It cannot be denied that one of the causes of this lies in the situation we have just described. At the Mission School, words of cautions against this are regularly given. Pastors should therefore, both in the congregation's and their own interest, eagerly attempt to counteract this risk by bringing in the laity into effective participation in spiritual work. And not just in the lesser important occasions or in the periphery of the congregation, but even in the general, main worship services, in the congregation's most distinguished venues, and especially at the larger meetings. Indeed, may God help us, may we watch and pray with open eyes for the risks we face, as well as be fully aware that our help is only in the Lord.—P.W.

THE DIVERSITY OF GOD'S CHILDREN

C.O. Rosenius, 1859

(*"Om likheten och olikheten Guds barn emellan"*)

We repeat once again, that the differences among God's children, which we have just been considering, come from God and are not at all something bad, but instead quite the opposite, something rich and beautiful. Indeed, this diversity and nuance is so characteristic of the work of God. If in a congregation all of the limbs were so similar to one another, that if one had seen or heard one of them, one might as well have seen or heard all of them, then this is not a good sign. For in a true work of God, the unity of the Spirit will manifest itself in a diversity of gifts, and each and every limb will work with a particular gift. Otherwise, it will be like a uniform human creation. It is so far from the case that we should need to be troubled by all of the differences among the children of God. And when we consider how God's providence allows the one person to be born and raised in one country, city, or race, and the other person someplace else, provides the one with certain spiritual teachers and writings, and the other with different ones, all the while directing each and every person through different experiences and sufferings and blessings, it follows that all of these circumstances produce even more differences among the children of God. These differences do not indicate anything bad, but first and foremost come from God, and do not need to arouse suspicion, contempt, or criticism. They should be observed, as has been said, with reverence for God, who is the source of a diversity of grace.

But these differences between the children of God, which we have observed so far are probably not the most difficult to understand and correctly observe. It is more difficult when we encounter differences in prevailing *opinions* and *lifestyles*, in which we regard ourselves as having received the clear word of God. But even these kinds of differences do not always discount the veracity of a person's faithfulness or their life of grace. The differences in question here could possibly either be dependent on spiritual maturity or on the progress of the work of grace. Or they could also depend on different interpretations of God's word, such as those passages which could be understood in two ways, with equally faithful research in each case. Or they could arise from the recently mentioned external circumstances, into which one has been born or raised. Or, finally, from different predispositions and tendencies in the person's nature. And this is not to mention the fact that also the devil can influence us in various ways, without snuffing out the life of grace. For example, you think that I have too strict of a spirit, preach too much law and admonitions, while I, on the other hand, think that you preach these things too little. Now, both of these things could be true. Both you and I could be found to be exaggerating, which would not be good, and could either be the result of some human error or, pure and simple, the work of the enemy. But also our *opinion* and *assessment* of one another could be incorrect, and the difference in our preaching might derive from our different calling, such as one might consider the differences between a John and a James. As another example, your conscience might be troubled by various things, which I can do with complete peace in my conscience and with thankfulness to God. Can even such differences take place among the children of God? [...]

But when we speak of the differences which arise from different insights and perspectives on God's word, we must remember in particular that this can be the product of different spiritual ages and stages of grace. It is altogether impossible that a person in every stage of life would be able to fully comprehend any given point of doctrine, in terms of sincerely holding it as true and taking ownership of it. No, a person must live into [*lefwa sig in i*] these divine truths. When it is a matter of simply imprinting them in the head, then one can learn all of the articles of faith at once; but if one becomes awakened and begins to investigate the matter in full, then the systems of doctrine are overturned, then one becomes like a child, ignorant, and must begin again with the basic alphabet. Then one learns, in a new way, one step at a time, as life and experiences move us forward; and then I might at one moment fiercely battle against one truth, while at another moment this truth might become my very life and blessedness [*salighet*]. The superintendent M. F. Roos, in his dissertation on "differences and agreements between the children of God in this life," describes this in the following way: "*The differ-ent degrees of Christianity also account for the differences between the children of God; and while it is partially God's will, that one would not comprehend everything at once, but instead first after proven faithfulness in the lesser stage reach a higher one, partially because the faithlessness and ineptitude of human beings hinder their progress from one stage to another, here one can infer that this difference is partially of God, partially from themselves. [. . .]*"

Other differences between the children of God arise purely and simply from different natures, for grace does not completely overturn these differ-ences in nature, but instead gives them a new, holy direction, as well as disci-pline and moderation. The same strong and lively nature, which contributed to making Paul, prior to his conversion, into a very fierce persecutor, also later contributed to making him into a very effective and energetic apostle. [. . .] It was without a doubt simply a difference of nature, which caused the beloved disciple John to remain in the boat when Jesus stood on the beach, while Peter immediately cast himself into the water so that he could come to his Lord as quickly as possible (Jn 21). But if Peter was intense in love, he was also intense in other changes of emotions, such that he lost control of himself more often than the faithful John did. [. . .]

With everything that we have seen regarding the differences that can arise between the children of God, it is usually the case that there is one difference that is particularly confusing, which is why we will conclude with a few comments about this. It is this difference which seems to most closely address the spirit and life, namely that there can either be an emphasis on the law or a more evangelical emphasis. The easiest way around this differ-ence is to simply hold up the one emphasis as the true one, and completely reject the other standpoint. This is something that many people do, but if this is based on the leading of the spirit of truth and the fear of God, this is only for the Lord to know. It is just as erroneous and thoughtless when people decide that everything spiritual is good and full of blessing, whether it is of the law or the gospel. Let us not be so hasty in dismissing such an important question. [. . .] Just as there are two kinds of emphases on the gospel: first those poor sinners, who truly live on grace and therefore have a sanctifying Spirit; and the second being those who are dead, who are all too glad to hear the word of grace, but who have neither discipline nor sanctifying grace; then there are also those two kinds of emphases on the law: those who are strong in themselves, and those who are poor in themselves. Let us not forget this!

Now since we have a tendency to either lean to one side or the other, then it is quite healthy for us to keep company with brothers who have the opposite opinion from us. It is healthy to listen to both Paul and James, though it can cause us to be conflicted within ourselves. Besides, it is the duty and wisdom of every Christian, as far as it is possible, to seek to unify and keep together this band of siblings, which is so often tempted to break apart. [. . .] Surely these people are our siblings in grace, even if they have different tastes than we do in many cases. But if they are a self-satisfied group of people, who only have use of Christ for their own sanctification, then this is another matter—then they are not siblings in grace, but instead enemies of the gospel, and then it would not help matters to be unified with them. But it is always highly necessary to seek to understand and love even these brothers we find peculiar, partially since we are so inclined to judge everything according to our own heads and our own tastes, and partially because we still stand to gain from our contact with one another, even if we remain separate. We also know how frequently the apostles admonished the Christians to preserve the unity of the Spirit through the bonds of peace.

And no matter how numerous or large these differences might be, which exist between the children of God on earth, there are still many greater and more important ways in which they are all one. The unconverted will not find much support from the differences of the Christians; for all of God's children and all the different Christian denominations are nevertheless unanimous in regards to the unconverted, namely they share the great common doctrine, that a person only may be saved [salig] through becoming a new creation in Christ. However different God's children are on earth, they are yet one in this greatest and most marvelous relationship of all: they are "one body and one Spirit, as you were called to one hope, when you were called: one Lord, one faith, one baptism, one God and Father of all, who is over all and through all and in all" (Eph 4:4–5). Let us with this great unity in mind, look past all of our differences and, as siblings for eternity, support one another during our mutual struggles on this journey to our common homeland and our Father's house in heaven! Amen.

TESTING THE SPIRITS

C.O. Rosenius, 1845

("Några de wiktigaste förswaringsmedel emot förförelsen af falska läror")

We have seen from the above how necessary it is for a Christian, if he is to remain "steadfast" in the truth, to not accept just anything that presents itself as good or as God's word, without testing the spirits before he believes this. [. . .] *"You shall know them* by their fruit." Yet, Christ did not say that every single person would be able to distinguish these different voices, but that it was his sheep who had this kind of hearing. *"My sheep hear my voice, but a stranger's they will not follow"* (Jn 10:5, 27).

Now there remains this most important question, which is concerning the *proper way* to test the spirits. First it is quite important to understand and differentiate between the two kinds of spirits that can be harmful to us. Some of these come from the true *wolves*, who with a variety of fabricated and misleading teachings, fall in among Christ's flock and are truly zealous to strive to convert them from the truth to "another gospel." Others are simply dead, unfit hired shepherds [*legoherdar*], who very well may defend their sermon, but do not have any specific objective other than that they derive their livelihood from this, and who very well may defend accurate doctrine to the letter, but who have the sole flaw that they are dead, that they themselves do not live according to their own teaching, as well as that they do not guard the flock with any diligence or faithfulness and so on. [. . .]

If someone has the gift of prophecy, then this will be in agreement with faith, that is to say, if someone expounds on Scripture—for prophecy here means (as in 1 Cor 14) the *exposition of Scripture*—then his exposition must be such, that it completely agrees with "the *main articles of the Christian faith,* founded on the *clear* language of Scripture [. . .]" (as doctor Gezelius speaks concerning this language). [. . .] But just as among the heavenly lights there is *one* sun, so too among all the articles of faith of the Christian doctrine that are clear and light our way, there is only one of them, which is the sun for them all, namely *Christ,* as the *world's only reconciler, our only righteousness before God,* indeed, *"the way, the truth and the life."* [. . .] In short, only the one who comprehends *Christ*—namely in his heart has a living comprehension of this great article of reconciliation and justification, as well as the articles which proceed from this great article (to God be praise and glory!), about which the Scripture is not dark, but bright and clear as the sun, however much other people may see this as dark—the person who has comprehended this main article, he has a great light, a sure guiding star, an unfailing touchstone, rule, and principle, against which he can measure, test and correct all doctrines in the world. Whatever conflicts with Christ must always be error, for *Christ* is the very center and star of Scripture, *Christ* is *"the way, the truth and the life."* So, if anyone wants to teach me that we will be made righteous by deeds, then I will answer: *"Then Christ would have died in vain,* your teaching is not in agreement with *faith."* If someone wants to tell me that the law no longer needs to be preached, then I will answer: "Then Christ would not be necessary, for *'I did not know sin except through the law,'* and where sin is not known, there one will not seek a reconciler." If someone wants to teach me that I can all at once become rid of all my inherent sin, then I will answer: "Then I would not need Christ to be *'a defender with the father'* (1 Jn 2:1), who *'always lives to pray for us'* (Heb 7:25); but instead, it would have been enough for him to once and for all have justified and sanctified me." If someone wants to tell me that Christ *cannot* give us his body and blood in communion, then I will answer: "Then he would not be almighty God," and so on. In short, the one who simply knows Christ as Lord can test and evaluate all doctrines, to see whether they are in agreement with faith or not.

This is excellently confirmed in Christ's words: *"My own know me— My sheep hear my voice—but the stranger they will not follow."* Look at how Christ speaks here, and note this well. "My sheep know *me,* hear *my voice;* they know my mind and heart, my method and manner with sinners; they know, how I usually speak and behave; whatever is in agreement with this, they will hear and follow; whatever is in conflict with this, they will flee." This is how these words must be understood, for *"the voice"—the voice of the shepherd*—must contain all of the things that distinguish Christ as the good shepherd, who gave his life for the sheep. [. . .]

But let us return to the subject of testing false spirits. Christ says: *"By their fruits you shall know them."* [. . .] Pay attention, therefore, not only to their words, but also to what proceeds from them, to the fruits! [. . .] *The fruit of the Spirit is love, joy, peace, patience, kindness, goodness, faithfulness, gentleness, and self-control.* [. . .] But if love is such an important sign, isn't it also appropriate to understand *what kind* of love this is that the apostle means! For not all love is the fruit of the Spirit. The partisan spirits also have love for their followers. We should therefore closely examine how the apostle himself describes this love. . . [1 Cor 13:1–3]. *Love is patient and kind.* If you find someone who speaks and teaches powerfully, has all knowledge and knows all mysteries, but who personally is the contradiction of patience and kindness, is *in general* intolerant and bitter, is quick to wrath and quarrelling, more often scratches and bites the sheep, than heals and cares for them, then it doesn't matter how good the words and office might be and everything else that belongs to the *"sheep's clothing;"* it is by the *fruit* that you will know what is *"inward"* (Mt 7:15). [. . .] *Love is not jealous.* Many seem to have love, are kind and peaceful, but only as long as their neighbor does not have more success, happiness, and honor; then they will have plenty to say against him. This is *jealousy.* This distinguishes the partisan spirit, that as long as he himself is the one and only or the highest master, then he will be pious and good; but if someone else is honored more, then he will become antagonistic. [. . .] *Love is not puffed up.* When someone is proud and arrogant over his gifts and attributes, his teaching or his enterprises, then he will lack love and will not improve, but instead the apostle's words will be confirmed: *"knowledge puffs up, but love builds up."* [. . .] *He will not be self-seeking,* seeking his own glory and advantage, but instead the glory of the Lord and the good of his neighbor, and can therefore, when he encounters opposition, calmly and gently say this: "Well, 'this is *your cause,* O gentle Lord'; and since you are allowing this, then it is good that this is not my cause, my failure." From this it follows then that *he will not be angered,* he will not begin by making commotion and accusations, but instead will commit the matter to God. *He will not keep a record of wrongs,* he has no inclination to present other people's opinions and inner condition in the worst light—nor does he *wish* the fall and misfortune of his neighbor. No, *he will not rejoice in unrighteousness.* There are people, who take joy and pleasure when they hear that a Christian has fallen or gone astray, since they now have something to share and talk about. This joy is rather closely related to the devil's malice over the depravity of human beings. Such a joy is not found in love. *But he will rejoice in the truth,* wherever it is to be found. *He will endure all things, he will suffer all things,* for the service of the neighbor and the defense of the truth. Those who, out of the lack of gratefulness they receive from other people, cease to do good, have not love. *He will believe all things, hope all things,* he will be a good child. If he, at times, becomes deceived in his good thoughts, he will yet be a loveable child. Those, who are never able to believe the best about anyone other than themselves, have not love.

Now, let these only serve as examples! It is based on these and other fruits, that one can test the spirits. [. . .] Therefore, here it will certainly be necessary, first and last, that one above all tests and practices *his own life* in Christ, and then *humbles himself before the Lord* and *prays*—prays for the gracious leading of the promised holy Spirit, who alone has the office, the power and the glory to *"lead us to the whole truth."* Such humble and faithful prayers are certainly necessary in this time in which we now live.

ON HOLY BAPTISM

C.O. Rosenius, 1846

("Om det heliga dopet" / "Några ord om barndopet")

There are many Christians who, in all of their life, have never derived any assurance or joy from their baptism, who do not even know that there is assurance to be found in their baptism. One might expect that all Christians would have been well educated about holy baptism, but nevertheless one discovers that many people are almost completely oblivious to it. This does not even include all those irreverent, ignorant people who regard all new birth as being already finished at baptism, and thus they do not want to hear anything about repentance and conversion. But there are also many serious Christians who regard baptism as being something belonging to the past, which does not need to be reflected upon any longer, or who do not regard baptism as a "practical" matter, that is to say something that a person can yet practice or participate in. The true situation is that even now one could never understand this enough, reflect on and remember one's baptism, its worth, its treasures and riches, and neither could one ever exhaust the potential to participate in its work.

In order to properly understand baptism, it is necessary first and foremost not to observe it solely based on what is seen externally with the eye or its outward appearance, but instead to observe it according to *God's word*. Here is the mystery, as well as the reason why people see it differently! This is the case with all of God's works. If one were to observe *Christ on the cross* only according to the outward appearance, then one would see nothing more than a wretched and condemned human being. But if one observes him according to the Scriptures, then one would see the power and wisdom of God at work, performing the greatest miracle. [. . .] This is how it is with baptism, as well. If one were only to observe its outward appearance, then one would only see water or an empty and childish ceremony, which might confound a thoughtful human being. But if one observes it according to God's word, in which Christ himself ordained and instituted baptism, reflects on the words that he [. . .] has connected with this water, then one will see this as a water of life, rich in grace, a water of health and heavenly salvation, a bath to new birth in the Holy Spirit, indeed, a bath to eternal life. [. . .]

In Matthew 28:16–20 and in Mark 16:16 we read that when the time had come, that the Lord Jesus was to leave this earth and return to his Father, he gathered his congregation on a mountain in Galilee. And when they now had gathered together, he came before them, and spoke, saying:

"To me has been given all power in heaven and on earth, go therefore and make disciples of all peoples, baptizing them in the name of the Father, and the Son, and the holy Spirit."

"The one who believes and is baptized, he shall be saved; but the one who does not believe, he shall be condemned."

From these words we have the three foremost teachings regarding baptism. First we learn here that baptism "is not of human beings," is not a human invention, but has its divine origin, and has been ordained and instituted by him, to whom was given *all power in heaven and on earth*. It is an institution and ordinance, which was to apply to *all peoples*—an institution, which has been made and sealed with the name of the triune God, the Father, the Son, and the Holy Spirit. [. . .] The second thing that we notice here comes from those words, that baptism would accompany the preaching of the gospel, as God's second agent of grace, to effect belief and new birth. "Make *disciples of all peoples*," said Jesus, "*baptizing them . . . teaching them*." Our abundantly loving Lord has foreseen and known our great lamentations and wretchedness, our slowness to believe. [. . .] Yet our gracious Lord also has come to meet us in our need, our weaknesses and sighs! This is precisely what he intended with baptism. Here he has given us an outward event in the congregation, in which he, in a specific moment and in a visible way, entrusts to the *individual* what the gospel proclaims and offers to *everyone,* so that we would be able to know that we have received and accepted this great treasure, as well as to know *when, where,* and *how* we have received this. For this reason, he has bound salvation with a visible and earthly element—water. [. . .] The third thing we learn from these words of Christ, is nothing less than what it means *to be saved. The one who believes and is baptized, he shall be saved.* What is meant *to be saved* once again entails being liberated from all one's sins, from the rule of death and the devil, and then entering into the inheritance of eternal life and its endless riches. It means being immediately restored to all the things to which we were created—to grace, to being children of God, to honor and glory—but which we had lost through the fall into sin. This is possible because Christ extends to us this right, made possible through all of his doing and suffering, indeed, through his death and resurrection. O, what a matchless counsel of love! This was Christ's intent as he spoke these words and bound and invested all of this into the water of baptism. Thus, with this visible sign in his congregation, he distinguishes the individual person who possesses this grace, and ultimately equips us to embrace this great, spiritual, invisible gift and take our assurance in it. The water of baptism, as lowly as it might seem to the eye, is nevertheless, an exceedingly rich and precious water. [. . .] Let us reflect on what Christ's words contain here. He does not say: "The one who believes and is baptized *can* be saved," or that he "*probably* will be saved." But instead he says decidedly: "He *shall* be saved, he *cannot*, may not perish; he shall enjoy everything that I have accomplished in my obedience and my suffering, my death and resurrection." [. . .]

Here there remains a question on this matter, which is perhaps the most difficult to understand, namely: "What use does one have of baptism, after one has broken the baptismal covenant and run away from God? And who of us hasn't done that?" As an answer to this question, take note of the following. The apostle Peter says (1 Pet 3:20–21), that just as Noah's house in the midst of the flood was saved through the ark and through the water, which carried it, and at the same time, the old, unrepentant world was drowned and killed in this same water—that this is a model for baptism. For after he says that "in the ark eight souls were saved through the water," and continues, "which now is a symbol for how baptism saves you—not as though in the removal of uncleanliness from the flesh, but instead as in the pledge of a good conscience toward God—through the resurrection of Jesus Christ." Reflect for a moment on this image. If anyone in Noah's household had fallen out of the ark, had fallen into the waters of the flood, the ark would not have been destroyed or sunken on account of that. Certainly the one who had fallen out of the ark would have been lost if he had remained in the water, but if he had once again taken hold of the ark and come back up into it again, this same ark would have saved him; for, as has been said, the ark did not break apart on account of his having fallen out of it. [. . .] Now as we have seen how baptism is *the ark of salvation*, which cannot fail, [. . .] this ought to all the more bring assurance to the believer against all of his daily infirmities, sins, and faults. Indeed, in every recurring distress and crisis of temptation [*anfäktning*], he can reflect and say to himself: "I am baptized all the same, not on account of myself and my own righteousness, but instead on account of Christ and his righteousness; if I were expected to stand on account of my own righteousness, then I would not have needed to be baptized to Christ." [. . .]

In order to understand the significance of baptism and its work within us, it is helpful to know that in the first era of the church, baptism was performed in this way, that a person was submerged completely beneath the water. This act of submerging and lifting up the person was to serve as a sign that "the old man within us shall through daily contrition and repentance be overcome and killed with all of his sins and evil desires, and that a new man would daily appear and rise up, which in righteousness and holiness will eternally live for God." [. . .]

How does this come about? The apostle says: "As now you have received the Lord Christ Jesus, so walk in him" (Col 2:6). Note this little word "so"—*as you have received Christ, so walk in him.* In the same way as this took place when you *received* it, at the beginning, when life began, this is how it is to take place in your *walking,* in the continuation, as life continues to grow. [. . .] However, this is not so that we might remain *lying* in our wretchedness, in slavery and powerlessness, but instead that the new man, "the mind of the Spirit, who is life and joy," also would daily appear and rise up within us, be nurtured and strengthened. This is also necessary that through the gospel we would constantly be assured and established in our conscience, be liberated from the law, and be glad and blessed in our Lord Christ. This is the very essence of our daily baptism or renewal. And in this way it becomes the *truth* of our sanctification, a sanctification that is *born* in us, not something that we *do.* It is a living sanctification by the Spirit, not one that is dead and superficial. [. . .] First after the foundation has properly been established in the inner life, then it is a matter of *the whole person,* that the flesh would be killed and the Spirit would reign in all circumstances. In baptism, all of the old man is sentenced to death. *We have been baptized to his death.*

*   *   *

You ask what one ought to think about the opinions of re-baptizers [*wederdöpare*], which have begun to circulate among you. [. . .] They say: "There is no commandment to baptize children; it is written: *Teach and baptize*—teaching ought to come first." They say: "When children receive baptism, they are in an unconscious state and have no benefit from it." They say: "Child baptism is the basis of all [false] security, in that everyone believes himself to be a Christian solely on account of having been baptized," and so on. You ask what we ought to think about all these things. Answer: first, we can read and consider what the great teacher Luther has to say about this, partially in the Postilla, partially in our symbolical books. Note that this question is not so simple, nor is it so easily resolved; and also that there is just as much support for child baptism, if not more. As you might imagine, it began already in the *first* century of the church and became *common in the second,* which is to say, at the height of the tribulations of the martyrs, that most healthy of times for the church, when God's kingdom was not comprised merely of words, but even in power. Child baptism was not an institution of any state church, nor was it introduced by Constantine, but instead it became a custom in the little persecuted church of Christ a century earlier, and it will always remain until the end of the age. [. . .]

When the Baptists say: "It is first written: 'teach,' then 'baptize'—first: 'believe,' and then 'be baptized'" (Mk 16:16), then I would immediately point out that this is a loose and false argument. For it is only natural that when the disciples would be sent out, they would have to begin with teaching—and no one should seriously believe that what the Savior wished to communicate with these words was that teaching would always come first. If one is to make this claim, that the order of the words has such a decisive significance, then let them read Jn 3:5; Eph 5:26; Tit 3:5. In all of these places, water is mentioned first and then the word and the Spirit. [. . .] When they say that the child is unconscious and therefore can have no benefit from baptism, then you can answer: "Poor reasoning!" The Lord says that the kingdom of heaven belongs to children; and when they have grown up, and need the assurance of the word and baptism, then they have just as much to gain from their baptism as they would if they had received it at a mature age. [. . .] Christ says expressly: "Unless a person is born of water and Spirit, he cannot enter into God's kingdom." Thus it is never a secure thing to allow a child to go unbaptized. If someone says that this statement is only binding for those who can hear and understand it, then you can answer that this is not what is written. Instead it is written: "Unless a person is born of water," etc. Take Christ's words as they sound. If there is still any ambiguity remaining about this matter, it will yet always be most secure to have simply [enfaldigt] followed the words of Christ, when it certainly will not harm the child. Say I were to deny my child baptism, and later it died, then I would have less peace, than if I had simply [enfaldeligen] given it baptism. [. . .]

Now, what is demonstrated by all of this ambiguity? Here is the point I wanted to draw attention to. The point is that through these controversies and ambiguities it is only demonstrated that there is not any definite prohibition in the word against child baptism. Just as there is no definite time mandated for the participation in communion, so too has the Lord left this question (on the time for baptism) to the freedom of Christians. [. . .]

The summary of all of this is, first of all, do not take it as having been so resolved, that whatever you see in the word is so decidedly the most correct interpretation. Each and every person believes his own eyes, but other faithful people also have their viewpoints. And if it is incorrect to slavishly depend on the insights of the saints regarding the word, then it is an even uglier and more unchristian thing to exclusively believe one's own eyes and one's own spirit. But the second point is that if—if you should still arrive at the conclusion that it is altogether incorrect to baptize infant children (which surely is the most proper thing to do)—if you cannot come to this conclusion, then you ought to have learned from Paul, that you ought to withhold your own individual insights, "keep it between yourself and God and not trouble the conscience" (Rom 14), as long as you still can believe that the faithful in Christ have life and salvation [*salighet*], even if they have been baptized as children. "Do not be too righteous," so that you with your zeal for what you regard as correct do not altogether forget what it is that is most beneficial, what love and wisdom demand—so that in your zeal against impurity you do not forfeit your crowns, or destroy what is much more important, namely faith, peace in God, and refuge in his love.

BAPTISM

P.P. Waldenström, 1898

(Dop och barndop)

Third Conversation: Is Baptism a Confession?

Timoteus: Well, now we should get to the main question, right? Or do you have any more preliminary questions to bring up, as a means of delaying the main issue at hand as long as possible?

Natanael: No, you can rest assured that I do not want to avoid it, but instead let's get down to it: Thus, what does the New Testament teach about the essence of baptism? And when we hereafter speak of "baptism," then we will always mean *Christian* baptism, unless we specifically refer to the baptism of John [discussed previously]. Agreed?

Timoteus: Yes, indeed.

Natanael: Then please tell me, what do you believe about the essence of baptism?

Timoteus: It is a holy act, in which the believer in obedience to the command of Christ, in a symbolic way, confesses his belief in Jesus.

Natanael: This is spoken clearly and honestly. Now it only remains for us to know where this is written.

Timoteus: Where this is written? It is not written in any specific place. But is derived from all of those places, which speak about the meaning of baptism, if one understands them correctly. [. . .]

Natanael: We will see about that. Imagine for a minute that there is a person who has become a believer. He comes to you and wants to become baptized. As far as you all can judge, his confession is true, and so he will be baptized. Correct?

Timoteus: Naturally, he would be.

Natanael: But now, you all are in no position to search the heart, and then later it becomes revealed that he was not truly a believer, but merely a hypocrite when he was baptized. In that case, how should one look upon his baptism? Was it a genuine baptism or not?

Timoteus: A true baptism, of course.

Natanael: But he certainly did not have *faith* when he was baptized; and then the confession that he made at his baptism was *not a true one*.

Timoteus: But *we* naturally could not look through to his heart; when he, *as far as we could judge*, was found to be a believer, then we had to baptize him. Otherwise, we would certainly never dare to baptize anyone.

Natanael: Entirely correct. But this shows, clearly and plainly, that you yourself do not believe that the *essence* of baptism is to be a confession. For if baptism is nothing other than a confession, then it *cannot* be a *true baptism* in those cases where there is no *true faith*.

Timoteus: This we cannot see.

Natanael: What you see or do not see is irrelevant to the matter. If I with my baptism confess something that is not true, then my confession, that is to say my baptism, is not true. And if this man of ours later were to truly come to faith, then he ought to be baptized again. For it would only be then that his confession was true. But would you really baptize him in that case?

Timoteus: No, we would not do that for someone who is already baptized. [. . .] Thus it must be seen as a true baptism. But if the man then were to truly come to faith, and then request baptism, "then such a request should not be granted" [citing Anders Wiberg, *Svar på lektor Waldenströms skrift: Barndopets historia*, 1882, p. 109]. For that would be re-baptism. [. . .]

Natanael: In that you are completely correct. But it is precisely this that demonstrates that when the apostles looked upon baptism, they saw something *wholly other and higher* than a confession. And that this other thing in their eyes was the actual essence of baptism, which they demonstrated in how they expressed baptism as being true, even where confession had not been true. But furthermore there is another matter, which I have never been able to get clear for myself. You all say that child baptism cannot be true baptism, since children are not able to have faith. But if a grown man is baptized with an untrue confession, then you say that his baptism was a true baptism, despite him lacking faith. Thus, baptizing a little lad, on whom the Lord Jesus himself would have laid his hands and blessed him, this would not be baptism, but only a superstitious abomination. But if the lad grows up and becomes a hypocrite and confesses and lies, such that he fools the whole congregation and is baptized, then he would be regarded by you as having been truly baptized in a Christian manner!? Baptism can "on God's part, not truly be extended" to him, while he is a little child—who according to the Savior's own words would belong to the kingdom of God—but very well could be after he had become a hypocrite, about whom the apostle says: "You do not share any part or claim to this word, for your heart is not right before God" (Acts 8:21). Aren't you astonished by a contradiction like this?

Timoteus: But he *said* that he had faith, and we had no reason to doubt that. God does not require that the one performing the baptism is omniscient (Wiberg, p. 110).

Natanael: But his confession was certainly not true, and of what worth was it? Or do you mean that an *untrue* confession of the lips can have the power to make *that baptism* into a *true* baptism? Don't you see, how you yourself—as well as Wiberg—deep down believe, that baptism in its essence yet is something other than a confession of faith? Isn't Wiberg self-contradictory, for that matter, when he, in the same book that you just mentioned (p. 26), uses Mark 16:16 to make the claim that *the preaching of the gospel and faith must precede baptism.* There he is stating of course, that faith is necessary for baptism. But when he gets into a tight spot, he throws out *faith* and sets in its place *confession of faith*, even in an instance where a confession is not true. Indeed, he states that "when the one performing the baptism has baptized an unfaithful person—note: an unfaithful person—on the basis of what was a probable confession of faith in Christ, *even in this instance he has dealt according to the commandment of God*" (p. 110). This is altogether as though the Lord in Mark 16:16 or in some other place had said: "The one who *confesses* faith," instead of, "the one who *has faith*" and is baptized, he shall be saved. No, brother, this is not at all tenable. If baptism is in its essence a confession, then it cannot be a *true* baptism in those cases where faith is not true. [. . .]

Eleventh Conversation: On Child Baptism

Timoteus: I hope that you now won't object if we turn to the question of child baptism. Even if the words of the New Testament regarding the meaning of baptism are ambiguous . . .

Natanael: No, they are not at all ambiguous, as long as one sets out to read what is written, and allows the words to mean what they say.

Timoteus: Well, well, be that as it may, it still does not give any credence to the validity of child baptism.

Natanael: No, in this you are certainly correct. Therefore, we may now take up this question in earnest.

Timoteus: And on this point, you won't make much headway. It is certain that the Baptists have the right idea. There are no instances of child baptism during the days of the apostles. This is an invention of the state church and a mother to the Babylonian captivity [*skökan*]. It has been designed to keep people from personal piety and from developing their own conception of religion [*Barndopets historia, fortsatt av W.P.*, p. 21]. People who find themselves in a perfectly unconscious condition, will also be bound to a certain confession.

Yes, I would like to place more emphasis on this matter. Worldliness, ambition, conflict, deception, persecution, massacre—these are the expressions we must use in order to characterize the terrible consequences of this invention called child baptism (Wiberg, p. 239). Through child baptism, one lulls people to sleep in a false hope of salvation (p. 251). Yes, child baptism is the very source of most of those errors and abuses, which throughout history have appeared within Christianity, and those bloody persecutions, whereby the worldly church has sought to root out the faithful witnesses of Jesus (p. 252). Ever since I have realized this, through God's grace, I cannot fathom how I ever could have slept in ignorance of this.

Natanael: All this sounds truly hair-raising. And if I were a little bit more easily startled than I am, then I would not hesitate one more day to seek out salvation by hurling myself into one of your baptismal pools. But let us calmly and soberly examine the situation. When do you believe that child baptism first appeared?

Timoteus: In the third century after Christ's birth—and that was in the church in northern Africa, which already had become quite corrupted. [. . .]

Natanael: Now Constantine lived in the *fourth* century after Christ's birth. And just now you said that child baptism arose in the third century, thus *one hundred years before anyone had any concept of a state church?* How does that hang together then? How can the state church have invented child baptism, when child baptism according to your own admission is one hundred years older than the first state church that ever existed on earth? Are you not aware, for that matter, that it was in the latter half of the third century and the beginning of the fourth that the Christian church had to endure its bloodiest persecutions from the side of the state, even in northern Africa. That child baptism is neither a prerequisite of a state church, nor that a state church is its only outcome, this is evident in recent times within the Methodists, Congregationalists and other denominations, which practice child baptism, yet have never been state churches.

Timoteus: Well, yes, in any case the state church can take delight in the fact that child baptism has been invented (Wiberg, p. 239). [. . .]

Natanael: You said that child baptism is designed to keep people from personal piety and from developing their own conception of religion, as well as lulling them to sleep in a false hope of salvation. How can you make this claim?

Timoteus: This is demonstrated by experience, and I hope that this is something that even you yourself can admit.

Natanael: By no means. My experience and earnest conviction is that a true conversion is not more difficult for a person who has been baptized in childhood, and yet has strayed from the Lord, than for one who has not been baptized. You yourself were also baptized in your childhood, but it has not at all been a hindrance for you in becoming a true and living Christian. And think of all the great awakenings, which during recent years have passed through our country—these have occurred mostly among those who have been baptized in childhood, and they have mostly been called forth through preachers, who have been loyal to child baptism. Even you ought to concede that the vast majority of members that the Baptist denomination now claims in our country, were won by this denomination not from *the world*, but instead from among *the believers* of child-baptizing denominations.—In regard to personal piety and developing one's own conception of religion, I think that among the believers of other denominations there can be found every bit as much deep and inward personal piety and spiritual independence as anywhere within the Baptist denomination. Experience, to which you appeal, therefore does not at all help your case here.

Timoteus: But you will probably have to concede that many ungodly people comfort themselves in their ungodliness with the fact that they have been baptized in their childhood?

Natanael: It can certainly be the case that there can be found people who do this. Yet I, for one, have never heard of anyone doing so—and I know my fair share of people. But if there are people who do this, that does not prove anything. I believe that also within the Baptist denomination there are many hypocrites, who comfort themselves with the fact that they are baptized, and I would expect that you would not see in this any evidence disproving the authenticity of your form of baptism?

Timoteus: No, not at all.

Natanael: [. . .] But you said that through child baptism the unconscious child is bound to a certain confession; what did you mean with this?

Timoteus: Well, it ought to be very clear. When people are baptized by you, they are baptized to be Lutherans.

Natanael: Is that what you say? That is something that I have never heard. I see well enough that Lagergren in *Evangelisten* (vol. 7, 1880, p. 224) says, that a person through baptism "is bound to the congregation in which one is baptized." But in the New Testament, I never see that anyone is baptized to the "congregation." That the Baptists observe their baptism as a baptism into the Baptist congregation, this I have heard from various people, but never before have I seen it in print. But among us this is not what takes place. At every child baptism where I have been present, the children have been baptized into the apostolic faith, but not in the confession of the Lutheran church. Neither have I ever heard of anyone, indeed, not even the most ardent defender of child baptism, say that the person who is baptized in the Lutheran church would break his baptismal covenant if he were to go over to another denomination. But if he had been baptized as a Lutheran, then of course his going over to another denomination would in reality be a breaking of his baptismal covenant. For my part, I can honestly say that if I had been baptized to Luther, then I would immediately go and have myself baptized to the Father, Son, and the Holy Spirit. But now I am not baptized to Luther, but instead to God and his Son and his Holy Spirit. And I may honestly say, that I feel just as little need of a new baptism, as I feel any need of any other God or savior than the one to whom I have already been baptized.

Timoteus: Well indeed, this is just sophistry. At any rate, the children are raised in the Lutheran doctrines and in that way are made into Lutherans, before they can evaluate what it is that is being communicated to them.

Natanael: I really can't understand you here. Do you mean to say that Lutheran parents should be forbidden to teach or to allow their children to be taught about the Lord already from the days of their infancy?

Timoteus: No, not at all; quite the opposite. I believe that they ought to do it far more diligently than they do.

Natanael: But what do you actually mean? If they were to teach their children about the Lord, then you certainly would have to concede to them the right to speak with their children about the Lord *according to the faith that they themselves have*? Or *would only Baptists* have that right? But in *all* instruction of this sort, children are taught from infancy various perspectives on religion, which they themselves cannot be able to evaluate, but simply accept in good faith. This principle that you take as your starting point would lead to the consequence that children would not be able to receive any instruction at all in spiritual matters, before they themselves could evaluate what was being communicated to them. And that, you must understand, would be nonsense.

Timoteus: Well, yes, this I can also concede. But that would not make child baptism right. [. . .] Indeed, just look at the state churches! How is the condition in them?

Natanael: Regrettable to be sure, but from this it does not at all follow that child baptism is the cause. Decadence can take place even without child baptism. Let us all mutually and honestly admit to the decadence which exists. We would all gain by doing so. I believe that there are upright Christians in *all* denominations who are living righteously and ethically, and that all hypocrites within all denominations are on a basic level unethical. You probably also believe the same thing. Thus, decadence has its root somewhere else,

that is certain. [. . .] Furthermore, if worldliness, ambition, conflict, deception, and such within the church are a fruit of child baptism, then certainly
these things would never appear within the Baptist denomination. But is
that the case? Is there really no worldliness, ambition, or conflict within
your denomination?

Timoteus: Of course, we would have to concede that there is.

Natanael: But here you contradict yourself. And it seems that you are destined to do this one point after the other. For my part, I believe that the
decadence within the state church chiefly has its root in the *conflation of
state and church* and *does not at all have anything to do with child baptism.*
[. . .]

Timoteus: Yes, but even if it is as you say, child baptism is still not right. It
is a superstition, which not even its most ardent defenders can explain. Just
ask them! The one says this and the other says that, and complete chaos
reigns among them without foundation in God's word. [. . .]

Natanael: No, you are completely mistaken. For me the matter is like this:
regardless of whether I can explain the meaning of child baptism or not, its
validity does not depend on that at all. *A thing can be true, even if no one has
been able to truly explain it.* It is a similar case with communion. It has been
the subject of many contentious and many fantastical explanations, but
nonetheless communion remains true. There once was a pastor in a Baptist
congregation who said to me: "What is all this with child baptism? I have
asked [Peter] Fjellstedt, I have asked Rosenius, I have asked other leading
men, and everyone has given me different answers." To this I responded: "Is
that to say that the Baptists are completely in agreement about the meaning
of baptism?"—"O," he answered, "there can certainly be different opinions
even among us." [. . .]

We can take [Charles] Spurgeon, for example. He is of course a well known
and respected Baptist preacher around the world. I have a book by him,
translated into German. There he speaks about the salvation [*salighet*] of
infants: *"children who die will without a doubt be saved; but note this well—
never has a child become saved through any other way than through the death
of Jesus Christ. They will all be* born again, *but not through the sprinkling of
conversion, but instead this takes place in all probability at the very* moment
of death *in a wondrous transformation in them through* a breath of the Holy
Spirit" (Spurgeon, *Bausteine zum geistl. Tempel*, 1861, p. 101). [. . .] I must
honestly say that I have never heard a more fantastical explanation of the

salvation of infants than this one by Spurgeon. [. . .] If the Holy Spirit can purify the infant child and cause it to be born again in the *moment of death* through a sprinkling of the blood of Christ, then I cannot fathom why he could not be able to do this at some other moment. Otherwise, then the moment of death would become a kind of sacrament of salvation for the child. It also seems peculiar that God would leave the child un-born-again, unwashed, unfit for entering the Kingdom of God, *as long as they remain alive*, but to the contrary, *if they die*, only then rush to them in the moment of death and cause them to be born again, without faith. O, brother, just think of how all this is fantasy and like so many shots in the dark—and this from people who make themselves out to be standing on solid biblical ground! [. . .]

Twelfth Conversation: The New Testament and Child Baptism

Natanael: [. . .] And how about this claim of yours, that whatever is not mentioned in the New Testament cannot therefore have taken place during the time of the apostles, and furthermore, that whatever is not expressly acknowledged there, is forbidden by default! How can that be?

Timoteus: You must be able to understand that the New Testament does not specifically mention *everything* which took place in the apostolic church.

Natanael: Certainly, that I have been able to understand for a long time, but it was you who needed some instruction in this regard. And the great lesson we can take away from this is that *just because a matter is not specifically mentioned, it is not the same as demonstrating that it has not taken place.*

Timoteus: But in that way, you completely negate everything that you your-self have spoken about the higher meaning of baptism.

Natanael: No, I am simply pointing out the end to which your reasoning would lead if one followed it to its conclusion. But let us now look at another matter, in which the same situation applies. Are you aware that the New Testament does not give any examples of any women believers taking part in communion?

Timoteus: There it is! I should have known that you would come out with that old, worn out argument again!

Natanael: Now, now, take it easy! The argument is old, to be sure, but if it is worn out, that I do not know. [. . .]

Timoteus: But anyway, Wiberg shows with the New Testament that women took part in communion (pp. 36–40).

Natanael: That is completely mistaken. He presents a host of situations, which make it believable that they took part—which is altogether the same thing that we do in the question of child baptism. [. . .] None of the women who followed Jesus, not even his mother Mary, were present when he instituted communion, although they were there in Jerusalem. [. . .] That men and women were baptized, that is written, but that women also took part in communion, that is written nowhere, and it puzzles me that you wouldn't find it peculiar that the one thing is not written, when the other thing is. That in Christ Jesus there is no difference "between man and woman," this would be something that would also apply to children: in Christ Jesus there is no difference between "the elderly and children"—that is, except for the difference *that children are the greatest in God's kingdom, and that the older people must become like children in order to be able to enter therein.* That there were women who were deaconesses, that is to say, females serving the congregation, this is written, but that they took part in communion, this is written nowhere, and yet you believe that they did this. [. . .]

Sixteenth Conversation: Laying Hands on Children

[. . .]

Timoteus: [. . .] But children of course do not understand what is being done with them, and then all of this becomes a superstition, an empty and dead ceremony and nothing else, altogether like when the papists baptize church bells and so on.

Natanael: But when a Baptist lays hands on his children and blesses them, do the children understand then what he is doing with them?

Timoteus: No, of course not. [. . .]

Natanael: You know what, brother, I thank God, that I was baptized as a child. I thank God for receiving the opportunity to present my children for baptism. If there are things I don't understand about the meaning of baptism, I will leave that matter to my Savior. Different explanations of baptism might be able to *confuse simple minds*, perhaps even *trouble their consciences*, but they do nothing to *invalidate the thing itself*. And as much as you consider it to be a superstition that I believe a great blessing is instigated in the lives of my small children through baptism, it could similarly be said that the very same superstition is demonstrated in the fact that you lay hands on your children and bless them. There is much that surpasses our natural understanding, but which nevertheless is true and right and full of blessing. And however "unconscious" our small children are, neither are they timbers or stones or church bells or soulless animals, but instead are true and genuine human beings, receptive to God's grace and blessing, and though equally unconscious of the sins of their parents, would be just as receptive to those things. Yes, I say it again: I will gladly present my children in faith through baptism to the Father, Son, and Holy Spirit.

Timoteus: And what I will do in the future with my children, only God knows. Thanks in the meantime for our conversations. Farewell!

COMMUNION

C.O. Rosenius, 1846

("Något att betänka wid Herrens nattward")

Now, you ask: "What has our dear Lord intended with this wondrous and lofty institution? What were his true purposes with this?" There are many Christians who have never gained a proper understanding of communion or how to appropriately enjoy it, nor have they been able to receive that assurance, happiness, and joy, which communion normally imparts, either because they have not known or have not perceived what Christ's intentions and purposes were with this institution. To say *everything*, that the Lord has intended, will only first be possible in eternity, when everything will be explained. Yet we can still understand some of it. We will begin by [...] reflecting on the characteristic of communion as a remembrance of the reconciling death of Christ.

The Lord said: "*Do this in remembrance of me.*" Now we should first understand that he did not institute this memorial for *himself*, but instead as a service to *us*; for everything that Christ did on earth, this took place for us, as he himself says: "The Son of Man has not come to be served, but instead to serve and give his life as a ransom for many" (Mt 20:28). So take note of his grace-filled purpose in what we can see already here, that he has instituted a remembrance of himself for us. In other words, Christ knew the weaknesses of his children, as well as the arduous road they would have to walk through this life's desert and vale of tears. He knew how they would often be close to the point of giving up on this road; he knew how they were weak and sensitive, had fearful hearts and would have a daily, incessant feud with the flesh, the world and the slyness and arrows of the devil; he knew that they would become tired, sick, wounded, exhausted and despairing. In addition, he knew that they would only be able to be revitalized and draw their assurance and strength from *him*; that only if they earnestly turned their thoughts to *him*, would they once again be able to receive new life, courage, strength, and cheerfulness to continue on their journey. He knew, furthermore, that what would most of all wear away at their courage, make them timid and anxious, would be their own *sins*, mistakes and infirmities; but also, that against all of these sins, nothing else would be of more assurance to them, than his suffering and death, his offering of his body and blood, which were poured out for the forgiveness of sins. And so he instituted this memorial to his reconciling death and said: "Children, gather here together often; when it begins to grow dark to your eyes, and you begin to give up, gather here together to enjoy my body and my blood, and think of me." In short, he wanted to set up huts along the road for our rest, where the weary wayfarers would be able to go in and be strengthened and revitalized by this bread of heaven, his body and blood, and by having their thoughts focused on him.

For although this memorial of Christ and his reconciling death could have been preserved in power in the congregation merely through the preaching of the word, it was yet in his eternal wisdom and delight in love to also institute a specific, outward and visible means, whereby this memorial would tangibly come to life and intervene in our weak, incredulous hearts. The Lord has always made use of such means as a way of supporting his people in faith. When they were under that most terrible slavery in Egypt, sighing and wailing, on the evening before Israel at long last was to be delivered, the Lord instituted the sacrament of the Passover lamb, as a memorial to this marvelous deliverance, which would always strengthen and enliven the people in faith and reverence for God. Now then: "Our Passover lamb has been slain for us" (1 Cor 5:7). The Passover lamb of the Jews was a model, a shadow (Heb 10:1) of the true *sacrifice of the Lamb of God* and the great *spiritual deliverance*, which thereby would be imparted to the whole world, as well as to the *eating* of this Lamb of God in communion. [. . .]

This memorial to the miracle of reconciliation, by Christ, by his bloody and pale figure on the cross, is certainly beneficial to all of our inward person. It awakens us from our forgetfulness and slumber; it cleanses our eyes from the dust, which has clouded them during the journey; it paints both sin and grace in their true colors; it offers assurance and solace to our dejected hearts, strengthens and restores the peace and joy of our child-like trust; it lifts our souls from earth and directs them toward heaven, and much more. But we also note this aspect: that Christ in his communion has not merely instituted a *memorial feast*, but instead that he also *gives us his body and blood to eat and drink*, as well as *those words* which he spoke, just as he passed the cup of blessing. Namely, this was an actual blessing that was his primary purpose here. His words were: "This is my blood, the new covenant, which will be poured out for you and for many to the forgiveness of sins." From these words we note that the main point was to offer *assurance to us against our sins*, to *grant peace to our burdened conscience.* For the one thing that he said about his blood was that it was *the new covenant*—and that it was *poured out for the forgiveness of sins.* Take note here of the Lord's purpose and disposition! It was not enough for him to simply pour out his blood to the forgiveness of our sins, but he also wanted, in the most powerful and profound way, to *convince us of our participation* in this reconciliation, he wanted us to be truly assured and glad about this. [. . .] In this blood, *a new covenant* has been established between God and you, not like the old one (Jer 31:31–34). The old covenant *demanded* and *condemned*; the new covenant *imparts* and *reconciles*. The old one said: "*Do, give*"; the new one says: "*Believe, receive.*" And the blood of the old covenant was the blood of goats and calves; the blood of the new covenant is *the blood of God's son.* And "this blood of mine is poured out *to the forgiveness of sins.*" See, this is what the Lord wished to say.

Here there is an inexhaustible wellspring of assurance for every soul, whose conscience is tormented by sin, if only she will just pause, calm down, be still, and ponder what the Lord is doing and saying here. Here thousands of traumatized and condemned souls have been awakened and found an endlessly abundant source of assurance and blessedness, when the Lord has been able to open their minds, so that they can perceive what is here for them. Consider this for a moment: you who come with a sick conscience and are trembling on account of your sins, who truly have the desire to be made well, believe, and follow your Savior, but have not been able to do it—note this well and consider that Christ has himself said: "*My blood will be poured out for the forgiveness of sins.*" [. . .] Indeed, if you did not have any sins, then you would never have a reason to come to the Lord's table, never would have needed to come, since then the Lord would not have had anything here that could cheer you and serve you; for the only thing he serves here is the assurance for the forgiveness of sins.

Dear soul, perhaps things have gotten quite bad for you now—perhaps you have been careless, indifferent, unvigilant; you have perhaps fallen into some sin, for you have an evil flesh, which is full of all manner of evil desires, which is like gunpowder to fire, easily ignited to all manner of sins; what is more, you are surrounded by people and situations which give you a thousand reasons to sin; besides, the devil is deceiving you in order to bring you down. In this situation there can be plenty of opportunity for misdeeds, sins, anguish, and worrying. If the situation for you now is so bad that you doubt that you could ever again find any assurance, all the same—pause, look, and listen! What do you believe about this meal? Can't you see what the Lord, the merciful one, has meant it to be? Do you not see that it was precisely his intention to offer assurance to poor sinners, when he instituted this supper, in which he gives us his blood and says: *"this is poured out for the forgiveness of sins."* See, this is what the Lord says, the one you have feared. See to it that you don't argue with him who is speaking to you, and that you don't also add to the pile of your sins that you also deny his grace, his precious blood, and his holy word. Or is it the case that his blood is no longer sufficient for the washing away of all *your* sins? Your sins could very well be grave and great, but against the *blood of Christ, God's Son* they become small and light, indeed, (as Luther says) *like mere sparks against the vast ocean.* [...] Truly, Christ poured out his blood, not merely for *some* sins, but for *all* of them, not for invented or imagined sins, but for real ones; not for small ones, but also for the great and grave; not for sins overcome and long past, but also for the sins that are mighty and close at hand. [...]

Now finally, here are some words on another marvelous thing, which Christ has intended and accomplishes with the distribution of his body and blood to our nourishment. This is namely the *inward union with him and his faithful followers.* About this he says expressly: "The one who eats my flesh and drinks my blood, he will *remain* in me and I in him" (Jn 6:56). And immediately after the institution of communion, he said: "You will understand that I *am in* my Father, *and you in me and I in you*" (Jn 14:20); "I am the vine, you are the branches; the one who remains in me and I in him, he will bear much fruit" (Jn 15:5). [...] O, this must be the crowning glory of this excellent sacrament. Isn't this union the most glorious thing we have here on earth! Indeed, when a soul has first received the great assurance against her sins, which this sacrament exists to impart, she often begins to burn with love for her Lord and Savior, that she well wishes she could take him up into her heart. [...] And see, the Lord has here created a way that precisely such a wish could be satisfied. If one wants to understand what the true foundation is for all of this, then one must remember that it was precisely the reunion of humankind with God that was the entire purpose for this counsel of salvation. Humankind was created to be in intimate union with God.

COMMUNION

P.P. Waldenström, 1891

(Guds eviga frälsningsråd)

This is my body, which is given for you (Lk 22:19). [. . .] It remains for us now to speak about the meaning of this holy supper, its outward institution and its proper use for spiritual upbuilding.

My body, *which is given for you*. Christ assumed, in his birth by a woman, a human body. The word became flesh (Jn 1:14). In his manhood, he lived and wandered around among us, full of grace and truth. He gave everything for us. He forsook his heavenly glory and became the most despised and rejected, wounded and afflicted (Isa 53). He became poor for our sake, so that we through his poverty could become rich (2 Cor 8:9). All of his time, his days, his hours and minutes he gave to us. All of his strength he gave to us. You will never discover a moment in his story when he was living for himself. For the Father's sake, he devoted himself to us in everything that he was and did. And now, he stood there prepared to give out his own life, his body. [. . .]

"*This is my blood, of the covenant, which is poured out for many for the forgiveness of sins,*" he says, when he passes the wine to them. Or as Luke and Paul relate: "This is the new covenant in my blood." With this he makes a reference to the old covenant. This too had its sacrifices and sacrificial blood, but all of it was merely a shadow of this good thing that was to come, and not the thing itself. For the Old Testament's sacrificial blood could never take away sin. But now, says the Lord, now the new covenant has come, and it is instituted in my blood, which truly cleanses from sins. [. . .]

When the apostle says: "*You proclaim the Lord's death until he comes,*" he thus makes it understood that in communion there is an expression of the believers' certainty and expectation that *the Lord shall come again*. In this holy supper, the believing person's spirit is stretched both backward and forward. In faith, he stretches back to Christ's first entry into flesh; in hope he is stretched forward to the second coming of Christ at the end of this age. While the Lord *was here*, this supper was not needed; therefore, he did not institute it until it was time for his departure. When the Lord comes again, it will also no longer be needed. At that point, it will cease and leave room for something higher, which we cannot imagine now, but which the Lord expresses with these remarkable words: "I say to you: I shall not drink of this fruit of the vine from now until that day, when I drink the new wine with you in my father's kingdom" (Mt 26:29; Mk 14:25). Communion is an *in-between* meal, in which we eat his flesh and drink his blood, until that time when *he comes himself.*

Concerning how often one should partake in the Lord's supper, by contrast, there is nothing commanded in God's word. The Savior stipulates no time, does not say *how* often, but simply, *"as often as you do this."* With that he leaves it to the disciples themselves to do it as often as they will. Neither does he stipulate any certain room, but instead leaves this also up to them. *"It is as though he wished to say: I am creating and instituting an Easter feast or supper, which you shall celebrate not only on the evening of this day each year, but instead enjoy it often, whenever and as often as it should please you, as it is opportune and necessary for each and every person, without being bound to any room or any time"* (Luther, in his larger catechism). Now this may take place publically in the congregation or privately here and there in the homes; about this there is no commandment or prohibition. As often as one does it and wherever one does it, one should do it in his memory only, in faith in him, the blessed Savior, whose blood cleanses us from all sin.

Concerning the form for the celebration of holy communion, we see from the institution itself that according to the Lord's arrangement, that it shall be celebrated with the eating of bread and the drinking of wine. Thus it is not acceptable to replace bread with something else, or to instead of the *fruit of the vine* use something else (for example, berry juice). Just as in baptism one may not use something other than water, so too one may not exchange the bread and wine in communion for something else. If communion was merely a symbolic event, then this would make no difference. [. . .] But as we have seen already, communion is not anywhere in the New Testament presented as merely a symbolic event. It is a means by which the Lord gives us his body to eat and his blood to drink. And in this case, one should keep faithfully to what the Lord has instituted. In the outward form itself, may Christian freedom prevail; but if one were to substitute bread and wine for something else, then it would be a different supper altogether. [. . .]

But *for whom* is holy communion instituted? This question is of great importance. Is communion instituted for all people or for some, for believers and the ungodly or only for the believers, and is it instituted for all believers or exclusively for some of them? If we now look to the New Testament, we immediately find that the Lord has instituted communion for his *apostles.* Then we find that the apostles celebrated it together with the believers, and finally that the Christian congregations, according to the arrangement of the apostles, celebrated it among themselves. [. . .] Thus it is for all of the disciples of Jesus that holy communion has been instituted, without differentiation between man and woman, rich and poor, master and servant. But it has not been instituted for anyone other than the disciples of the Lord. [. . .] But *even though* Judas Iscariot was present at the institution of holy communion, it does not follow in any way that holy communion has been instituted for blatantly ungodly people. The Lord did not separate Judas from the circle of the disciples, despite the fact that he knew well enough that Judas was secretly a thief. But from this it does not follow that the Christian congregation should accept or retain blatant thieves or other criminals in its membership. Secret hypocrites, whom only the Lord knows, these people have to be allowed in the Christian congregation. [. . .]

Indeed, if in his simplicity, some believing Christian, because he believes that it pleases God, celebrates the Lord's communion among the children of the world, does this mean that for him this holy communion has been nullified, such that he is not partaking in Christ's body and blood? Answer: No, not so. The Lord's institutions do not stand on such loose foundations. [. . .] Even though the validity of the event is not based on the merits of the participants, it is nevertheless of importance that the bounty of God's holy table is administered by the right people. [. . .] Even though the people in your company cannot, by their lack of faith, take away this holy bounty from you, it is still of importance that *as far as it is possible*, the right people are gathered together for this supper; and the right people are the disciples of Jesus. It is for this reason that holy communion should remain a communion and fellowship of believers. It is a fellowship, on the one hand, between them and the Lord, and on the other hand, mutually between each other. It is for them that this supper has been instituted and not for others, as we have already before extensively seen.

Thus when it has reached the point in the large church denominations where all of the spiritually dead world, blatant blasphemers, drinkers, lechers and others of the sort are permitted indiscriminately to holy communion, then this for the Lord is certainly an abomination. People make the excuse that it is impossible to achieve a pure congregation, but this is altogether the same as when the individual, ungodly person excuses his gross, apparent ungodliness by saying that there has never existed anyone in this life who has managed to become perfect. But such an excuse is nothing more than those fig leaves, with which Adam and Eve tried to cover their nakedness from the Lord after their fall. It would be better for people to wake up, confess their sins, and mend their ways. To make excuses and cover up transgressions, this leads to ruin and condemnation. [. . .]

You, who need Jesus—this supper has been instituted for you. You have many dangers to pass through, many difficulties and sufferings. So then, make use of this holy supper. It will be help and strength to you. [. . .] Perhaps you feel tempted and tormented by all manner of impure thoughts and desires, wrath, bitterness, greed, pride, fornication, and so on. Indeed, perhaps you are like so many of God's children, so tormented by these things that you do not dare speak about it with other people. You think that no one can be like you are. Now then, come here, eat and drink! [. . .] Yes, it is you—precisely you, who should come to this table. This table is set not only for strong and exceptional disciples, but also for the weak and miserable ones, for people who need to be lifted up, bandaged, and strengthened. [. . .] "Eat, drink, and take your strength, my son, my daughter! This is what I have to give you, until I come to you myself."

It is a terrible seduction of the devil, when he frightens simple souls, on account of their weaknesses, away from *the table of grace*. It is altogether as though this table had been intended as a reward for the strong, and not a help to the weak. When the king invites guests to his table, then he does it as a way of honoring those who are deserving and outstanding. But when Jesus invites people to his table, he does it to bless, console, strengthen, and aid the miserable and weak. The impoverished, who have no helper, who have no money, who do not dare to lift up their eyes—even these people he wishes to see at this table. If they are unworthy, they are yet in need, and he is a savior to those in need. Therefore, come and come often, as often as you need. Jesus will not cast you out. And if the devil attempts to do so, then boldly show him the door.

We turn now to some beautiful words on this matter from Rosenius: "[. . .] *What do you believe about this meal? Can't you see what the Lord, the merciful one, meant it to be? Do you not see that it was precisely his intention to offer assurance to poor sinners, when he instituted a supper, where he gives us his blood and says: this is poured out for the forgiveness of sins. See, this is what the Lord says, the one you have feared. See to it that you don't argue with him who is speaking to you, that you don't also add to the pile of your sins that you also deny his grace, his precious blood and his holy word. Or is it the case now that his blood is not sufficient for the washing away of all your sins? [. . .] Truly, Christ poured out his blood, not merely for some sins, but for all of them, not for small ones, but also for the great and grave; not for sins overcome and long past, but also for the sins that are mighty and close at hand."*

When the word becomes dry and powerless, and when it seems to you that you are reading and listening, but not grasping any strength, no blessedness in it—when "it tastes like dry wood" (Luther)—when prayer becomes dry and lackluster and the practice of devotion becomes mechanical and superficial, such that it causes you worry, then come to the Lord Jesus' table, eat and drink his body, which he has given for you, his blood, which he has poured out for you. And say: "Lord Jesus, my dear Savior, I do not understand myself; it feels as though I am without faith, without love, without strength, without life. Therefore, I come to you in my great need. You are life, make me alive; you are all-powerful, make me strong; you are holy, allow me to partake in your holiness; you are love, enlighten my heart with your love." And your prayer shall not go unheard.

COMFORTABLE CHRISTIANITY

P.P. Waldenström, 1893

("Beqväm kristendom")

Comfortable Christianity, it is indeed, when a believer lives for himself. He does not want to be a part of the congregation, as one of its members. He sticks to himself. He calls it "being free," and free he wants to be. If the congregation builds a meeting house and furnishes it nicely and secures for itself a good and talented preacher, then he will go there and listen and feel good. But being involved and bearing the burdens, taking part in the responsibilities and tasks of being a member in the body of the congregation, which makes all this possible—that he has no desire to do. He will perhaps lay a mite in the offering occasionally, and this will likely never add up to much. If difficulties of the economic sort come up for the congregation, then he is glad that he stands off to the side, and can avoid placing his shoulders under the burden in order to help carry it. Instead he goes in the other direction to someplace that is more rewarding. This is splendid, and he feels that he is so free. How things would go if everyone were to do the same thing—he does not think about that.

If difficulties of the spiritual variety appear in the congregation, for example through sin, in this case he will also be glad that he stands off to the side. To be part of the congregation and share in its sorrows and concerns, wash feet, correct immoral practices, search to find the lost and restore the fallen—to this end he feels no calling. Quite the opposite, he thinks like this: "God be praised, that I do not belong there!" This is indeed splendid, and he feels that he is so free.

If the congregation's preacher is not that talented or begins to become burned out, then Mr. Comfortable goes to some other place, where people can provide him with a better preacher. And now is when he really feels the benefits of being free. To be part of the congregation and help lift up and support the preacher—no, his spiritual insight and his Christian love do not extend so far, that he realizes or feels that he might have a duty to do something like that. If the preacher becomes old, sick, or feeble, such that the congregation needs to support him, then Mr. Comfortable can of course complain to the congregation when they do not do that right. But for he himself to be involved and help carry the burdens, to that end he feels no obligation. He of course does not belong to the congregation; he only went there as long as they had something to offer that he liked. Now he goes and eats with other people, until he happens to find yet another place, where he can eat even better without any cost or inconvenience or worries.

When the kingdom of God appears, he is perhaps expecting that the Lord will say to him: "You good and faithful servant, who defended the true evangelical freedom, go on into the drawing room and find yourself a seat right in the middle of the sofa."

This is a highly serious matter. May God help all Comfortable Christians to a right mindset!

PRAY FOR THE PREACHER AND THE CONGREGATION

P.P. Waldenström, 1899

(Den kristna församlingen)

As you prepare to come to a gathering, you should first *pray for yourself, for the preacher and for the congregation*. Many a Christian, who complains that he has not gotten anything out of the sermon, has only himself to blame. He has not prayed to God to receive anything. Very often this is the case. But people don't think about this. One would rather blame the preacher. "He is dry," people say. That can also be the case. But it can very often depend on the fact that you and the other believers *have not prayed for him*. And then, whose fault is it?

It often happens that the one believer might receive the greatest of blessings from a sermon, while the other believer does not experience anything. This cannot depend on the preacher. No, it depends on that the former has come, hungering and thirsting for the word of life and praying to God, both for himself and for the preacher. The latter, on the other hand, comes sluggishly and indifferent without any spiritual hunger, without any prayer. But can anyone rightfully expect that he has been thinking about this, confessing his sins, and praying to God for forgiveness? No, instead he perhaps will say with a sigh: "O, if only God would give us another preacher, for there is nothing to hear from this one."

"But can it be the case that the preacher and his sermon might be flawed?" you ask. Indeed, preachers are very flawed and frail in relation to the heavy responsibility, which rests on them. But therefore, you should, with your prayers and your interest, help them to improve. Do you do this— *do you*? And then you should also pray for yourself, that God might give you the ears to hear. For the one who is deaf, will not even hear the rumbling thunder, but will think that everything is completely silent. You should pray that God would give you a true spiritual hunger. For even the best and healthiest food will not taste like anything in the mouth of the person who is not hungry. But if a true hunger is present, then the simplest and homeliest meal will taste like heavenly manna.

The old man of God, Rosenius, told me once about an occasion when he had preached so miserably that he was embarrassed to show himself in public afterward. And so he stayed in the vestry, until the people had dispersed. But nevertheless, he couldn't avoid the company of the well-known composer [Oscar] Ahnfelt, whom he had invited home to dinner. While they were walking, Ahnfelt went along crying silently. Rosenius thought: "Now he is probably crying because of how miserably I have preached." After a while, he gained the courage to ask: "Why are you crying?"—"Well," answered Ahnfelt, "something has happened for me today, which seldom happens, that God's word has moved me to tears." Astonished, Rosenius asked: "Are you joking with me, or have you not noticed, what a terrible time I have had of it in the pulpit?" Now it was Ahnfelt's turn to be astonished. But they soon understood the situation. Ahnfelt had come there, praying, hungering and thirsting for the word of life, and God had, through a worthless sermon, satisfied his soul. How can this be? Perhaps you have something to learn from this story?

Don't believe that the preacher can just shake a sermon out of his coat sleeve, such that he has no need of your prayers. On the other hand, don't believe that you are so spiritual, that you don't need to pray for ears to hear and the heart to understand and receive. O, how much of the noble seed of the word is spilled on the road, even for the believers, just because they have not seriously taken this important matter to heart! The preacher needs your prayers. Even the apostle Paul requested that the believers would pray for him, that the word might be given to him so that he could "proclaim the mysteries of the gospel with all fearlessness" (Eph 6:19). And you yourself need to prepare yourself to receive God's word, so that it will be a real blessing to you. [. . .]

But it is not just for yourself and the preacher that you should pray, but also for the congregation or the audience in general. Praying for them is mission work. We are not able to explain how the prayers of the one person can come to influence the other, but it is nevertheless a reality. Most of the realities that we experience are inexplicable, but are no less real because of it. Such is the case with the blessing of intercessory prayer. It is a great and blessed reality, that I can through my prayers influence the people I am praying for. There is a mysterious, spiritual connection between people, and this is because no human being stands alone isolated. Each and every person comprises a limb in a connected whole, altogether as the limbs in a body stand in relation to one another and influence one another through the body to which they are joined.

Therefore, in the simplicity of your heart, say: "O, Lord God, help the preacher to preach. Help me to hear and help this crowd of listeners, that everyone might have the eyes to see and the ears to hear and the heart to obediently receive what it is that you are speaking to us."

THE BLESSING OF SONG

C.O. Rosenius, 1850

("Låten Kristi ord rikligen bo ibland eder")

"With hymns and songs of praise and spiritual songs, sing in grace to the glory of the Lord in your hearts" (Eph 5:19). Here the apostle challenges us that even songs can be used for our upbuilding. And isn't song full of blessing and a means to awaken, uplift, and collect our scattered thoughts, calm and cause the heart to rejoice amidst the troubles of the vale of tears! How many times have not the thickest clouds been dispersed through an upbuilding song! How many hard and cold souls have not been warmed by a delightful song and awakened to reflection! How often hasn't it been the case that many precious lessons have been planted deep in our hearts by songs, long after the sermons are forgotten! Luther's enemies complained that he did more damage (to the pope's church) through his songs, than through all of his sermons. And on the merits of song, Basil has made the following thoughts (Homil. in Ps. 1): *"Since the holy Spirit realized how difficult it would be for the human mind to allow itself to be drawn to what is good and holy, since we are very willing to do things which are delightful to our nature, what should he then do? For this reason he combined the delightfulness of song with the nutrition of doctrine, so that in this way we might receive the beautiful sustenance of the word before we even realized it."* [. . .]

But the most important remark that the apostle makes here, sounds like this: "And sing to the glory of the Lord in your hearts." By this, of course, he did not mean to say that we should not sing with the mouth, but he challenges us that we should not merely allow this to be a song of the mouth and for other human beings. Instead, as the apostle says in another place: "I shall make praise with the spirit (in my heart, for the Lord), but I shall also make praise with the mind," that is to say with such a voice, that even others will hear and understand it (1 Cor 14:15). Just think, when the hymn contains expressions of prayer, thanksgiving, longing, and more, and you allow it to only proceed through the mouth, instead of bringing this before God in your heart, then this of course is a clear hypocrisy. It is a great danger, particularly in some places, where people make a great fuss about the harmony of the song, of practicing the parts and such things, that in the end it becomes—just a song!—without heart, without meaning and spirit. O, how easily our rebellious hearts drive us off onto the wrong road! If we could only be vigilant and upright, we would soon take note of this and confess it. Many seek to be seen by others as being grounded in spiritual communion when they sing spiritual songs, while at the same time their *hearts* do not participate in the very thing that they are singing with their lips, even if they in their *thoughts* are in agreement with it. For human beings, such songs might be nothing other than something beautiful, as religious entertainment, but for God it is a nauseating hypocrisy, when it had been intended to be regarded as sincere. Lütkemann has correctly remarked: *"Christians ought not use song in any other way than how they use prayer itself, namely with true devotion and fear of the Lord."* And the church father Augustine says about this (in Confess.): *"If I were to sing in such a way that I found more joy in the delightful tone and sound, than in the contents, then I confess that I thereby would have sinned most truly and would need discipline. I would much rather not sing or hear singing, than that no devotion would be present in it."* This is what the apostle means, when he adds: "And sing to the glory of the Lord in your hearts."

Now, what a rich blessing it is if we also in this way, through upbuilding, delightful songs of devotion allow the words of Christ to richly dwell within us and among us! What a peace and joy in the spirit, what a strength against all manner of temptations, if a Christian in the midst of working, as the occasion allows, even allowed himself to be built up by this! He would thereby, without himself being aware of this, build up and do much good for his listeners. Isn't it delightful and upbuilding to hear how a farmer in the field, or a craftsman in the workshop, or a servant amidst the stillness of the day's chores, lightens this labor and the heart with a beautiful spiritual song! Doesn't a Christian do right by himself when he, whether at home or out in the countryside, sings a song of praise to the Lord, instead of allowing unhealthy thoughts and sorrows to distract and trouble his heart! The early Christians had such healthy practices as these. And when the love of Christ is burning warmly in the heart, these will rise up on their own. "If someone is in good spirits, let him sing hymns," says the apostle. It is only where a legalistic spirit reigns, where the "yoke of slavery" weighs down the mind, where one does not hear songs of praise. But when an evangelical spirit begins to reign, there these happy songs rise up on their own. It is about precisely this kind of blessed moment and upbuilding practice that Hieronymus says quite beautifully (in epistola 17 ad Narcellam): "*No matter where you turn, the man in the field behind the plough will be singing a joyful hallelujah. The busy harvest worker will take delight in a song of praise, and the vintner pressing grapes will be singing a psalm of David. These are our love songs. The shepherds of the fields resound with them, and with them our countrymen arm themselves.*" See, this is something we should constantly do, even during our work, and in this way have fellowship with Christ, that his word would richly dwell among us.

CITIZENSHIP IN HEAVEN

C.O. Rosenius, 1853 & 1852

(*"Guds folks borgerskap och umgängelse i himmelen" / "Alla trognas saliga hopp"*)

"*Our fellowship* [umgängelse] *is in heaven,*" writes the apostle, "*and we wait for the Savior from there, the Lord Jesus Christ, who will transform our lowly bodies, so that they will become like his glorious body*" (Phil 3:20, 21). Consider the confidence with which the apostle speaks here! He expresses the most confident certainty of his divine calling, so that already for this reason these words do our hearts good. Thus we see here that it is not impossible already in *this* world to have *certainty* regarding the grace we have received, and not simply that, but also concerning the life to come in heaven. [. . .] And we should not simply fix our eyes on this marvelous destination of ours, but know that it is a great and actual reality—which is just as certain as that we now exist on this earth and once were created by God—so that our faith and hope might give *strength* to our heart and to all of our life.

This true Christianity is not a system of doctrine among others that is cordoned off from the rest of life, as the blind children of unbelief often claim. No, this is the most wonderful "strength of God to salvation," which creates new human beings on earth, and with its sanctifying Spirit pervades their entire being. Because of this they already enjoy a heavenly fellowship here and now, as the apostle says: "Our fellowship is in heaven." And if one asks about the foundations and sources of this heavenly fellowship, they are the following: first, *certainty regarding a great inheritance that is already won*; next, *a daily experience of the living Lord*; and finally, *the glimpse of hope for the glory which God shall give.*

Paul in Rome describes himself as *a prisoner* and yet free, *oppressed* by the world and yet *triumphant* over it, and despite facing a constant threat of death, he is fearless and full of joy. And in the second letter to the Corinthians he says: "We are in every way hard pressed, but not crushed, perplexed but not in despair, persecuted but not abandoned, struck down but not lost, as though dying, and behold, we live, as chastised and yet not dead, distressed and yet always glad." Listen to these riddles! Isn't this the expression of a peculiar and mysterious essence? Such is the essence of a Christian: oppressed and yet triumphant—distressed and yet glad—poor and yet very rich—sinful and yet completely righteous—miserable and yet marvelous—a transient on earth, but with a heavenly citizenship! [. . .] For Paul, the sun rises first in the evening, and when it grows dark down here, then he lifts himself up to the light of paradise up there. He has a double life: he is a transient here on earth, but his citizenship is in heaven. He belongs to a higher order of things and lives with his heart in this higher, true fatherland of his. "Our fellowship," he says, or literally, "Our citizenship [*borgerskap*] is in heaven."—It is, as he says, not "what shall be"—and thus he indicates something that is already present. O, what Paul is explaining here is something completely different than that which the world means with its hope "of a life to come." Paul knows already, while he is walking here on earth, that he is a citizen of heaven—and what happiness, what a treasure this consciousness is, which no other human idea here on earth has ever been able to match! But from where had Paul received this certainty of his faith? One might very well ask this. Indeed, Paul knew Christ! This is the entire secret. [. . .]

Our *citizenship* is in heaven; our *fellowship* is also there, for the apostle adds: *"we wait for the Savior from there."* And we wait not simply for the great day of his return, but we wait, we sigh and cry out to him *day by day and moment by moment.* This is something that is characteristic of God's children and the heirs of the kingdom of heaven, first, that they have received the spirit of being an elect child, in which they can cry out, "Abba, Father," and that they begin to confide with God, as children with their father;

and second, that if they are not able to confide with him in this way—for such weakness and powerlessness often befalls them—then there remains in their heart a sighing and waiting for the Lord. The Savior, his grace and presence, is the vital need of their souls, such that this waiting for the Lord is the very breath of the new human being. [. . .] But do not think that you will always be able to see and perceive that he is near. Quite the opposite, it is characteristic of his household, that he often hides himself from us and allows all manner of evils to appear and be felt, such as sin, powerlessness and the most terrible attacks of the devil. Then we may think that the Savior is thousands of miles away and that evil spirits alone have us in their power, along with our own evil and that of the world. [. . .] But as surely as God himself declares to Zion: "In wrath I am hiding my face from you for a time, but with my eternal grace I will have mercy over you," and as impossible as it was for Christ to remain away from the weeping Mary at the tomb or the two disciples, who were walking to Emmaus and who thought that he was forever lost, it is just as impossible that any solitary soul now can wait for the Lord and cry out to him day and night and nevertheless come to shame in her waiting. No, this goes against the very essence of God's being. God leads his own in mysterious ways, but always with an eternal faithfulness. And regardless of how things stand with your sins and your situation, when your soul yet waits for the Lord—even if you cannot bring yourself to utter a single prayer from your lips, but instead your tormented heart in powerlessness and indescribable sighing waits for the Lord—even then it is impossible for him to remain at a distance. [. . .]

We wait for the Savior, the Lord Jesus Christ, from heaven; and then he shall also "transform our lowly bodies, so that they will become like his glorious body." So, may all the joys of earth gladly be taken from us! For this reason we are exceedingly happy as we wait for this blessed day, when the Lord shall come with the angels of his power and with the trumpet of God, in order to exalt his saints and be worshipped by all those who believe. Then all the darkness and half-heartedness of this earthly life, its frailty and lamentations, shall meet their end; all sin and fears, uncertainties and sorrows, indeed, all the evil and torments of the heart shall meet their end; we shall "see him, as he is," the faithful Savior, who was here following us invisibly, who heard our prayers, who forgave our sins, and helped us in all our distresses. [. . .]

Even the shabby tents of our bodies will be transfigured like his glorious body. Not simply our souls, but also our bodies shall be exalted and filled with blessedness. If you ask how this is possible, then here is the apostle's answer: "According to the power, whereby he is able to bring all things under himself." It is the almighty Creator who shall do all this! What could be easier for the Almighty than to do everything he wills to do? And if someone asks how we ought to understand the resurrection of our bodies, then the apostle leads us to a field sown with grain, and shows us how the Lord already there has demonstrated for our eyes an annual example of the resurrection. [. . .] Consider now, when the sower in the autumn casts out his grain into the earth, and upon it falls many dreary downpours of rain and snow, and the earth freezes hard as stone during the winter's long, dark months; then it seems as though all of this seed was discarded and lost. If we were not accustomed every spring to seeing how this seed returns in multiplied measure, then we would have just as much cause to be distressed about the return of this seed, as we now wonder how all those people who have been laid down in the earth shall once again rise up. O, this foolish human heart of ours! We see constant works of wonder from God's almighty hand; but if it pleases him to prophecy one single thing before he has shown us this, then we are immediately ready to call him a liar, without any better cause to present than that *we* do not understand it, and that *for us* this is an impossibility. Consider this: he, who does not allow the insignificant grain of wheat, which is cast into the earth, to come to nothing, but instead grants even to it a day of resurrection, would he allow the most precious thing he has created, all those thousands of more priceless, noble, and artfully-crafted seeds, the human body—which he has so highly honored when he took this upon himself as his garment, and then redeemed it along with the soul—would he allow this priceless seed to come to nothing?

*   *   *

In the second chapter of the letter to Titus (2:11–13), the expectation of the Lord's return is presented, not as something monstrous and unfruitful for the godliness of the Christian, but instead as the culmination and crowning of a Christian life. *"God's grace teaches us that we should forsake all ungodliness and worldly desires and live self-controlled, upright and godly lives in this world and wait for the blessed hope and the great appearance of our God and Savior Jesus Christ."*

Already in the above testimony from Scripture it is sufficiently established, not only that this marvelous return of Christ to the judgment of the world and the deliverance of the faithful is to be the proper object for all of our common, blessed hope; but we have even seen that already the apostles and the first Christians had hoped to experience this return of Christ. And from this we find that when these same disciples predicted these great events that would precede this return of the Lord, they did not mean such an immense extent that these things could not be completed within their lifetime—since they themselves, of course, hoped to experience the return of the Lord, indeed, were waiting every moment for the Lord to come down from on high. From this we can observe that neither do we have any cause to wait for world events of such a great scale, which would thus preclude us from expecting the appearance of the Lord at any given moment. This is how the Lord himself spoke, when he invited those with whom he was speaking to never be so confident that they might not be taken by surprise by him "as a thief in the night," saying: "Keep watch, for that reason; for you know not when the master of the house will come, either in the evening, or at midnight, or at the crow of the rooster, or in the morning; keep watch, that when he comes suddenly, that he will not find you sleeping. But what I say to you, this I say to everyone: *Keep watch!*" (Mk 13:32–37). It is because of such clear and unambiguous admonitions of the Lord himself and his apostles, that we do not preoccupy ourselves with the more murky and ambiguous things, but instead set these things respectfully aside. So we, for example, do not at all speculate about any so-called thousand year kingdom of peace, which will precede the last judgment, or the general conversion of all human beings—indeed, we do not even occupy ourselves with the question of the conversion of Israel, when the fullness of the heathens will have come. We respect the Scripture's word about these things, fully confident, that they will be fulfilled *in the way* that the Holy Spirit intended them to be fulfilled. But we note that among the interpreters, there are such divided opinions about their meaning, that we do not regard any of these different opinions as containing something as sure and as certain, as that which the Lord himself has expressly and unambiguously explained, namely that we all ought to be prepared to wait for his return, and that the situation of the world when he comes will resemble the situation in the days of Noah, when the flood came.

But in addition to this, the Lord and his apostles have also given us various signs that point to his return, which most of all should awaken his friends to vigilance and hope. These signs can all be summarized under a short title, namely: *an extraordinary battle of spiritual powers.* On the one side, there will be evil, unbelief, blasphemy, and the denial of all things holy, accompanied by an extraordinary unfettered and diverse ungodliness, which will distinguish the time for the Lord's return. On the other side, there will be the preaching of the gospel, a zeal and a working for the kingdom of God, which will be just as distinguished. [. . .]

When one reads the second and third chapters of Peter's second epistle, as well as the epistle of Jude, one could well believe that they were written in our own time and with particular attention to current circumstances. The bold denial of the Lord, who has bought us; the false teachings and delusions; the mockery of the way of truth; that out of greed and by deceptive words, people make their (earthly) profit at the expense of ignorant souls; the wandering after the flesh in all manner of impure desires; the contempt for authorities and the mockery of power; the obliteration of all feeling of reverence and healthy fear of divine and human governance; [. . .] all of this and more, which in particular characterizes our time, we can find described in detail in the apostles' letters named above.

[. . .] Yet even Christ and his warriors are on the move and unusually active. When one looks back to days gone by, and compares them to the present-day zeal and activity for the kingdom of God, both for the spreading of the gospel among the heathen, as well as for the awakening of the children of the old, slumbering Christendom, then one has to admit that there are great preparations for battle under way in the camp of Immanuel! More has been carried out in decades, than previously was accomplished in centuries. And just as before the end of Jerusalem, so too shall be the case before the end of the world that there will be this significant sign: *The gospel shall be preached for all nations, and then shall the end come* (Mt 24:14; Mk 13:10). As already has been said, the one who recognizes what is going on in the world, has to admit that we live in a time of great significance. The greatest and most profound of life's questions in religion, concerning God and the way to life, concerning Christ and reconciliation, about the truth and the meaning of God's word—questions, which before either were slumbering in the stillness of the confessions and preaching of the church, as though they were already decided, or had shyly and dejectedly crept into the most obscure corners of the anxious hearts of the few—these questions have now emerged into the open battlefield and become the object of general study, commotion, and debate, which has hardly left any baptized human being in peace. [. . .]

We do not deny that we have generally embraced the teaching about the return of the Lord as an *article of faith*; but from this it does not automatically follow that we have also embraced the return of Christ as our *hope*. The question is not: "do you believe, that the Lord shall return?" but instead: "*are you living in this hope*, in a true *expectation* of his return?" And to this question, not many among us would be able to answer "yes!" If it were so, that all believers were walking in the hope and expectation of our glorified Lord's return, then this hope would all the more appear in our sermons, in our Christian conversations, in our entire lives. [...] Every *hope* is predicated on a *wish*, and every wish has its root in what we *love*. [...]

Take heed of this, O mortal, time is short! If something joyful is happening to you, rejoice in moderation [*lagom*], it will not last long, you will soon leave it. If something distressing is happening to you, mourn in moderation, it will not be long, time is short. If you take a wife, if you receive acreage, be of such a mind that you might soon leave both. This "silly flesh" of ours incessantly seeks to raise up its head and carve out for itself a paradise down here. This is insanity—it will be so short! O, that those Christians who are engaged in such eager preparations in this world, with their earthly goods, their business, and their building—O, that they would restrain themselves in time, before the last spark of their spiritual life has been extinguished and their god-fearing spirit has completely vanished! Let your hands work; but be honest in your self-examination—where is your heart? Do not lie, on your soul! Where is your heart? Is it in heaven, from where you wait for the Savior? Or is it in your earthly well-being? Be honest! [...] O, that we would be ready and awake and have oil in our lamps, when the cry is heard: *Behold, the bridegroom comes near!*

THE KINGDOM OF GOD AND THE CONGREGATION

P.P. Waldenström, 1882

(Guds rike och församlingen)

The Savior presented this parable [Lk 19:11–27], "while he was near Jerusalem, and they thought that the kingdom of God would be revealed at once." The disciples were thus expecting that during this visit in Jerusalem, Christ would establish his kingdom. That they really held such an expectation can be seen from their song upon his riding over the Mount of Olives, about which the evangelist Luke writes in 19:37–39: "But when he had already come near the place where the road goes down the Mount of Olives, the whole crowd of his disciples began to rejoice and praise God with loud voices and all their strength, because of all the miracles which they had seen, saying: 'Blessed is the king, he who comes in the name of the Lord; Peace in heaven and glory in the highest!'" But notice how he presents this parable precisely as a means of dissuading the disciples from this expectation that the kingdom of God would be revealed at once.

The parable is inspired by the historical situation at the time of the birth of Christ, in which it was the tradition for the kings in Palestine to be appointed by the Roman emperor. The one who wished to occupy an empty throne had to travel to Rome in order to "receive the kingdom" from the emperor. And when he had received this, he returned, took control of the government, held judgment over his opponents, and so on. Who here does not clearly see the parallel image of how Christ would return to the Father in order to receive the kingdom from him and then to return to establish it, as well as hold judgment over his servants (verses 15–26) and then over his enemies (verse 27)? During the time of waiting, he had given his servants minas to manage. Some of them are faithful, others are unfaithful. But when the kingdom comes, the faithful ones would receive the compensation for their faithfulness and enter into the kingdom, but the unfaithful servants would be punished for their unfaithfulness and be cast away (Mt 25:30). But his *enemies*, who during the time of waiting had lived in peace and not feared any harm, would be judged and be put to death when the Lord came into his kingdom.

Matthew relates the same parable within a context that even more sharply presents the same thing. There the Savior says namely to the disciples: "Keep watch, for you do not know the day nor the hour. For as a man, who was leaving on a journey. . ." (Mt 25:13–14). According to Matthew's expressed words, Christ is presenting this parable to stress the importance of their waiting for his return. *To wait for his kingdom is thus the same as waiting for his return.*

In Mt 13 there are several other parables about the kingdom of God. After the Lord had first explained, in the parable of the four planting fields, the different ways in which the word of God is received by human beings in the world, he then transitions to the parables of the kingdom of God. In verses 24–30 he says: "The kingdom of heaven is like a man, who had sown good seed in his field." [. . .] What is presented in this parable to represent the kingdom itself? Is it the sower? No, for the sower is, according to the Lord's own explanation, an image of the Son of Man. This gives us immediately a very important clue in interpreting many of the Lord's parables. When the Lord similarly in verse 45 says that the kingdom is like a merchant who sought after pearls, then it is *not the merchant*, but the pearl, which is presented as the image of the kingdom. In the same way, when the Lord in Mt 22:2 says that the kingdom of heaven is like a king, who prepared a wedding for his son, then it is *not the king*, but the wedding, which is the image of the kingdom. When the Lord says that the kingdom of heaven is like a man who sowed, or a merchant, who sought pearls, or a king, who prepared a wedding, this is to say that *with the kingdom of heaven, the situation is like a man sowing good seed, or like a merchant seeking pearls, or like a king preparing a wedding.* Mark expresses this the same way, when there we read: "*Such is the kingdom of God, as when a man casts out seed onto the earth. . .*" (Mk 4:26).

In the parable of the weeds and the wheat, neither is it the field, which is the image of the kingdom, for according to the Lord's own explanation, the field is an image of *the world*. Neither is it the growing seed that is the image of the kingdom, but instead this is *the children of the kingdom*, as the Lord explains the matter. [. . .] The question to ask is what it is in this parable, which depicts the kingdom itself? [. . .] What then is the Father's kingdom, in which the believers shall "shine forth as the sun"? Is it in the Christian congregation or in "the New Testament's spiritual world order" or in some "heavenly powers of salvation" where they will shine? No, it will be in an actual kingdom that they will shine forth as the sun, and this will not be a kingdom that exists now, but a kingdom which will come at the close of the age. The establishment of the kingdom is thus, as in the Savior's parable, *when the weeds are burned and the wheat is gathered into the barn.* Compare here John the Baptist's words about when the threshing floor is cleared (Mt 3:12) as an image of the coming of the kingdom. When the kingdom comes, then the ungodly will be cast away, but the righteous will shine forth as the sun in their Father's kingdom. This corresponds perfectly with everything that the Bible otherwise has to say about the kingdom, in particular with the parable just drawn from Luke 19. Even here God's kingdom is presented as something which is to come. [. . .] The kingdom is prepared for in the preaching of the gospel (sowing of the seed) and bears fruit in people's conversions. But when the time of the harvest comes, that is when the kingdom comes, then the grain is gathered into the barn and the chaff is cast away. The current age is a time of preparation for the kingdom of God, altogether as the time of sowing and husbandry is a preparation for the harvest. [. . .]

Now the invitations to the wedding are being made, now the people are being gathered in the wedding hall (congregation), but the wedding itself has not yet come. When it comes, among those who have been gathered in the hall, only those few among them who have wedding clothes on will be allowed to come. The others will be sent away. The wedding belongs to the last things, as John saw, and about which he heard a voice from heaven crying out: "Hallelujah, for the Lord our God, the almighty, has been made king; let us be glad and rejoice and give honor to him, for the marriage of the Lamb has come" (Rev 19:6–7). Thus the parable points to the future, and has the same lesson to give as so many other parables, that when the kingdom comes (when the wedding begins), then those who have superficially received the invitation and taken their seat at the table, shall be separated from the others, and that those, who do not have their wedding clothes, shall be sent away. The groom exists now, the wedding hall exists now, the wedding people exist now, but the wedding is not yet here. This parable does not speak about *the bride*. The believers are presented here in the image of the wedding people who are clothed in their wedding garments, or the wedding guests. [. . .]

The image of the leaven also teaches us that as the leaven permeates the fresh dough as a leavening agent, so too does God's kingdom increasingly permeate, *with his power and his character*, the chosen people, who now in faith await the kingdom. In this way, the power of God's kingdom was already at work in the Old Testament and shall remain at work through all of the present age, until the chosen people have matured for the kingdom. And then shall the kingdom come. (This is, as one in scientific language might call the *potential* presence of God's kingdom, like for example, how the tree is potentially present in the seed.)

"THE HIDDEN DISTRICT" FROM SQUIRE ADAMSSON, OR, WHERE DO YOU LIVE?

P.P. Waldenström, 1863

(Brukspatron Adamsson, chapter 12)

Translator's note: By this point in the allegory, the main character, Squire Adamsson, has changed his name to Abrahamsson.

In Evangelium, life was proceeding along as it usually does. [. . .] But one day, something happened that caused a great deal of commotion and would become the subject of much confusion and speculation. Namely, there came to Evangelium three poor creatures from [The Hidden District], who were admitted to the great hospital. They were called Miserable, Depraved, and Fallen. Anyone who looked on them in their wretched state, bodies emaciated and suffering extremely, could not help but shudder. Even Mother Simple had started to believe that such wretches as these had never been brought to the holy city before. But a serious discussion with Conscience soon managed to convince her that she did not have any reason to boast about herself in front of them.

[. . .]

The city was in a commotion, the news traveling from mouth to mouth. [. . .] After a while, a couple more people arrived from the same place, Vile and Wretched. A short time later, still more arrived. They too were vocal in their praise of the mercy which had been shown to them. They thought, in those first overwhelming emotions of grace, that they were altogether liberated from their misery.

Many of them, furthermore, would later go on to be immediately healed. Though for others, by contrast, the sickness began to reappear after a little time had passed. They lived in The Forgiveness of Sins, were attended to in the hospital, they bathed in the [River of Blood]—but nothing seemed to help. Of course there were certain times when they did get better. But then the attacks would break out again, to their own horror and that of the others. Earnestly they prayed to Immanuel and begged for his presence, but it seemed as though he did not want to help them. They began to doubt themselves, as well as Evangelium and Immanuel. Among the other residents, there was no one who was able to give any advice or was able to inspire renewed courage, except for one person. This was Mother Simple. Faithfully sitting by their bedsides, she encouraged them to *have patience and wait, as well as to remain diligent in believing in grace;* "for," she would say, "there is nothing else, after all, which can help."

"But Watchman said that we would soon be healthy again!" they objected, one after the other.

And so this progressed over a long period, and watching these poor people in their mourning and grieving was heart-wrenching. They paced about their rooms, tossed and turned, they sighed and they screamed. But when the attacks came, they lost their senses, and the storm winds bore them away.

Yet, after a year there began to be a slight change that appeared. Miserable became entirely healthy. This caused many to rejoice. "This comes as proof," they said, "that grace is powerful." But this caused the others who were sick to become even more disappointed. They had already been aware that many people, upon arriving in Evangelium, had become healthy; now they saw that even Miserable after his long struggle had become completely free from his sickness. Therefore they had made up their minds that it was all over for *them,* since *they* had not received this kind of healing. And Abrahamsson, along with many others, also began to be convinced that things had never actually been right with them. If things continued to go this way for them, then eventually they would need to be on their way and leave Evangelium, he thought.

"This cannot be good in the long run," he told them, once again.

But in a situation like this, no chastisement would help. This only increased their suffering. Heavy sighs and anxious lamentations were the only response that he got from them. Deeply saddened and without a clue as to what he should do, he sought counsel with some of the others. They came to the conclusion that people should earnestly pray for these people and try to surround them with love. But all efforts seemed to be in vain. Sometimes it would appear promising, as mentioned before, and everyone would rejoice. But then the attacks would come again. Then people would agree that someone ought to tell them, in no uncertain terms, that they should not go around making claims of having received grace, as long as they remained in such a condition. On this point even Miserable agreed. People explained that giving them these admonitions would prompt increased seriousness and greater efforts. This message was communicated to them one evening, and the result that it had could already be seen the following morning. Namely, during the night, Depraved and Vile, who could not stand any more of this, had both set out from the city, the former on his way to The World and the latter on his way to Loose Living. What had been keeping them in Evangelium thus far and had maintained their spirits were the words of assurance that Mother Simple had been so earnestly speaking to them. Now they found themselves instead under a terrifying judgment, and this was something they already had plenty of experience with from before. When they were not allowed to depend on Immanuel's grace, then they just could not endure any more of this. As soon as word reached Abrahamsson's ears, he rushed off to tell Mother Simple.

"Oh!" he exclaimed, "what are we supposed to believe about these people, who have been lying here like this for three years without becoming healed?"

"Well," answered Mother Simple calmly, "if you ask me, it is high time that the Squire ought to start thinking about himself, and let Immanuel take care of those who are sick."

"But their wretchedness is in stark opposition to grace!"

"And why is that?"

"Because it is so horrible and so foul!"

"And when is sin so beautiful, that it is not in opposition to grace?"

This question Abrahamsson was not prepared to answer. But scrambling for words and avoiding a direct answer, he shot right back:

"Are you trying to defend sin?"

"No, that is the last thing that I would ever do! But I do wish to defend grace."

Abrahamsson was completely bewildered. "Defend grace?" he asked, "What do you mean? Defend it against whom?"

"Against the Squire and other people of the same mind," answered Mother Simple hastily. "All of you simply will not allow grace to be as high as the heaven is over the earth. You do not allow it to overflow and cover every sin."

"Is that so? Then I imagine you are indifferent as to whether people sin or not, and would like to rush to the defense of each and every person who is living in sin. That is quite a remarkable doctrine!"

"I wish that the Squire would go and think about this matter, and then come back when his senses have returned. Or what is it exactly that the Squire himself thinks he can boast about? Go ask Conscience, he will surely tell the Squire. [. . .] Has it gotten to the point now with the Squire, that he has started to excuse and try to diminish his own sin? Oh, then the Squire is already in a much more dangerous place than these poor people, for whom he has so much concern. For know this—that even the sin that seems most innocent can be fatal, if one tries in some way to excuse or make light of it, in such a way that it seems to be far better than the sins of another person. This is the sort of thing that directly challenges grace. But when the sinner sticks to judging himself for his sins and begs for grace, no one shall ever be able to rob him of grace or drive him out from The Forgiveness of Sins, even though there will still come times when he is caught off guard by recurring moments of wretchedness. In these cases, one must return to the words of the old apostle: 'If a man is overtaken by any sin, you who are spiritual, restore such a one in a spirit of meekness.' The kind of spirituality that is hard on the weak—which breaks the bruised reeds and extinguishes the smoking wick—this is an immature spirituality. The proper spirituality is to have mercy on them and help them. I would much rather be weak than to be a bully to the weak."

"Is that so? You think that every conceivable form of wretchedness can stand alongside grace?"

"No, of course not; but on the basis of the word of truth, I do believe, more firmly than I ever have, that even the worst form of wretchedness can indeed stand *under* grace, just as I believe that nothing, not even the most innocent of sins, can stand *alongside* grace." [. . .]

"Well, you must admit that these wretches ought to, at some point, be made well."

"Dear Squire, do not start talking about 'wretches.' That can have a negative effect. We have not yet seen the end. Of course, I agree that they ought to be made well; and I have never seen anything that has caused me so much confusion as all of this. Even Bankrupt Faith is also bewildered. But what does that matter? There is no other advice to follow than to try to support them with grace."

"But remember, you yourself said, that the sin that is in opposition to grace, is the one that one tries to diminish?"

"Yes, of course, for when one tries to excuse or diminish sin, then one tries to defend its place alongside grace, and that is a falsehood."

"Now, how do you know that Depraved and Vile aren't exactly this sort of people?"

Mother Simple became uneasy, for she sensed something, but she could not put her finger on it.

"Tell me," she asked anxiously, "what exactly is the Squire getting at? Has something happened?"

"Well, they would not tolerate a healthy word of instruction and a serious word of warning."

The little old woman became even more anxious, for now she understood that Abrahamsson had done something terrible. Therefore, she asked him once more if something had happened to Depraved and Vile.

"Yes," answered Abrahamsson, "haven't you heard that sometime last night they left Evangelium? They made clear that it was because I, following the mutual agreement of several of us who have no tolerance for the flesh, finally told them the honest truth. That is what they could not endure."

At these words Mother Simple burst into a flood of tears.

"May Immanuel forgive the Squire for what he has done!" she gasped. And upon this she made haste to the hospital, without waiting for Abrahamsson's answer. When she arrived there, it was confirmed that Depraved and Vile had gone, and what pained her even more was to hear the mourning of both of the others. The judgment had also hit them hard, and Wretched himself was just getting ready to move out of the holy city. For not only had he begun to lose confidence in Immanuel's grace, he had also that morning received a letter from an acquaintance, who was suffering from the same sickness, but who had moved to the city Self-Righteousness, where he said he had become completely healthy. Poor old Fallen. He did not know what he was going to do. His despair exceeded everything imaginable.

"If I may not believe in grace," he exclaimed, in the midst of bitter sobs, "if I may not believe in grace, then I am lost. Tell me, Mother Simple, can I believe in grace?"

"Yes!" exclaimed Miserable, who at that moment came in and heard these last few words. "There is nothing preventing you from believing in grace. But in the condition in which you now find yourself, there is no room for grace, and thus you can have no benefit from it. . ."

Engulfed in a blaze of zeal, Mother Simple swung around, and the dead-serious look in her fiery face reduced Miserable to silence.

"Who has given you the right to drive people out of Evangelium?"

With that she made her way to the beds of the sick and now, sparing no pains, gave them words of assurance regarding Immanuel's unchanging grace, which was wholly independent of all their being or doing. [. . .]

"Why can't I also get well?" [Fallen] sighed. "Immanuel is not concerned about me. He has withheld his mercy out of wrath." [. . .]

It goes without saying that in Evangelium there were many people who remained quite confused in regard to Fallen, and who also thought that Mother Simple was not all that wise. She ought to restrain herself when it came to all of these unqualified assurances of grace, they reasoned. Of course they had no desire to pass judgment on poor Fallen—they did not really dare—but to emphatically assert that he was covered by grace, this they thought was going too far. Because of this, one of them came to speak with Mother Simple one day, none other than Councilman Cautious. [. . .]

After he had first greeted them and emphasized his heartfelt appreciation for all of her care for these wretches, he added:

"But don't you think that one ought to be a little more careful about presenting grace to Fallen as freely as you have? I believe that we, in this peculiar case, must keep our personal opinions to ourselves and leave him to the mercy of Justus All-Powerful."

"What is the Councilman saying?" objected Mother Simple with astonishment. "Oh, if I did not allow myself to be left to the mercy of Justus All-Powerful, then I would be lost."

"Don't misunderstand me," interrupted Cautious, "I did not mean that. It is clear that we all need to throw ourselves before the mercy of Justus All-Powerful. But what I meant was that we shouldn't try to make any particular evaluation regarding Fallen, nor relate this to him. We ought not judge him, but neither should we try to make any assurances to him regarding grace. We should leave him to the mercy of Justus All-Powerful."

"It is impossible," answered Mother Simple, "for me to understand what the Councilman is really trying to say here. Does the Councilman mean that I may not tell him for certain that Immanuel's blood was shed for all of his sins?"

"Well, that is clear; what has been done, that has been done and may freely be preached. But one needs to be careful about saying this to a man in his condition, as if this applies to him and that he has some claim to this word."

"Oh," exclaimed Mother Simple, "Is that what you meant? Then the Councilman wants us to not give this poor man *any firm word of grace to* cling to, but instead means that he should be abandoned to *doubt and uncertainty!* And the Councilman explains this as 'leaving him to the mercy of Justus All-Powerful'!"

The good councilman became rather troubled by this exchange. He did not know for sure how he might get himself out of this. For he must have realized deep down that this plan he had articulated—of leaving Fallen to the mercy of Justus All-Powerful—would in reality be the same thing as leaving him to uncertainty and doubt. And that this was a bad example of pastoral care, he could not deny. Yet, he had soon collected himself and retorted:

"But look at Wretched; he has certainly become healthy, while Fallen is still lying in bed."

"Yes, I can see that well enough," answered Mother Simple. "But was it through doubt and uncertainty that he was healed? No, most certainly not! I know that much, I being the one who watched as it all happened. But if now Wretched has been healed solely as a result of these certain and confident assertions of grace, why should we then try to heal Fallen through uncertainty about grace and by withholding grace? And this method of healing him will not be made any more effective by calling it 'leaving him to the mercy of Justus All-Powerful'?"

Now the councilman was stuck once again and did not know how he should answer. After a moment of silence, he said:

"But you must understand that if these kind of ideas of yours start to spread, then some people might find cause to live freely in sin and rest on the assurance of grace. Think how terrible that would be!"

"Well, if hypocrites misuse grace to their own ruin, then that would not be the fault of grace. If anyone reads the story of the thief on the cross and thinks: 'Oh, I think I would like to be a thief, and then in the last moments before death become converted,' then that is his own business. No one can blame the thief for that, nor should they tear out his story from the Bible. For this story has been a source of salvation for a countless number of souls. And there remain countless souls who still need to hear it. There were many people who drowned in the flood that saved Noah." [. . .]

"But you know you have an obligation to admit, that it is grace that is necessary to treat sin?"

"Yes," answered Mother Simple, "that is exactly what I am doing, and if the Councilman himself were to admit this, then he would be acting the same way I am."

"What?" exclaimed Cautious, "aren't I admitting that? That is what I have been trying to do."

"In words, yes," answered Mother Simple, "but when the Councilman attempts to heal Fallen by *withholding grace,* then he is demonstrating the opposite. Whatever people might now be saying about Fallen, what is certain is that *if we take away* grace, then that cannot possibly cure him." [. . .]

"That is a question that we will have to leave to Justus All-Powerful," answered Cautious, though overcome by indecision.

"No," interrupted Mother Simple, "*it is we* who need to know your answer to this question. For if anyone, despite being a true resident in Evangelium, can still be thrown into Gehenna, then we are all lost. Then we have no hope. Or has the Councilman by now conquered all his sins, such that he can never fall for any of them anymore?"

"No, God knows I have not," answered Cautious.

"And despite this, the Councilman expects that he will still be counted among the righteous, even if he were to depart this life today?" Mother Simple chimed in.

"Yes, through Immanuel's grace."

"Well then," continued Mother Simple, "then that would mean that the Councilman was allowed to be counted as one of the righteous, despite the fact that he has not yet conquered all of his sins? Tell me, do these qualifications for righteousness only apply to the Councilman, or may other people also be judged by these standards?"

"Of course," answered Mr. Self-Wise, who had just then entered and heard these last words: "Of course, other people may. But for someone like Fallen, who is openly living a life in the flesh, this simply does not apply."

These words threw Mother Simple into a fury. With a flash in her eyes, she answered: "Yes, I see that you, who is living his life in the flesh in secret, has made this sport of trampling on the wretched part of his own path to righteousness. But," she added, now turned to Cautious, as Self-Wise angrily left the room, "I have witnessed enough to be able to conclude this: however it might be regarding Fallen's life, this one thing is certain: he is not *living* a life in the flesh. No, I have seen him *fall* into, but never *live* in sin. If he has fallen, it has been as though into fire or water. He has never been able to remain lying there." [. . .]

"God be gracious to me a sinner!" exclaimed Cautious, and he departed from there, fully animated. But Mother Simple hurried off to Fallen in order to tell him that it was indeed for certain that his sins were forgiven. And that is what she considered "leaving him to the mercy of Justus All-Powerful."

After about a year had passed, still Fallen had not yet been healed from his wretchedness, and over and over again this surprised and defeated him. And then an event occurred that quickly sent a wave of alarm throughout Evangelium. Fallen was called to Holiness. The summons had to be obeyed, and so Fallen set out. Hardly anyone could escape feeling some emotion of dread at this news. Everyone was forced to wonder how his case had gone for him. [. . .] Mother Simple and Wretched hoped for the best for their departed friend, particularly when Bankrupt Faith pointed out to them the passage in God's Word where it says: "But to him who does not rely on works but believes on him who justifies the ungodly, his faith is accounted as righteousness."

And when they compared these words with what Immanuel once had said, "Whoever believes in me shall never die," then they became almost certain that all had gone well for Fallen.

Immanuel Church, Stockholm

5

Invitation to Experience the Life of Faith

THE SPIRIT AWAKENS US TO LIFE

C.O. Rosenius, 1852

("Den tid, då du war sökt")

When Christ for the last time entered Jerusalem and viewed the city from the Mount of Olives, he wept over it and expressed once more the righteous judgment, which rested over this beautiful city. And now he explained the reason for this judgment with the words: "Because you did not recognize the time, when you were visited" (Lk 19:44). [. . .] Was it not possible for Jerusalem to convert themselves, whenever they wanted? No, here we see otherwise. Here it is written: "The time when you were visited." Thus, there were other times, when they were not visited. [. . .]

Every person is by nature spiritually dead. The profound words about our fall—that "you will surely die"—have so permeated all flesh, that humankind would lie forever as a dead and decaying corpse, unless God's own living Spirit comes down into this dust of earth, begins to move and awaken her to life again. If this does not happen, then the human being will remain dead for eternity. As impossible as it is for a physically dead person to make himself live again, it is just as impossible for a spiritually dead person to be raised to life without God's Spirit. You may as well expect sunlight without a sun, than that spiritual life would come without the Spirit. From this it follows that no one can convert himself whenever he wishes, no one can come to Jesus, without the Father first drawing him to himself through the Spirit.

And thus it is an astonishingly important time, this "time when you are visited." This is the decisive time for your eternal wellbeing. O, that people would be able to understand and perceive this, that in not all moments is it so crucial, how we respond! Not all moments in your history are of equal importance. There are long periods, when neither God nor any understanding person can expect you to convert—namely, in those times when you are not visited. It is when the Lord is visiting you that conversion must happen, now or never. [. . .]

You, who are reading this, perhaps it is right now that is the time when you are being visited. Or when will it come to pass, that you will "be visited?" How will your invitation arrive, to the banquet of grace? Answer: Sometimes God visits an entire country, a city, or a congregation, as when Jerusalem and the Jewish people were visited through the coming of Christ in the flesh, or otherwise in those frequent moments when a prophet appeared, as one crying in the wilderness. Such things still happen. When a country, a city, or congregation has for a long time experienced a stiff formality in its services and ceremonies, as in Jerusalem, and also when within the minds of the people everything has been dead and still, but then, all of the sudden, awakening comes as faithful leaders begin to cry out in the wilderness: "Repent, for the kingdom of heaven is near!" Then it is this city's, this people's time of visitation, when these children will be collectively moved by the faithful Spirit. Is it not already apparent for everyone, that right now there is such a time of visitation in *our country*, when awakenings are being reported in almost every province, and people from every rank and class are beginning to inquire about the way to life?—Jerusalem! O, that you too would recognize the time of your visitation!

But otherwise, when it is not a time of collective visitation, then the faithful Spirit seeks out individual souls, and through the voice of the word, speaks to their hearts and exhorts them to repentance. In a Christian country it is surely the case that there are few people, who do not at some point perceive a visit from God's Spirit and a knocking on their heart—at least in the years of their youth, when they have newly broken the blessed covenant with God and departed for the foreign country of sin and vanity, but have not yet strayed so far, that the faint voice from the Father's house cannot still be heard. But even afterwards, the good shepherd will pursue the stray sheep in its errant path. [. . .]

The Spirit of God speaks according to his audience. To the rich, strong, self-contented people he may send troubles; to the poor souls and the grave sinners, who walk around with secret self-loathing, he may only offer grace, a grace which they never could have expected, and which will melt their hearts. But God's Spirit also uses all manner of ways to bring these voices of invitation to people's hearts. Sometimes he may strike them with misfortune, sorrows, and illnesses. In order to bring the prodigal son to reflection, there was a great famine in the country, and he began to experience need; then he reflected on his situation and remembered his father's house. At other times, the Spirit may send a friend, who out of the fullness of a warm heart will speak to you in the language of love. At still other times, he may allow a terrible death to occur before your eyes, as though a mysterious hand were writing on the wall: "God has numbered your days. . ." or "Get your house in order, for you too shall die!" He may allow an intense awakening to occur among your neighbors in order to make the truth apparent to your eyes that there is a kingdom of God on earth, and that there is such a thing as what Christ called *new birth*.—O, faithful Spirit of God, you wondrous, most mysterious friend! This is how he moves around in the darkness of this world and knocks on people's hearts. He moves among the houses and in the church pews, at the communion table and among the beds of the sick, indeed along the highways and the farms, where you are walking alone. And he whispers to your soul: "Where are you? Where are you headed? Where is your path leading?" [. . .]

Consider this analogy: Since you know that it is the nature of trees to stand still, when nothing is moving them, but then you see that the trees begin to move and crack, when no visible being is moving them, then you immediately say that it is the wind that is blowing. And similarly you do not see the wind. This is how it is with God's Spirit. He has come before in visible forms, as in the likeness of a dove of the Lord and as tongues of flame over the apostles, and as a "mighty wind, which filled the whole house where they were sitting." Now he comes in invisible ways, but carries out the same work in people's souls, gives them the same "sting in their hearts," that they now, just as before, ask the question: "What shall we do to inherit eternal life?" It is because of things like this that you will recognize the same Spirit and know, that he still is moving and at work on earth, calling and awakening to repentance and salvation. And then consider how much of a misfortune it would be, if you were to resist him, to cause him grief and drive away this faithful Spirit. The apostle says: "Do not grieve God's holy Spirit!"—Just imagine! To have received a personal visitation of this exalted guest, but to have turned your back on him, indeed, this would be terrible! [. . .]

When you have the will to follow this counsel of the Lord and in the true order of grace, have the will to repent, believe and abandon sin, *but do not make use of those means*, which God has given us for this purpose, namely *his holy word*, and you do not use your quiet moments to read, hear and reflect on these things, then you are "testing God, and quenching the Spirit." Take special note of this last point: Say you have the will to repent and be converted, but only attempt to do so with your own work in your heart. You pray to the Spirit for grace and help toward this, without making use of the means that the Spirit gives you. In this way, you will never receive what you are asking for. God has never promised this. No, God, has given us his *word*, and it is *here* that he wants to meet us, here he wants to dwell and work, but not without the word. To have access to the word, to Christian teachers or the fellowship of brothers in faith and so on, and nevertheless to show contempt for these means of grace, but yet still ask for repentance and faith, this is a form of *testing the Lord*. This is as though someone were to request that God would sustain his physical life, and yet refuse to eat what God had provided us. That person can wait for as long as he likes for the miracle to take place, and "wish this until he dies," as Scripture says of the lazy person. This is how it will go for the person who wants to have the Spirit work in his soul, but does not make use of the means the Spirit provides. [. . .]

All sin brings grief to the Holy Spirit, even that which is most hidden in your heart, such as prideful thoughts, evil desires, jealousy, falsehood, and others. But here it is necessary to point out, that it is only when one has fallen *so grievously*, that one begins to *excuse* and *praise* sin, that God's Spirit is driven away. However, in those cases where someone is punishing himself on account of his sin, is suffering, struggling, sighing, and praying against it, this is when the Spirit becomes like a doctor in a hospital. When he is surrounded by illness, infirmities, wounds, and lamentations, this is when he is in his true element and most effective. It is for this reason that God's Spirit is able to dwell in a sinner's heart. [. . .] If this were not the case, then not one single Christian would be able to retain God's Spirit for a single day. [. . .]

O, my God, allow me to become poor, indeed, even a beggar; allow me to become sick, blind and deaf; just don't allow me to become hardened! "Do not cast me from your countenance, or take your Holy Spirit from me!" See, the one who continues to fear for himself, who still is able to be moved by God's word to be concerned about repentance, and retains some desire to believe and be a child of God, this is evidence that he has not been abandoned to a hardened heart. [. . .] No, just because sin continues to assail us, this proves nothing; all believers will continue to experience hardships and complaints, as long as they remain in the flesh. As long as you allow the Spirit to discipline you, and you are seeking deliverance and always keeping close to the seat of grace, as well as seeking and hearing the gospel and, despite all reason and emotions, are believing in the blood that cleanses eternally—then the Spirit is still dwelling within you, as in his proper workshop. His entire office is to care for sick sinners. If you were to become completely free from every sin, then he would have nothing left to do within you. The kingdom of Christ is a kingdom full of sinners. Therefore, do not allow yourself to be led astray! It is only those who "do not allow themselves to be disciplined by the Spirit," whom he must abandon—May God graciously preserve us from this! God, *God*, do not take your Holy Spirit from me! Do not take your Holy Spirit from me!

JESUS AND THE SAMARITAN WOMAN

C.O. Rosenius (with Amy Moberg), 1868

("Andra Söndagen efter Trettondagen")

[Text: Jn 4:5–26] Once more we see here how the Lord revealed his glory for the Samaritans, when he, at the well of Jacob outside of Sychar, spoke at length with a Samaritan woman who was there fetching water—to which he compared and praised the living water, which he had come to give—until that point when her spiritual eyes were opened, and she understood that she had found the Messiah and in him the eternal life, through which the marriage of heaven began in her soul. [. . .]

Jesus was tired from the journey, which is why he sat himself down by the well, while his disciples went into the city in order to buy food. Not merely hungry, but also thirsty, he said to the woman: "Give me something to drink." But, as we shall see later, all of his bodily hunger and thirst was nothing compared to the hungering and thirsting in his heart to save sinners. For as soon as his speech had made an inroad into this woman's soul and through her to the people in Sychar, and Christ had thus seen the field begin to ripen for the harvest (verse 35), then he forgot his hunger, so that, when the disciples later came with food and said: "Rabbi, eat," he answered: "I have food to eat, which you do not know." Such was the disposition of his heart and his primary objective, when he entered into conversation with this woman. However, to this lofty love, her first response was one of natural darkness, as she replied: "How can you, who are a Jew, ask for something to drink from me, a Samaritan woman? For the Jews have nothing to do with the Samaritans." From his garments and dialect she could perceive that he belonged to that people, who because of their spiritual prejudices had the most profound contempt for the Samaritans, who both in religion and their blood were a mixed, heathen people. Instead of now entering into this old argument between the Jews and the Samaritans, Jesus simply answered: "If you understood this gift of God, and who it is who says to you: 'Give me something to drink,' then you would have asked him, and he would have given you living water." If you understood this gift of God, this gift of eternal life, and how this is only to be obtained through the one who now stands before you—if you understood this, then you would begin to ask me—ask, that I might give you the water of life; that is to say, all the spiritual goodness, which is granted to human beings through Christ, the forgiveness of sins, life and salvation, the Holy Spirit with all of his work of new birth and solace to a new life of peace and regeneration for your soul, which now silently languishes in its distressed conscience. But like Nicodemus in the previous chapter did not understand this talk of new birth, but instead answered with those crass words about entering into his mother's womb and being born again, so too, this woman did not understand these words about the living water, but instead answered: "Lord, you have no dipper, and the well is deep; where do you have this living water?" Instead of humbly asking what these profound words about the living water might mean, she begins with a cold and offensive comment: "Certainly you cannot be greater than our father Jacob, who gave us this well, and himself drank from it with his children and his livestock?" See here, this unbroken, fleshly mindset! This is what the burning mercy of Jesus can expect to receive in return from sinners. But Jesus answered in steady tenderness: "Each and every person who drinks of this water, he will be thirsty again; but whoever drinks of this water, which I shall give him, he shall not thirst for all eternity, but this water that I shall give him shall become a spring of water welling up within him with eternal life." Not even these words, which so tangibly pointed to something spiritual, were able to awaken her rough, fleshly spirit. Instead she answered again: "Lord, give me this water, that I might not thirst or need to come here to fetch water." She did not want to pause and reflect on this talk of eternal life; she wanted to keep at a distance and evade this with a few silly words about earthly things. But the Lord knew one way to break through to her, he knew a more sensitive point, which he now wished to bring up. He said simply: "Go, fetch your husband and come back." The woman answered, probably desperate to avoid this: "I have no husband." Then Jesus said to her: "You are right when you say that you have no husband; for you have had five husbands, and the one, you have now is not your husband; what you say is true." What Christ here said to her, touched upon something so worthy of punishment, that, as we can see from verse 29, her conscience was stricken down by this, that she thought that he had said "every" bad thing she had ever done, although he had only spoken of one single relationship. For without entering into the question of the five husbands she had had, whether they had died, or she had in some inappropriate way been divorced from them, nevertheless there was surely something unlawful about it, since Christ confronted her with it in order to bring about her contrition, which he effectively accomplished. The most certain thing is that the little comment: "The one, you have now, is not your husband," indicated an unlawful relationship. That she had him, must mean such a life together, as if he had been her husband; and either she was not at all married to him, or one or another of her previous husbands was still alive, whereby her life with this man properly constituted adultery.

Now the woman's joking came to an end. Now she exclaimed: "Lord, I see, that you are a prophet." Nevertheless, she still attempted to avoid the question regarding herself, and tried to bring in yet another contentious question and said: "Our fathers have worshipped on this mountain, and you Jews say, that Jerusalem is the place, where one ought to worship." To this comment, the Lord now gave her a word, which partially contained an answer and also was designed to awaken her to reflection about who he was, who was speaking with her. He said: "Woman, believe me, there will come a time, when you will worship the Father neither on this mountain, nor in Jerusalem. You Samaritans worship what you do not know; but we worship what we know; for salvation is from the Jews (Isa 2:3). But a time is coming and is already at hand, when true worshippers will worship the Father in spirit and in truth; for the Father is also seeking such worshippers. God is a Spirit, and those, who worship him, ought to worship in Spirit and truth. Then the woman said to him: I know that the Messiah, who is called Christ, shall come; when he comes, he shall proclaim everything to us." [. . .] This thought about Christ had been awakened in her now, which caused her to begin to sense: "Might he not be the Christ?" Therefore she received this definite answer: "I, who am speaking with you, am the same." This is how far he had now come, that he expressly said to her, that he was the Christ, the promised Messiah. And the effect that all of this had on her, we can see from what follows: "Then the woman left her jar standing there and went into the city and said to the people: Come and see a man, who has told me everything I have ever done. Could he be the Christ?"

Here there are several things that we can learn. When the Lord Jesus is here presented as being "tired from the journey," as well as hungering and thirsting, we see him as a true human being, subject to all the natural needs for the sustenance of the body. It often happens for us when we observe his marvelous deeds and his divine essence, which we see in the signs and wonders that he performed, that we forget that he was also a true human being, that he has been here on earth and through his own experiences, perfectly understands all human weaknesses and suffering. This is something that we ought to remember, as it too, in its time, can also serve as an assurance. As exalted as he is at his Father's right hand, he is certainly high above all things, yet not so high, that he cannot understand and suffer with us in our weaknesses. "He was tired from the journey." You Christian, who also have become tired of your journey here on earth, consider this, that Jesus became tired from the journey for our sake, indeed, that he even became poor for our sake! He has known what purely natural hunger and thirst is. You, who now suffer from the same, can with full certainty believe that he, who was just as truly a human being as his mother Mary, shares with us and wishes the best for us; for according to his human nature, he is just as truly human as she is. Jesus was tired from the journey. In Mark there is an account of one time when he worked so diligently during the day with his preaching and the curing of the sick that his friends were afraid these over-exertions would cause him to "go out of his mind" (Mk 3:21), and attempted to lead him away, so that he could find some rest. O, Jesus, if you have become tired during your journey on earth and your work for us sinners, how much would we gladly wish to be able to repay you and delight your gracious heart!

The second thing we see here is the patience of our Lord Jesus Christ, which we ought to regard for our salvation. Here we can see his tender-heartedness and tolerance, how he seeks a lost sheep and will endure with all meekness this poor sinner's natural wickedness and intractability, if only he can win her in the end. But in addition to this dear subject, so we also learn here what it is that is most effective in bringing an unfaithful naysayer and despiser of Christ and the testimony about him, to belief and obedience for the divine truth of the word, namely the conscience when it becomes disturbed. As long as the conscience is sleeping, and the sinner is able to sustain himself with merely superficial matters and questions of debate, then it is common that no proof will be sufficiently strong to quiet his objections of disbelief or convince him of the truths of the gospel. But a moment will come, when all of the objections of reason and disbelief will be scattered like smoke before the storm. It is in that instant when the conscience will be awakened, and God's righteous judgments will stride forth before the soul. Then all of God's gospel will soon become so true and tangible. The same doubter, who before was not able to believe the truths of the gospel, but instead always found them to be insanity (1 Cor 1:23, 25), the same person will immediately receive another mindset, which now will find in the gospel the very height of wisdom and truth.

The fourth thing that we see in this woman's awakening is a biblical example of the remarkable occurrence, when a human being in the midst of the everyday tasks and duties of her earthly vocation, is all of the sudden awakened to spiritual concerns. The woman was walking that day like every other day with her jar to the well, just to fetch water for her household needs and never thought that anything new or peculiar would happen to her that day, like so many others. At the well she sees a man, whom she assumes is an ordinary Jew, which she derives from either his clothing or his speech. That he requested water from her, she regarded as completely natural, since the well was deep, and travelers are often thirsty. The only thing that gave her pause was that he as a Jew could request water from her, who was a Samaritan woman, since the enmity between the two peoples was such, that a Jew never wanted to have anything to do with a Samaritan. Least of all was she able to think, that this tired traveler would on this day open for her the kingdom of heaven. But nevertheless, this is what happened. As she left this conversation she returned with a whole new world before her eyes. The Messiah had come, and was found by her! And he had told her everything that she had ever done. For since the Samaritans possessed the five books of Moses and thus the ten commandments, which they revered as God's word, therefore she also knew the sixth commandment and her own crimes against it. But the Lord had now spoken to her in such a way, that, together with the raging storm in her conscience and the judgments of the law, undoubtedly there was some spark of belief in grace that had become lit in her dark soul, this grace that had been promised through the Messiah and was to shine forth in all of his delightful essence. Her belief had to some degree already been lit, this we can see from its fruit, which immediately demonstrated itself in her diligent love for the people in the city, to whom she immediately ran with this first message about Christ, and why also the Lord, because of her opened mind, received such great joy that he forgot his hunger. All of this now happened completely unexpectedly at the well, where she stood with her jar and spoke with the tired stranger, whom she had learned to know as Christ, the Savior of the whole world. [. . .]

What an indescribable and unforgettable moment in the life of a human being, when her soul is thus awakened out of the sleep of spiritual death, and she all at once is able to see, what she previously, despite everything that she had read or heard from God's word, never had seen or perceived, namely her sin and judgment, as well as the splendor of grace! In this relationship with the man who was not her husband, the woman in our text had never seen anything which had troubled her peace or awakened her to seek the Messiah. But in one moment, this became the most important thing to her, such that she forgot her errand, left her jar standing there and wanted nothing else but to speak with this man, who had told her "everything she had ever done." Now this question of the Messiah became her only important question. So it continues to be true today, when a human being in the midst of all of her practices of devotion and religious observances has been asleep the whole time, and suddenly either through a word from some instrument of the Lord, or through recalling the word of God heard previously, which only now gains significance and meaning for her conscience, wakes up to see things, which she had never before recognized, asks questions that she has never asked, and goes on errands, on which she had never before gone. These are indescribably important moments, in which a whole new world opens up for a human being, when she is overwhelmed by concerns, which she never before had perceived, and catches a glimpse of God's gifts and supreme happiness, which she never before had glimpsed! [. . .]

But now—if it remains for you to simply pause before the voice of Jesus right here and now, then you will experience a never-ending series of objections. If the sleep of security is still weighing heavily on your eyes, then you will not see any reason for urgency in seeking grace right now, but instead you will beat around the bush like this woman with all kinds of non-essential questions and objections in order to avoid arriving at the most pressing business regarding your very own soul. But if you were to suddenly be awakened to see your sin and culpability, and the legitimate judgment of God that awaits you, then all of the gospel you know might not suffice to give you enough assurance to now go forward and request grace for everything. Then the sins might still be too many, too grave and unmentionable—in particular your long-held contempt for grace, since you have known well enough what the will of God is, but have always resisted and resented God. You might not be able to expect anything else, than that he also would have resentment for you. And even if you were to believe that the great reconciliation in Christ's death and blood is more than sufficient for all of your sins, then you might still be stopped by your objections and your faulty remorse and prayers, and think: "I am not only the most unworthy of sinners, but also completely incapable of receiving God's kingdom, through the fact that I do not properly have remorse for my sin, am not truly contrite, am not truly serious and diligent in prayer." [. . .]

But now if you wish to hear and believe Christ and know the disposition of his heart, then look to this day's text, look at this woman at the well, and how gracefully the Lord Jesus works with her in order to win her soul. Look, how many detours and objections he has to endure on account of her. I do not see her coming with much remorse and contrition and confessing her sins; no, she wanted to talk about anything else, but not about her sins. It was first when she was essentially trapped by Christ's speech about this man who was not her husband, that she realized that she was in the presence of the kind of prophet who could see through her entire life; it was then, finally, that she confessed that he had spoken the truth. But we do not see much of her remorse and contrition and her prayers. No, we see that Jesus was moved to want to save her long before any single prayer or confession of sin had passed her lips. We do not see either that there was any deed or service that she had done, which caused him to be gracious to her, but instead that Jesus, like a true Savior, was seeking her simply on account of her distress and misery, without there being any deed or service of hers that had moved him to this. [. . .]

Behold here the very nature of the heart of our Lord Jesus Christ, and what grace is, and be on guard against the snares and cunning of the cruel enemy of the soul, and do not think anything about Christ other than what he himself has demonstrated in these examples. Be on guard against forgetting or despising this main teaching of the gospel, that we are saved by grace alone. *And if it is by grace, then it is no longer by works, otherwise grace would no longer be grace; but if it is by works, then it is no longer grace, otherwise work would no longer be work* (Rom 11:6).

FAITH SHALL BE TESTED

C.O. Rosenius, 1852

("De skärande motsägelserna emot wårt barnaskap hos Gud")

How peculiar is not the kingdom of Christ and the life of God's children here on earth! Here the most strident contradictions are intertwined: The greatest glory and the most lamentable wretchedness. [. . .] Truly, in and of itself and for God it is certain and secure, this fact of our status as children of heaven! It is also undeniably great and marvelous! But do you believe that you will always see and feel this way, see and experience for yourself these marvelous things in the midst of the dark moments of your everyday life? If you need to feel and see, then take your leave at once from this kingdom! The kingdom of Christ is a "kingdom of *faith*." Here there is a founding principle, that *faith shall be tested*; for this reason, you will often see and feel the opposite of everything that God has told us. Truly, no Christian shall be able to retain faith in the grace he has received and his status as a child of heaven, without bracing himself for the most strident contradictions to this claim. Indeed, he will need to brace himself for the one blow after the other in crises of temptation [*anfäktningar*]; *externally* through sorrows and horrid misfortunes and long periods of unanswered cries; *internally* through sins and persistent temptations and a lamentable helplessness, which, despite all praying to the Lord, seem to become worse and worse. [. . .]

When John the Baptist was born and was to be circumcised, Zechariah sang with prophetic joy to the Lord, the God of Israel, how he now, "as he had spoken through the mouths of the holy prophets, would save

us from our enemies and out of all of the hands of those who despise us."
Yet this same man's son, John, would later have his life ended at the hands
of enemies in Herod's prison, where he had been sitting, long forgotten in
his imprisonment, as though God and his angels had altogether forgotten
him, and finally have his head fetched from the executioner and placed on a
platter in mocking jest! [. . .]

In whatever form it might take, we all must pass through this kind of
testing whenever we pray for something without receiving it. In these times,
it seems as though God does not keep his own word and promises. God has
certainly everywhere promised to hear our prayers. Now imagine I come
into distress, bodily or spiritually, and take God at his word, and pray for his
help, praying long and earnestly, but the evil only becomes worse and worse.
Then I might say: "Where now is the Lord and his promises concerning the
hearing of prayers?" It is in this way that many believers have landed in the
most horrible doubts concerning all of God's word, indeed, even doubts in
God's existence. But, be still, poor heart! The Lord has also said: "What I do,
you do not understand now; but henceforth shall you understand it." The
Lord has therefore taught us to pray: "Not my will be done, but yours." And
you cannot be certain that what you are praying for in that moment is in
accordance with God's will, though it might be spiritually good. Paul, too,
once prayed for deliverance from the angel of the devil, even praying intensively on three different occasions, but was denied. And afterward he came
to understand that this weakness was just as beneficial to him as strength (2
Cor 12:8–10). [. . .]

But of all our discouraging experiences and the contradictions to our
status as God's children, there is nothing so difficult and faith-testing, as
when I, on account of some constant, inherent sin and obvious shortcom-
ing, believe that I ought to give up, that all of my Christianity is false, that I
am most definitely headed down a wicked path and that it is also impossible
to make any change. [. . .] Then I look to God's word, and how it speaks
of the freedom and power that is brought when we are born of God, and
then—then I become anxious, then my assurance is shaken. And neither
can I change the unfortunate situation! I take refuge in God, who promised
to hear my prayers, and pray night and day for help; but no, I am not heard.
[. . .] This is truly the most bewildering and faith-destructive kinds of temptation crises. But in these cases one shall learn to "take heed of the word"!
[. . .] We have heard a hundred times, and even thought that we believed
this, but nevertheless have never seriously understood this, that a Christian,
throughout his whole life, must battle with the sin that continues to dwell
within him; and that he will certainly never be completely free from this
thing he is battling against. We have heard, but never truly understood, that

within a Christian there are two battling natures, Christ and Adam, the new man and the old man, the Spirit and the flesh. Everything that Scripture has to say about the freedom of a Christian and victorious strength deal with those times, when God sends this strength—times of joy and peace, "the joy of the Lord shall be your strength." But a Christian will also experience other times. In this way, he will not have received such strength that he can manage on his own and be strong, whenever he wills, but instead he will yet live in a dependent relationship, as a child under his father, and each moment will have to pray for those gifts and the strength he will need. There will also come times of all manner of testing, and "if so must be," times of darkness, temptation, and lamentable weakness, when it seems that sin and the devil alone reigned and all strength and help were gone—as we see all of these things in the example and witness of the saints. See, when a Christian does not realize this, that he has two different natures and forms, and that in the time of temptation and weakness, it is impossible for him to feel strong and holy, then it is natural that he will feel bewildered, become ensnared and be imprisoned. [. . .]

The main explanation for why Christ became a riddle in the face of all reason, "a snare and a net for the residents of Jerusalem," such that the great, enlightened chosen people of God rejected their own long awaited Messiah, and his faithful disciples finally "took offense by him"—the explanation is that Christ had two highly conflicting forms and different natures, namely his exalted divinity and the lowliness of his manhood. [. . .] Even today, this is how it goes for us, when it is a matter of *Christ in us*. Even today, we make the same mistakes and land in the same bewilderment, when we are confounded by the Christ who is hidden in ourselves and in our brothers, and are not able to believe, that he is dwelling there, where we see and feel only so much wretchedness. We read in the word about how the true Christian does not only have a holy mindset and heart, but also strength in the Lord and victory over all evil; we see that faith is a victorious strength, which conquers everything that is in the world—that through it "the former weakness became their strength, and they became mighty in battle" (Heb 11:34). [. . .]

Do you think that a right-minded Christian never feels the evil, never is taken hold of by temptations, never becomes weak and wretched in the face of sin, but instead is always strong and holy? The witness of the saints shows the exact opposite to be true. The strongest have become the weakest, "have been taken prisoner" by sin, have been overcome, and have fallen. They have in some cases endured their entire lives trying to resist some specific temptation, so powerful that they often have not been able to feel anything other than that they altogether are slaves beneath it. [. . .] O, what hard battles and pitiable experiences we need, so that the deeply-rooted delusions of Adam regarding our own strength and righteousness can be killed in us! O, how profound and diverse this process is, as we must be made destitute before we are able to learn to fully take this seriously, that it is only in the Lord that all our righteousness and strength lies! [. . .]

Take heed of this! If I were free, then I would be perfect! No, I am taken prisoner by the law of sin in my limbs. But the flesh or sin is not in control, as long as I do not abandon the holy way of the Lord, as long as I do not make a pact with sin and abandon myself to being its servant, but instead persist in battling against it. As [Johann] Arndt rightly says: *"As long as this battle continues within a human being, sin does not have mastery over her; for that which one still battles against, that does not yet have the upper hand."* Luther also comments: *"In a battle, the victor is not decided by small attacks and defeats, but it is decided by who holds the field at the end."* In this way it is demonstrated that the Spirit continues to reign as the master of the house, whenever I am not straying from the way of the Lord, but always remaining the same Christian and, as often as I have the misfortune of being overtaken by my sin, continue to stand up in repentance and faith, continue to be troubled by sin, to discipline and condemn myself, but yet seek forgiveness and peace with my God through Christ, as well as continue to pray intensively for nothing other than strength and the deliverance from sin. No, such a soul is yet free in spirit, despite the fact that the flesh continues to love sin and battle against the Spirit. O, what a peculiar life the Christian must live!

THE FUNCTION OF DOUBT

C.O. Rosenius, 1848

("Om de hemska twiflen på allt heligt")

But what purpose can God have when he allows the soul to be abandoned to herself and to the devil, and thus be sifted and tempted [*anfäktas*] by doubt? [. . .] O, it is in these moments that she learns to properly understand what it is to be a *human being*, what human understanding, light, strength, and free will amount to on their own! It is then that she learns to understand what the consequences of the fall truly were. Then she learns to value every little crumb of grace from the bread of life, which comes down from heaven— instead of becoming accustomed to abundance! Indeed, then she learns, so that she will remember it, that *faith comes not from human strength*, but instead is a *gift* of God. One might have believed this before, since one can be quick to give assent to and rather easily recite this confession, that we are nothing, are capable of nothing, "are not even capable of *thinking* anything, on our own." But one will never be able to say this and truly mean it, until one has learned this through trials of temptation [*anfäktningen*]. [. . .]

As a way of illustrating this, we might have something to learn from the testimony and confession of a man, who has experienced what we have been discussing. As he tells it: Through the sheer mercy of our God, I had been living in union with my Savior for eight years. This was a blessed life, full of mere childhood exercises, struggles, and developments, when finally in 1839, all of this heavenly kingdom of mine suddenly seemed to have been wrenched from me, and I entered into a deep, hellish torment, into the most terrible doubts about everything holy. Certainly I had once or twice before this had attacks of the same temptation [*frestelse*], but these had been briefer and had soon passed over. I can remember in particular one occasion, three years previous, when I had preached in a country church, and many pious souls from the nearest town had journeyed out there, and even expressed their great joy after my sermon. Then that evening I received such a mighty crisis of temptation [*anfäktelse*] of doubt in all of God's word, such that I became so powerless, that I was not able to stand on my legs, but instead had to lie down. But the situation improved after a few hours, and I once again was able to see God's glory. What this had meant, I understood afterwards from 2 Cor 12:7: "So that I would not become conceited because of these surpassingly great revelations, I was given a thorn in the flesh, an angel of Satan to torment me. . ."

But now, three years later, in this long-lasting, utterly devastating darkness of doubt of mine, this is what happened. I was living as a private tutor [*informator*] on a country estate 1 ¼ [Swedish] miles from Stockholm. This was a horribly dark place, and I had gone for an entire year without meeting a single soul who was seeking after God. For a long time, I was having a hard struggle about this, in that I had been praying to God about a matter, which I regarded as being decidedly God's will, but yet my prayers were going unheard. During my time in Uppsala, I had previously also prayed much about this matter, but now it had become my first and last prayer every day for an entire year. To conclude by saying: "Father, not as I will, but as you will," this I regarded as hardly Christian, since I was praying with all my strength and ability for something, which I thought was God's own decided will, of course. As long as I continued to go without receiving this strength, I remained in a constant state of distress, not just because I was lacking this strength that I had been asking for, but also because of the doubts that arose due to the fact that my prayers were never being answered. There must not be any God, the Bible must not be the word of God, since I was not being heard in a prayer like this. This is what I often thought. And the doubts about my own receipt of grace, as well as whether or not a God existed—I did not even want to talk about those things. It was certainly clear that *I* at least had been abandoned by the Lord. O, God! I could not believe it, that you could play such a cruel game with your child! Thus, I forgot your word: "My thoughts are not the same as your thoughts!" [. . .] I lay one evening on my knees in prayer in my private chamber. Suddenly, I shivered at the thought of what he was doing, leapt up from my prayers and uttered a blasphemous thought, along these lines: "Alas! This is insanity! With whom do I think I am speaking, here! Do I imagine that God is here, in my cramped chamber! O, no! This is insanity!" and so on. With this, I threw myself onto my bed in the midst of my dark, horrible thoughts, and lay there until I fell asleep. In the morning I woke up—without God; I lived a whole day—without God; I went to bed once more—without God. Whether or not the existence of God could entirely be ruled out, I could never entirely make up my mind. I now had a great question to resolve, day and night: *did a God exist or not*? In this most serious episode, my doubt did not remain for long. One evening, I received a lighter moment, when I even found enough joy and marvel to write some lines of verse:

> Sun, moon, stars, and planets in the skies,
> And even earth so richly dressed
> These shapes whirl before my very eyes
> All these to me their God attest.
> For the world did not itself create
> They point to someone else's fame
> Who guides their courses, governs their fate
> And *God Almighty* is his name.

> [*Sol, måne, stjärnor, wärldar, himlar*
> *Och jorden i sin rika skrud,*
> *Ja, allt hwad för mitt öga wimlar,*
> *Allt säger mig: Det finns en Gud.*
> *Ty ej har wärlden skapt sig själfwer;*
> *Det måste finnas någon ann,'*
> *Som allting skapat, styrer, hwälfwer,*
> *Och* Gud Allsmäktig *heter han.*]

But my second great question became: Whether the Bible contains the word of this great God? With this question in my heart, I now sat, day after day, staring into the wind, examining, but thinking crosswise, everything that I knew from history, philosophy, and theology, in order to find some solid case *for* or *against*, if only I could find *some* conclusion and decision in this question. But everything was equally fruitless. The proofs and constructions that I built one moment, collapsed through some new maddening objection the next. My mind was like a clay vessel that had been smashed in many bits, and which could not contain anything. I lived in this state for several weeks. The boys, whom I was tutoring, were on their own for the most part, for the soul of their tutor was off in some distant country. Sometimes I descended into tender and bitter sorrow over my unfortunate state, in particular when I thought back to those happy years, when I had been living in the most intimate union with my Savior, had tasted and seen how good the Lord is, understood and believed the most marvelous truths of the gospel. For in those first years of my life of grace, I had many delightful experiences of my Savior's grace and presence, had spent the breaks between the school terms with a group of siblings of grace, who were in the midst of the warmth and excitement of a first love, and I had made use of the summertime to spend entire days in the woods, with a bit of food and a book, in order to be able to be completely undisturbed with my Savior in the most honest conversations and prayers. Finally, I had begun working for a few years rather earnestly for the awakening and enlightenment of others, and to be an instrument to many people's blessedness [salighet] in Christ. That former blessed life now became for my soul like a lost paradise; I viewed my life as though I were a backslider and a disgrace to the people of God. [. . .] In particular, I was reduced to sorrow and tears, whenever I would receive letters from those very dear friends, my siblings, parents and children in Christ, or wrote to them myself. And it was peculiar, that no matter how dilapidated my faith had become, however terrible my doubts felt to me, I nevertheless still managed to send these believers the warmest words of encouragement, and embrace them as God's angels, happy and lovable. It was only for me that all was lost. [. . .]

But about that same time I had started to hear about a spark of spiritual activity, which was out of the ordinary, and which provoked the murmuring of the world's disdain—both good signs. There was namely an English priest by the name of Scott, around whom this activity was gathering. This man, I thought, knows what pastoral care is [själavård]; he ought to be able to understand my troubles; I want to hear, what this man has to say about these things. With such thoughts, I traveled in to Stockholm and sought out this English priest. Driven by my distress, I came in to meet this man I had never met, and in short order had explained to him my whole situation. To this he initially responded with a few simple and light-hearted remarks concerning the general nature of trials of temptation [anfäktningens art]. Then he said: "The gentleman has probably studied and knows the evidence for the divine origin of the Bible, which is generally presented by theology?"—Yes.—"But am I to understand that this does not apply now?"—No.—"One thing that

I'd like to propose is something that is very simple and, precisely because of its simplicity, rather powerful, which is namely this: If the Bible truly does not contain the word of God, which it assures us that it is, then whose word is it? Was this book compiled by evil or pious people? Is it possible, that evil people have written a book, which with such spiritual richness, powerfully and profoundly condemns these very same people and the essence of their being? But it is just as impossible that pious people could have been able to write this book, if it is not true; for could pious people be able to stitch together lies and pass them off for God's word? Note, that this would mean that for century upon century, each person would have kept adding to the fabrications of another, creating one gigantic, coherent lie; fabricate events and miracles, which all point to the same great main theme—all of this being lies—and then present this as God's word?! Does this correspond with the holy, powerful and lofty spirit that appears throughout the holy Scriptures? In short: The Bible contains sufficient testimony in itself, possesses such a spirit, that the one who knows her, but yet does not want to believe that she contains the word of God, must settle for the most serious improbabilities instead." This is what the English priest had to say. At this, a beam of light and assurance coursed through my soul, and a couple of joyful tears appeared in my eyes—it was a moment of such solace, that I had not received for many weeks, indeed months. I could not protest, but instead sought merely to retain this insight that I had gained. Now he encouraged me to press on, and with prayer to God for his mercy, to continue to read the Bible.

But even then, my hour of deliverance had not arrived. I came home, thought and thought for one more week and was once again in the same darkness. An incessant and unreasonable "who knows? who knows?" made everything uncertain for me. All of my soul was in such a thick darkness, in such confusion and sifting, that I could not see the smallest thing, nor could I retain it, even if I was able to perceive it for a moment. After a week, I returned again to the good Englishman. He asked how it had gone, if I had emerged from my temptation [*frestelse*]. No, I had answered, everything is just as uncertain for me. Now, he gave me another, rather peculiar bit of advice. He said: "I suppose that it is not merely objections to the Scriptures, which are arising in your heart, but that there are sometimes also better thoughts, which contradict the former?"—Yes.—"Now then, take both the former and the latter and write them up and then ponder them carefully. In these temptations, the enemy's power lies primarily in transposing and confusing your thoughts. He is the spirit of darkness, does not love the light, nor serious and profound study; by being dragged out into the light, he is disarmed. Write down everything on paper, which occurs to you, both *for* and *against*, and then see which list weighs more."—With this peculiar advice, I left. And the Lord blessed this exercise so wonderfully that three days later, I came to such a certainty about the Bible's divine origin and the truth of *everything* that is written therein, that I was both amazed and rejoiced, and in glad excitement, I trembled and wept for a long moment in my chamber. Everything is true, altogether true, divinely true, and everything remains, these things that I had been grieving over as though they had been lost! This was how I spoke. It was not only that I was seeing everything again that I had previously seen, but instead it was as though my eyes were renewed, such that I saw everything more clearly than ever. It was now the case with my soul as it can be out in nature, when the land has been covered by thick clouds, rain and storms for several days, and then the skies suddenly clear, so that there is not a speck of cloud that remains, and the air is so purified and the sun shines so marvelously on the wet, glistening leaves, that one thinks that one has never seen such a beautiful landscape. Now what had been destroyed was restored again, this long-absent childlike trust in God. I received grace to once again believe in the forgiveness of my sins, and could now embrace my Savior anew, the God of my life, and with Thomas, exclaim: O, my Lord and my God!

WHAT IS FAITH?

P.P. Waldenström, 1891

(Guds eviga frälsningsråd)

"Faith is a secure assurance about that which one hopes for" (Heb 11:1). In these words the apostle describes the true essence of faith. And as we have seen in the previous sections what an importance has been laid upon faith, such that it is only through it that we are able to be made righteous before God and saved, then it is natural that in many people's hearts the question would arise: "What then is faith?" This question is all the more important, as there are many people everywhere who mislead themselves with a false faith. Namely, when one is aware of such things, then an upright soul cannot avoid searching to find out to what extent her own faith is of the right sort or not. [. . .]

But before we go and see what the right faith is, we ought to set aside various misunderstandings about faith. First and foremost we observe something, which may strike some people as strange, namely *that faith in Christ is not the same as faith in the Bible*. There are without a doubt many who regard themselves as believers [*troende*] whose faith [*tro*] is comprised in nothing other than that they believe [*tro*] in the Bible. But this is still not at all the same as faith in Christ. A human being could of course be so certain about the truth of the Bible, that she would be ready to risk her life to defend it at any moment, yet this is still not an indication that she has faith in Christ. Indeed, a great number of those *who are the enemies of Christ and his kingdom*, nevertheless also believe the Bible and never doubt that it is the word of God. For this reason it is never written in God's word: "Believe in the Bible, so shall you be saved." [...]

Further, we observe that faith in Christ is not the same *as having a proper knowledge of or conviction about Christ*. You may well have such a proper knowledge and conviction about Christ, as any angel ever had, but still be without faith in Christ. Many people have sacrificed their strength, their possessions, and their lives for a pure doctrine about Christ—indeed, many still do so—but in their hearts they have been lacking faith. They have had a proper belief [*tro*] *about* Christ but have lacked a proper faith [*tro*] *in* Christ. Therefore the Scriptures never say, "If you have a proper knowledge *about* Christ, so shall you be saved." For with such a faith one could still be lost, that is for sure. The devil also has a proper belief about Christ and is yet condemned. On the other hand, there are many who have a very incorrect belief *about* Christ, who yet truly have faith *in* Christ. Before Christ was exalted and the Holy Spirit poured out over the apostles, they had in many regards an incorrect belief *about* Christ, to which the gospel writers give witness. They did not know anything about Christ's death, nothing about his resurrection; when the Lord spoke with them about these things, they did not believe, indeed once Peter even rebuked him for such speech. But beneath all of this in their hearts they yet had faith *in* him, as well as were his true disciples then, just as they would be later. Their knowledge was different, but their belief in him remained the same. And it was through *faith* that they were disciples. Many are those, as well, who now have a very clouded and jumbled knowledge about Christ, but who yet are living children of God in their faith in him. The one person believes incorrectly about him in one aspect, the other in something else, and from this there arises countless differences of opinion and debates, but all the while they could, despite all of these debates, all still have faith *in* Jesus. Nothing can therefore do more harm than this, that one regards faith in Christ *as belief in this or that doctrine about Christ*.

Further we observe that faith in Christ is not the same as *believing in the forgiveness of sins*. One could believe in the forgiveness of sins, but still not have faith in Christ. Indeed, the whole world goes around believing in the forgiveness of sins, but does not have faith in Christ. In contrast, a soul can certainly have faith in Christ, while she does not yet dare to believe that she has the forgiveness of sins. Indeed, there are probably many sinners, who are in this situation. Therefore it never says in the Bible: "Believe in the forgiveness of sins, so shall you be saved." It does not even say: "If you do not believe in the forgiveness of sins, then you will be lost." No, with such a belief one can still go lost, and without such a belief one can yet be saved through faith in Jesus. [. . .]

Further we observe that the proper faith is not the same as *believing that one is saved*. Therefore, if you ask how it is with this and that person, and receive the answer: "He believes that he is saved," then you have not yet received an answer as to whether or not he believes in Christ. No, one can believe that one is saved, without this being an indication of whether one actually is, and one can truly be saved even if one does not yet know this or dare to believe this. [. . .] A *certain* or a *secure* belief is not the same as a *true* or *proper* faith. The Pharisee Saul even had a *certain* and *secure* belief, when he persecuted the Christians, but a *true* faith, this he did not have. The children of this world often have a *certain* and *secure* belief, while they are wholly lacking the *true* faith. [. . .]

But what then is faith in Christ? Answer: Faith is, according to the apostles, *an assured confidence* [*en viss tillförsikt*], and faith in Christ is thus *an assured confidence in Christ, a heartfelt and inner reliance on Christ, as the one who is Lord and Savior*. Such a heartfelt reliance on Jesus can exist in the midst of very poor and very incorrect knowledge. Even small, simple children, who do not understand much, can yet have such a faith. Indeed, it is children like these whom the Lord presents as the very pattern of faith. It is such a reliance that we find among all of those people in the New Testament who are called believers, as we shall soon see. If one were to have tested them according to our catechisms and spiritual textbooks, then they would surely not have performed well. But in their hearts they placed their reliance on Jesus, and that was faith. It was through this that they were saved.

It is a highly remarkable situation, that when Christ or the apostles preached faith in him as the way to salvation, there was no one who asked what it meant to have faith. What it meant to have faith, this was something that they knew from before, and with the coming of the gospel they did not learn a new way to have faith, but instead they learned who this God was, and who this Savior was, in whom they should have faith. Even the heathens have faith in their gods, that is to say, they place their reliance on them, as well as expect from them help and salvation in all distress. When the gospel comes to them and preaches faith in Jesus, then they do not receive a new way to have faith, but instead they get to know who Jesus is, on whom they ought to have faith. On this matter Luther says concerning Jn 14:1 the following instructive words: "*When a rich man relies upon and builds up his estate, then it becomes apparent that he is resting on his money bags, and this makes him enterprising and proud. Another person places his hope on this or that good friend and thinks: If everything else goes wrong, I will at least have that friend left. This is what Scripture calls 'relying upon [flesh]' (Jer 17:5). But if it is upon human beings or princes that one relies, then this makes them into an idol, because one is building one's hope on them and will become proud and confident, as though one had a god and everything, and did not need the true God. From this and other such idolatry one sees and learns how these two things, reliance and God, are related to one another. What a heart builds and relies upon, this becomes truly and completely its god, even though it is an idol. [. . .] Thus, Christ wants to encourage us to learn from the idolatrous world how our hope and our faith in the true God ought to be constituted.*" [. . .]

O, if only simple souls would heed this example and allow themselves to be freed from so much unnecessary worrying and anguish! But when now this question arises: "What is a proper faith, and how shall I know if I have it?" then it often happens that their thoughts are carried this way and that, looking for *what* they should believe, and they fear, that if they have faith or if they have an incorrect belief about this or that aspect of doctrine, then their faith will be false and not withstand death, and so on. When they hear about various doctrines, therefore, they come as though they were approaching the rack, as though their eternal life hung on this or that aspect of doctrine. But if you are being afflicted by fears like this, then look up here with both eyes—The more correctly you believe *about* Jesus, so much the better, but the faith that will save you is based on whether you, in your heart are *placing your reliance* upon Jesus. Where you have gone wrong in terms of knowledge about him, that will be corrected in heaven if not before, but your life, your salvation, your status as God's child shall not depend upon these things. When all of these debates about doctrine leave your head feeling so confused that you do not know *what* you should believe, then know at least *upon whom* you should have faith, namely Jesus. Go therefore with all of your worries to him and say: "Lord Jesus, I understand little to nothing of your word, have a weak grasp of all of these debates, but this I understand that *you are my Jesus, whom God has sent to save me*; therefore *I place my reliance upon you*, Lord Jesus, do not fail me." See, in this way when you hold fast to and rely upon Jesus with all your heart, then you have a proper faith in him, and whether you are Lutheran, Reformed, Catholic, or whatever else, then you are yet a Christian. Even if you are an ignorant Christian, then you are yet a Christian. [. . .] For each and every person is a *true* Christian who relies in his heart on the *true* Savior, Jesus, God's only begotten Son, who for the sake of our sins has been given and for our righteousness' sake has been raised.

GOD IS MY ASSURANCE

P.P. Waldenström, 1912

(Gud är min tröst)

On earth there is nothing, which in truth can offer assurance to a human being. For on earth there is nothing that is permanent. In 1 Sam 2:2, [Hannah] says to God: "There is no one besides you, and no rock like our God." And in 2 Sam 22:32, [David] says: "Who is God besides the Lord? And what rock exists apart from our God?" *Wealth* cannot offer assurance to the heart. Even the richest of the rich have often been the most unhappy of people; indeed, they too are plagued by economic worries. It is very common, that the poor are jealous of the rich and imagine that they live especially good days. But they may not feel this way deep down, and "good days"—days that can *truly* be called good—do not have their basis in external circumstances, but in *the heart*. The rich are often far more unhappy than the poor. Many a proud factory owner [*brukspatron*] is far more unhappy than the poorest of his workers; many country landowners are more unhappy then their poorest tenants. [. . .] Near Brooklyn, N.Y. in America there is unusually striking burial place, called Greenwich Cemetery. Once, when I passed through there, the coachman pulled to a stop near one hill that was full of graves and said: "Here there are buried seven millionaires, and all of them took their own lives." Directly afterwards, I bought the day's newspaper. The first thing I noticed was an article that communicated that a millionaire in New York had, that very night, ended his own life with the shot of a revolver. [. . .]

Power cannot offer any assurance either. The most powerful of people on earth often have been extremely unhappy. Those who think that emperors and kings and other powerful men are happy, they are mistaken. Their power gives them more anxiety than peace. The emperor's crown is much heavier than the worker's cap. And what is this power in reality? Merely a soap bubble. The emperor Napoleon was for a time the most powerful human being that had ever lived. Every kingdom trembled before him. And in the end, he wound up as the most miserable prisoner on a remote island out in the sea. There he had occasion to ponder the insecurity of all human power. Today, one might be the most powerful, tomorrow, the most powerless, today emperor, tomorrow prisoner. During the latter half of the past century, there were many kings and emperors and presidents who were toppled from their thrones. In America, three of the noblest presidents have been assassinated. Those who sit there now, they will eventually be toppled by death. And what will they have then?

Friends cannot give any true assurance either. Today one has them, tomorrow they are gone. Often it happens that the person who one day is your dearest of friends, another day can become one of your bitterest enemies. And even if their friendship remains constant as long as they live, they will not live forever, of course. Just as one has them, one will have to leave them and see their dead body be carried off to the grave. There one will stand, grieving. But no tears, no cry of lamentation can bring life to these dead bones. The one who has built his assurance on them, will be brought to shame.

Human favor cannot offer assurance either. It can, for a while, *intoxicate* you, but that is no assurance. "Do not place your trust in princes," says David, "they are human beings and cannot help" (Ps 146:3). And again: "It is good to place your trust in the Lord and not trust in princes" (Ps 118:9). But if the favor of *princes* cannot be trusted, if *they* cannot help—and often they cannot, even if they wanted to—then who is there to trust? When *the mountain* cannot hold, what is there that can? No, *all* flesh is *hay*, and all of its splendor is like grass in the field. The blade of grass is sufficient for neither cane nor crutch. Human favor, whether of princes or the people, is among the most unstable and undependable things on earth.

A good standing in this world, as judged by human beings, also cannot give any true and lasting assurance. The one day one has this, the next day one will not. And the joy that comes from this will later be turned into a sorrow just as bitter, as the joy before had been great. One of my acquaintances had through a business venture come into a very good standing. "Now my fortune is secure," he exclaimed triumphantly to a friend. A few days later, he lost his life through an accident. In short: on earth there is nothing, as we have said, nothing, which can give a human being a true assurance. [...]

"*In God alone my soul finds its peace, from him my help comes*" (Ps 62:1). David had much of those things that human beings generally regard as worth striving for, and about which they imagine that they would be very happy and have much peace if they owned them. But David did not find his peace in any of these things, but instead he says: "*In God alone* my soul finds its peace." Everywhere in his psalms we can also see that his heart is constantly keeping close to the Lord. In distress and desire, he turned to God. If he is glad, then he sings: "Praise the Lord, my soul, and do not forget the good things he has done." If he is in trouble and distress, then he pours out the sorrow of his heart before the Lord and cries: "How long, O Lord, will you forget me forever? How long will you hide your face from me? How long must I be troubled in my soul and anxious in my heart every day?" (Ps 13:1–3). Such is a true mindset of reverence for God. [. . .] In God there is true assurance to be found. The word, which in our new Bible translation appears as rock [klippa], is given in the old one as assurance [tröst]. Assurance is the same thing as security [trygghet], or resting against something. This security depends upon there being something constant to rest against. While now a rock is the most constant thing that exists on earth, this is why it is so often used as an image for God. Everything else on earth is inconstant in comparison to the rock. Flowers will last for only a few days or weeks; then they whither. Trees can stand for decades or hundreds of years; then they rot. The most formidable of human buildings will sooner or later collapse into ruin. But all the while, the rock will stand immovable, even if she stands in the midst of a stormy ocean. [. . .]

Let us not only take our assurance in God's goodness, but let us also make this known. David says: "In the morning I will sing of your strength and rejoice over your grace, that you have been a fortress for me and a refuge, when I was in distress" (Ps 59:16–17). And when Mary had experienced God's goodness, she said: "My soul magnifies the Lord, and my spirit rejoices in God, my Savior" (Lk 1:46–47). [. . .] If you are experiencing God's goodness, then strive to also make this known for other people. People need to hear this, and hear it again, that God is good. The ungodly need to hear this in order to become God-fearing. The troubled need to hear this in order to receive assurance. The believers need to hear this in order to be strengthened in faith. The fallen need to hear this in order to be raised up, and those, who are already standing, need to hear this in order to be able to run off on God's errands and carry his message. That is to say, speak about God's goodness and grace! It is the best service to which you can lend your tongue. David says: "I have made known your righteousness in the great congregation. Your righteousness has not been left hidden in my heart, about your faithfulness and your help I have spoken; I have not hidden your grace and your truth from the great congregation" (Ps 40:9–10). Whatever the heart is full of, this is what the mouth will speak, says the Lord Jesus. This has always been the distinguishing trait of the children of God, that they have gladly wanted to speak about God's goodness and mercy, and to thereby also make this known for others. [. . .]

Do you feel sinful and like a criminal, and is the devil tempting [anfäktar] you so that you think that you have been cast away from the face of God? Then do not be afraid. If it were to depend on your own worthiness, then you should never even imagine that you could be saved. But do not be afraid. Your salvation is a charge, which God has given to the only begotten

Son. And he is up to the task. When he is allowed to complete his work, then he shall even restore you as pure, righteous and holy before his Father's sight, and then you, too, with all of the company of the saved will sing his praise. Therefore, do not fear!

Jesus says about his little flock: "No one can pluck the sheep from my hand. For no one can pluck them out of my Father's hand" (Jn 10). His hand is the same as the Father's hand. Christ is the hand, with which the Father holds and preserves the little flock. There are people who, because of their faith, have been persecuted by their parents. But the Lord has preserved them. There are fathers and mothers who have surely wept over their children; they have attempted with every means possible to bring them back to the world. But they have not succeeded. No one has been able to pluck them from the hand of the Lord Jesus. There have been women, who have had ungodly husbands, who have tormented them terribly. God, who hears every sigh and counts every tear, has seen them. And no one can pluck them from his hand. There have been innumerable people, who for the sake of their faith have been thrown into prison, martyred, and killed. But they have stood fast. The Lord has helped them, and no one has been able to pluck them from his hand. There have been innumerable people, who have been very weak and infirm, very frail. The devil has knocked them around. They have a thousand times been on the verge of despair. But the Lord has once again raised them up, assured them, purified them, helped them. Then the light has dawned for them again. For all of these sorrowful things that have happened to them, nothing has yet happened to cause the Lord to grow weary or fail them. In this way, they have persevered year after year. Neither sin, the world, death, nor the devil have been able to overtake them. They have been weak, but the Lord has been strong in their weakness. [. . .]

Recall the most blessed moment you have ever had. This moment is a foretaste, but just a foretaste, of what you will have to expect in eternity, a little sip of the cup of bliss, out of which you will drink in the kingdom, "blessedness like a stream" from eternity to eternity. Indeed, there everyone who has believed on Jesus shall "shine like the sun" (Mt 13:43), and this includes you. There they shall all sing of victory, and this includes you. For such is the delight of the Lord. [. . .] That you are weak, this is of no consequence. Persevere! If you fall, then get up again. If you come into darkness, then cry out. Look always upward, always forward! It is God's good pleasure to give you the kingdom. Persevere, "day by day and with each passing moment."* Don't weigh yourself down with multiple days at a time, but say for each day: "Lord Jesus, help me make it through to this evening." Then you will see, how well it can go. And soon you will stand among the host singing praises at the throne of the Lamb, where you shall complain no more.

There you will receive the answers to all of your questions of "why, why, why." There you shall also be able to say: "Thank you, Lord Jesus, that I did not get my will on this or that occasion, although I thought that it was what I needed. Thank you, that you heard my prayers, that you did not give me what I asked." Indeed,

More secure is no one ever

Than the children of the Father;

Not yon star on high abiding,

Nor the bird in home-nest hiding.**

*"en *dag och* ett *ögonblick i sänder*"—from hymn by Lina Sandell-Berg

**Also by Sandell-Berg: *Tryggare kan ingen vara / Än Guds lilla barnaskara; / Stjärnan ej i himlafästet, / Fågeln ej i kända nästet.*

PRAYING FOR DAILY BREAD

C.O. Rosenius, 1855

("Fjärde bönen. Wårt dagliga bröd gif oss i dag!")

This subject to which we now turn is one that has been viewed from a variety of perspectives. Some people's situation is elevated so high above the question of daily bread, that they even find it surprising that anyone would want to take up this subject in a spiritual text, or that Christ has taught us to pray for this, right in the middle of such a spiritually-profound prayer as the Lord's Prayer. There are others who are wholly consumed by questions concerning daily bread, such that their souls are in jeopardy. Whatever God's word might have to say about conversion or faith, law or gospel has no effect on their hearts, because of this question of daily bread. This does not mean that the latter are so much more unfaithful, or that the former are so much better believers. In most cases it has to do with the fact that their trials are different, and this in turn seems to depend on differences in natural disposition or external circumstances. The happy-go-lucky youth, for example, who still eats at his parents' table, is not very familiar with concerns for daily bread. [. . .] Even among those who are responsible for a family, there are those who, thanks to a good economy or a light-hearted personality, do not worry over daily bread, nor do they think that they need to pray for it, but satisfy themselves simply with thanking God for his goodness. And of course they should! But if they have the spirit of Christ, they will come to see that even here there is something to pray for.

First we will say something to those who have worries and temptations regarding daily bread. Have you considered the significance of this, that the Lord Jesus himself taught us to *pray* for daily bread and turn to our heavenly Father with all of our earthly concerns? The most certain guarantee that the Lord wants to give us something is when he *says that we should pray about it*. For in the first place, he has said that receiving this is dependent on *him giving* it to me, and that it is not in *my* power to acquire it on my own. In the second place, he has shown me how it can be received, so that I do not need to languish in uncertainty about what I should do. [. . .] But we now turn to the third reason, and learn that the Lord has invited us to pray to him. One can easily imagine how cruel and contradictory it would be to say to someone: "ask me for this or that," and then when he had followed your advice and came to ask you for it, you didn't give him anything. Anyone who understands how cruel a trick like this would be can certainly not be so base as to believe that God would act like this. It is precisely because he has taught me to pray for whatever I need that this is the strongest assurance that he also will give me these things. [. . .]

This already becomes an abundant assurance when the Lord says: "Therefore do not worry, or ask: what shall we eat, what shall we drink, with what shall we clothe ourselves? Your heavenly Father *knows* that you need all of these things" (Mt 6:31–32). But as we have seen, it is an even greater assurance when in addition to saying this, he also teaches us to pray as we can in this prayer. When we take him on his word, and pray as he himself has taught us, how can we imagine that he would fail our trust and break his own word, his own truth, his own honor, and not give us the help that he himself has invited us to pray for?

"But," you say, "belief in God's blessings alone does not keep me fed and clothed. Neither are my children or my creditors satisfied with my faith alone. Neither does this satisfy those people who have loaned me money. I also would like to see to it that I actually get what I need and what I have prayed for. Whenever I do not see these things, what help is it then that I have believed all of these words of assurance?"—This is a rather bold way to speak with our Lord. Watch out, watch out, that you don't say the same thing that James says about false people: "If a brother or sister lacks clothes or is lacking food for the day and someone of you says to them: Go in peace, keep yourselves warm and eat well, but you do not give them the things that are needed for the body, what help is that?" (Jas 2:15–16). We ought to think twice before we imply that our faithful Father in heaven would deal in this way. This is no joke, but in fact quite serious, and sometimes this can lead souls to despair, so that they even rage against God and all of his promises, whenever they assume that they have clear proof that he does not give what he has promised. Now, although all temptations have their basis and source in the evil that is found in the devil's heart and the hearts of fallen human beings, still this temptation has other origins. It can be the result of the fact that a human being has developed certain ideas about *how much* she ought to have of the good things of the world. When she doesn't receive everything she imagined she should, then she thinks that our Lord God has not kept his promises, when he had actually prescribed a completely different objective for this prayer and never promised to give us everything that our fallen hearts might desire. Therefore, let us reflect on how the Lord has really taught us to pray here, so that we might know what he has actually promised to give us. And then we will see whether or not he has kept his promises and might not in the end be "found righteous in his words and prevail in judgment" (Rom 3:4). He has taught us to pray like this: "*Give us this day our daily bread.*"

What is meant by *our daily bread*? [. . .W]e pause with the first word, "daily." This word that in the original text has been translated as daily, can certainly be an ambiguous and obscure word, but all interpretations nevertheless present it as indicating something *essential* for our existence—not whatever the heart desires, but instead the essential. This actually means things that have to do with the maintenance of our being, which is why some people associate this prayer with spiritual bread or the food for the soul. What is more, Christ also adds the word "today" or "day by day," as it also can mean, in which we recognize the same idea that he expresses immediately afterward in the same speech, namely in Mt 6:34. [. . .] Have you not, up until this day, received what was necessary for your subsistence? And if you haven't received everything according to the plan for your life that you have charted for yourself, you have nevertheless received everything that *he* has promised, he who knows what is best and what is most wholesome for you. Or, do you know exactly how much discipline in the form of poverty and troubles that you need to endure for the sake of your eternal soul? In a case like this, a Christian who is not only poor, but even weighed down by debt, might answer us: "There is another aspect to this, compared to which all poverty is nothing, namely the trial of having to be beholden to other people. It is when I am not able to deal fairly with all, and I risk becoming a song in the mouth of the tempter, and a mockery of the gospel." Answer: In so far as you do not show any apparent tendency toward pride, which would necessitate a return to humility, and in so far as you are not "putting the Lord to the test," whether by negligence or idleness or through vanity and wastefulness of his gifts (Jas 4:3; Jn 6:12), but instead are a good steward, humble, diligent and faithful in your calling and continue to pray this prayer in simple faith; in this case you have all of the Lord's promises and assurances that he will give you so much that you do not need to be ashamed as a bilker, but instead shall be able to deal fairly with all. [. . .] To the extent that many of God's children through sickness or other circumstances are not always able to provide for themselves, but instead must depend on the mercy of other brothers, then this of course comes as a humiliation to our proud nature, but nevertheless can be part of the Lord's instruction for some of his children. [. . .]

We are so blind and forgetful that we see neither our own wretchedness nor the gifts of God, his goodness and power. Therefore, the Lord has a tendency to first place his children in the midst of worries, before he reveals his grace and power. Consider this, for example. When Jesus saw a crowd of more than five thousand people in the desert, he turned to Philip, this poor, clueless disciple, to answer the great question of how to feed such a large crowd. He says: "Where shall we buy bread, so that these people might eat?" But see what John writes, following this question: "*This he said in order to try him; for he himself knew what he intended to do*." Shouldn't we pay attention to such an example, that the Lord would give such a troubling question to a poor, clueless disciple? [. . .] But it often is the same way with us, as for Philip and Andrew, that we do not understand the intentions of the Lord, but instead begin in full seriousness to calculate the obstacles and do not believe that there is any help, do not believe that we have anything more than what we can see with our eyes. Philip thought and calculated quite accurately, that "bread for two hundred denarii would not be enough for them, so that each person could receive a small piece." He probably knew that in their money purse, which was managed by Judas, there was not any more than that. Andrew also wanted to participate in the worrying and points out something even more simplistic: "Here is a lad, who has five loaves and two fishes; but," he adds, "what could this provide for so many people?" This was the extent of the disciples' advice. But was it also the end of the Lord's? No, now it was his turn—he said: "Let the people sit down," and then he distributed, not as much as they had, but *as much as was needed*. [. . .] We ought to learn from this phrase, that the Lord passed out *as much as was needed*. [. . .] It costs God every bit as little to make us rich as to keep us in poorer circumstances; he has all of creation in his hand and could very easily let all the riches of earth rain down upon us, just as he allowed it to rain on the Israelites (Num 11:31–34; Ps 78:26–31). [. . .] What manner of mighty temptations might not accompany abundance? Consider, the terrifying words that the Lord has spoken about the rich! "It is easier for a camel to go through the eye of a needle, than for a rich person to come into God's kingdom." [. . .]

"Consider the birds of the air! They do not sow or reap or gather up into barns, and your heavenly Father feeds them. *Are you not much greater than they?*" (Mt 6:26). Think, open your eyes, and look at all of the endless diversity of living creatures in all of nature and how *he*, who has created all of these, cares for each kind with all of their particular needs. [. . .] The bird lives happily on God's providence, but the human being is racked by the grief of disbelief. Isn't it so true, what Luther has to say regarding this text, that when a bird flies over our heads, cheerfully chirping, we ought to lift our hats for him and say: *"My dear Herr Doktor, I confess that I do not know this art of yours; you rest so calmly at night and are not disturbed with worries for the coming day, and when you wake up, you first sing a glad morning praise song to your Creator, and then fly down, look for your grain and find it—and I, an old fool, allow the devil to so torment me, that I am consumed by worries concerning my sustenance."* May we pray to God against this foolishness, that he would open our eyes so that we, with thankfulness and deep humility, realize how the Lord, the God of our life, has poured out every grace and blessing over us from the very first morning of our lives. [. . .]

But this fourth prayer also has a lesson for those fortunate people, who know nothing of such concerns for livelihood and do not seem to need to pray for daily bread. There are two words in this prayer, which people like this ought to pay attention to, two words which indicate one and the same thing, namely the words *our* and *us*. If you have the mind of Christ, then you should also meditate on these words. He does not say *me* and *my*—give *me my* daily bread, but instead *our* daily bread give *us*. Do you believe that God has given you all of your good things, so that you alone shall live on those things according to your pleasure, or that you should gather up treasures only for your children? What does the Lord say? *"Make an accounting of your stewardship, for you can no longer be my steward."* Consider what God's intention is here, that he gives some people so much in this earthly existence. Have you ever considered why God has dealt so differently here on earth, that the one person is so rich, and that he has much more than he needs, and the other is so poor, that he does not have the essentials? The secret of this peculiar and uneven distribution is that we have different callings; those who have received more than they need, must be the Lord's stewards, who must distribute his gifts for him. He allows the poor to crowd around them, and to test them daily, to see if they will honorably distribute his gifts as stewards, or if they seek to bury their pound in the earth and make idols out of it, for themselves and their children. May we never forget the great principle: "Whoever has been given much, from him is much expected! And the one who has been trusted with much, from him will even more be required," as well as the royal commandment: "Love your neighbor as yourself." Do not forget the many poor, sick, weak, frail people around you, who are stretching out their hands for bread. In your prayers for all people, you should not think: *me, mine,* but instead *us, ours.* Furthermore, you are not to pray as a hypocrite, so that you in your prayers say *ours,* but then deal with the good things that you receive as though they were *yours.* No, you are merely a steward. And we are to be stewards gladly, because of Christ's love, so that he can say about all the good we have done: "You have done this to me." [. . .] Besides, the Lord can quickly take away the good things that we currently own, which is why you always have good reason to pray for his grace to preserve you, and for a daily outpouring of daily bread. Confessing our constant dependence upon the Lord in this way is a rather healthy thing for us as Christians.

LORD JESUS, MAKE US MERCIFUL LIKE YOU!

P.P. Waldenström, 1891

(Guds eviga frälsningsråd)

"The one who gives to the poor, he shall not be lacking, but the one who turns away his eyes, he will draw upon himself many curses," so it says again in Prov 28:27. David speaks about this in Ps 41: "Blessed is the one, who allows himself to care for the poor. The Lord will help him on the day of misfortune. The Lord will preserve him and keep him alive; he shall meet success on earth, and you will not give him over to the wiles of the enemy." And Isaiah says: "If you give your food to the hungry and feed those in distress, then a light shall go up for you in the darkness, and your midnight shall be like midday. And the Lord shall lead you always, and feed your hunger in the desert itself, and he shall make your bones strong, and you shall be like a watered orchard, and like a spring of water, which does not run dry" (Isa 58: 10–11). These are such clear promises, that one ought to certainly take hold of them. Do you really believe that it is the faithful and almighty God, who has spoken these things? And what, for your part, have you ever risked on them?

The days of misfortune will continue to come as in days of old, and descend upon cities and peoples. One time it will be a plague. Then the Lord will remember them who have served him through the poor, and he shall preserve their lives. Another time it will be a famine, so that the land will resemble a desert. Then the Lord will remember them, who in their good days were merciful, and he will make it so they will at least have food. When times are dark and full of despair, and for others it seems as though it were deepest midnight, then the Lord will allow these people to have light as though it were midday, and so on. It was not simply from a divine revelation that David and Isaiah spoke these words, but also from experience. And you of course can also try this for yourself. [. . .]

Each and every one of us is concerned about our children. Parents truly live for their children. For this reason they are also anxious, that their children might, if possible, inherent something from them after they leave this world. The one who has a farm strives as far as he can to leave it to his children someday, as debt free as possible. The one who has a home does the same. The one who has a business works to always make this stronger and improve it in order to one day leave it behind as an important source of income for his children. Still other people will make greater or lesser deposits in the bank for their children and so on. All of this can certainly be done in the fear of the Lord, as the apostle says: "It is not children who save up treasures for their parents, but instead parents for their children" (2 Cor 12:14). May everyone in doing these things have an awakened conscience before God. But the *most important* and *most secure* source of income that you can prepare for your children, is what you through benevolence to the poor have entrusted to God. Never forget this!

But it does not end here. The blessings of charity shall follow into the kingdom of heaven. "Their deeds will follow after them," it says of the believers (Rev 14:13). And the Lord says: "Make friends for yourselves by means of unrighteous wealth, so that when it has run out, then they might receive you in the eternal tents" (Lk 16:9). By unrighteous wealth, he means earthly property. And he exhorts his disciples to use these things in order to make for themselves friends, so that when their earthly property has run out, that is to say, when the Lord returns, they may be received in the eternal dwelling places in the Messiah's kingdom. Here he teaches his disciples to use these earthly possessions *with regard to the coming blessedness at the end of the age.* And then the return will be so great, that we will surely be put to shame by its extravagance.

About the same matter, the Lord speaks in Lk 14:13, when he says: "When you hold a banquet, invite the poor, the crippled, the lame, the blind. And you will be blessed, since they have nothing to repay you with; but the return will come to you at the resurrection of the righteous."—It is certainly no great effort to invite blind, poor, and miserable people to a banquet. Even more expressly does he say this in his words about the last judgment, when he says: "I was hungry, and you gave me something to eat; I was thirsty, and you gave me something to drink; I was sick and in prison, and you visited me" and so on (Mt 25:35). Even such small things as these, which someone has done in his name, he will remember on that great day, when he before his judgment seat shall gather all of the people of the earth.

About the same matter the Lord speaks in Lk 6:38, when he says: "Give and it shall be given to you. A good measure, packed, shaken, and overflowing shall be given in your lap."—Even in these words he indicates the eternal reward in his kingdom. However poor and frail our good deeds might be, it is sure that they will have a great significance for our place in the kingdom of heaven. This concerns what the Lord says elsewhere: "Whoever gives one of these little ones a cup of cold water to drink in his name by a disciple, truly I say to you: He shall not at all lose his reward" (Mt 10:42).—On that day, when the kingdom comes, you shall surely wish you had done much more for the Lord through the poor and the miserable. But then—do it now, what you on that day will wish you had done! *And let this amount to something!*

It will be of even greater significance, on the other hand, when a person considers how the Lord speaks about the judgment which will pass over those who have not been merciful. In Lk 16:19 he speaks about the rich man and Lazarus. The rich man lived for himself. He clothed himself lavishly and took delight in his opulence every day. "Am I not entitled to do with my things, as I will?" he thought. "Is it not rightfully my property? Should I not be glad about the employment that I provide for so many people through my stately lifestyle?" But at his door there lay the poor man, Lazarus, covered with sores, who in vain attempted to feed himself with the crumbs which fell from the rich man's table. What did this man have to do with him? "The poorhouse can take care of him," he surely would have said, if he were living in our day. And many people would have agreed with him. But soon the tables turned. In the realm of the dead, Gehenna, is where this unmerciful man wound up, and when he lifted up his eyes, what did he see? Well, it was Lazarus lying in the lap of Abraham. And then he begged in vain, that Abraham would send Lazarus, so that he might dip the tip of his finger in water and cool his tongue. The Lord has surely not told a story like this lightly. James understood this when he said: "Judgment without mercy shall pass over the one who has not been merciful" (Jas 2:13). See to it, that this judgment does not one day pass over you!

What now has been said about generosity, this applies to all forms of benevolence. The believers do not belong to themselves, but instead belong to the Lord, and the Lord has placed them here in order to serve him, precisely through their service to those who are suffering, and not only for those who are believers, but also for those who are not believers. He allows his sun to go up over both the wicked and the good, and lets the rain fall over the righteous and the unrighteous. Therefore it is also his will that his children would reflect beams of his own light and grace for all people.

May God, according to his great mercy, help all of his children to take this matter to heart! Lord Jesus, fill us with your grace and make us like you! Amen.

THE BELIEVERS' FREEDOM FROM THE LAW

C.O. Rosenius, 1858

("De trognas frihet från lagen")

Translator's note: this reflection followed a series on the Ten Commandments.

As we have now for several months been observing what God in his holy law demands from human beings, it is now necessary [. . .] to also observe what the Lord God wants for those who have been brought to contrition by the law and who fear his word. It is not only to the right that one can stray from the Lord's true way, but also to the left. [. . .] We have from God's own mouth heard what is lovely and pleasing to him, and on the other hand, what displeases and angers him. And we could never praise God enough for the light he has given to us, so that we are able to know what God's will is and what is pleasing to him. We have also seen the majesty and the grave seriousness of the Lord's law, the burning fire of zeal, with which the Lord God has pursued the transgressions against his holy commands, when he with his eternal wrath and vengeance threatens all those who show contempt for him, and on the other hand, his promises of unceasing grace for those, who love him and keep his commands. [. . .] May we in all our days remember this! For God's commands and warnings are no idle joke, but instead have this majestic seriousness and constant nature to them. What God has once hated, he will always continue to hate; what God has once loved, he will continue to love even today, so true it is that God does not change. This ought to awaken every human being to reflection. O, may the Lord have mercy! The very words of Christ himself, and his most perfect explanation of the law, was not able to prompt the Pharisees to become contrite sinners, neither was it able to awaken his disciple Judas from the allure of the devil. The one who so wills can always keep his heart closed and hide from the light of truth. [. . .] We should therefore also beware of the hidden hazard that often is most attractive, that a soul begins to look to herself alone, loses all sight of the covenant of grace, sinks down into a spirit of slavery and ends up in unbelief. Therefore, it is our wish, with God's grace, to take up a very important, remarkable, and assuring topic, something that is one of the lesser known and least talked about subjects: The believers' freedom from the law. [. . .]

Those who have been condemned and killed by the law, to the degree that they have sought and found their salvation only in Christ, have been altogether freed from the law's requirements for salvation, and the bondage of keeping the law as a means of seeking righteousness and salvation. By this they have also been freed from all condemnation of the law, and are free from the curse of the law (Gal 3:13). They are also, in correlation to their faith, free from the reign of the law in the conscience, or what the apostle calls the "slavery of fear" (Rom 8:15), and the "yoke of slavery" (Gal 5:1), as well as from anguish and suffering, when they in their Lord and guarantor see all of the fulfillment of the law, eternal forgiveness, life, and salvation. That the believers are free from the Jewish ceremonial and civil law, is already granted, since this law even in the days of the old covenant was not binding for other nations besides the Jews. But now it is a question of the moral law, or the ten commandments. Even here the believers are free from this law, namely that they no longer stand under its requirements for salvation, no longer shall be judged as they are before the law, but instead according to the perfect righteousness that they have in Christ. Therefore, they live under a constant grace, in a kingdom of grace, which will continue to reign over them, so long as they in faith remain in Christ. So much better is the covenant that Jesus has founded! (Heb 7:22). Praise the Lord, my soul, and all that is in me! [. . .]

It is thus only as a light and guide in the question of what is sin and what is holiness, that the moral law retains its eternal importance and strength for the believers, and serves as a guide for the willing spirit and as a chastisement for the wicked flesh. For as was said before, what God has once loved, he will always love, and what God has once hated, he will always hate; so true it is that his holy essence cannot change. Therefore, we see that the same apostle Paul, who spoke most about our freedom from the law, nevertheless also charged the Christians to keep the commandments of the law as a guide. For example, he says: "Do not allow freedom to give occasion to the flesh, but instead through love serve one another; for"—note this addition—"for the whole of the law is fulfilled in one word, in this: You shall love your neighbor as yourself" (Gal 5:13–14). There we see that he presents the commandments of the law as a guide. And John says: "This is love for God, that we keep his commands." [. . .]

In this way, the situation of the believers is that they certainly have a constant guide in the commandments of the law, but they will never be condemned for the greater or lesser shortcomings in following this guide. They will surely be chastised for their sins, corrected, cleansed, and made contrite, first by the law, later through "the rod and torments," "if it must be so"; but never condemned under the law. [. . .] This is why we even see how Christ, too, disciplined and corrected his faithful disciples for their sins, but never shut them out from grace, but instead even in the midst of his chastisement, spoke of their place of honor in heaven (Lk 22:24–30). [. . .]

But freedom from the law also means that through faith my conscience is liberated from the yoke of slavery to the law, so that I have received not the spirit of slavery and fear, but instead the spirit of an elect child, which calls out: "Abba, Father." [. . .] But this freedom of the conscience is an imperfect freedom, for this is dependent on my faith, and my faith is never perfect. Within the heart of God is an eternal satisfaction with the work of the Son alone, an eternal grace, an eternal delight in what the only begotten Son has done. But in my heart there is a constant shifting and conflict between faith and disbelief, a constant shifting between light and darkness. In heaven there is an eternal song of praise to the victory of the Lamb, but down here on earth, there are only short moments of light, joy, and praise. In God's great book, my account is eternally stricken through and settled, but in the little account book of my conscience, it is seldom really so clear and settled. For we have an enemy, who constantly records our debts anew, in order to cause us anxiety and to terrify us. But praise to God that the covenant of grace is perfect in *his* heart, fast and immovable, and that *he* does not count our sins against us, that *he* does not judge us according to the law, even though we continue to do so. [. . .]

The apostle says expressly in Gal 2:19: "I have through the law, died away from the law." Words like these contain the mystery of our question. He also says this in Rom 7:4: "You have also, my brothers, been killed from the law;" and again (Rom 7:6): "dead to what once held us prisoner." [. . .] What do words like these mean, that "I have become dead through the law," or that sin "killed me through it"? If you go to the bottom of this question, you will find a precious light. What "death" is the apostle meaning here, when he in this context says: "I have become dead through the law"? The catechism speaks of this death in three ways: bodily, spiritual, and eternal. But here this is a fourth kind of death that is being described, for the apostle was of course spiritually dead already before this, before the message came. What can he mean here with the word "dead"? Those with experience know this already, while others do not believe it. Well, this is how it goes, when the law truly strikes down a human being, when God's holy eyes begin to pursue her thoughts and the heart's designs. It is then that she is killed, and the more seriously she becomes attacked, the sooner she will be killed. It was the old Pharisee, Saul, who needed to be killed, before there could be a Paul. Jacob's hip had to be worn out in the nighttime wrestling match with the stranger, before he could say: "I have seen God face to face, and yet my life has been rescued." Then he received a new name, and afterward never walked straight again. In short, if you take the apostle at his word, then you will see who it is that became dead. He says: "*I became dead.*" It was his *self*, his self-active, self-righteous, self-holy *self*, which fell in the battle with sin under the law. The law instigated this battle, which pursued and drove him on with its demands and claims, while that deep-seated misconception of our own strength, which defines the soul of the old man, attempted to hold fast to the feeble hope of making progress in the battle; but all the while this contributed to exhausting and killing him. All of this he expresses like this: sin "pursued me and killed me through its message." Now it is broken, this old misconception of one's own strength and of the law's ability to make a human being upright and holy; now the human being lies there, lost, help- less, and powerless, indeed "dead." But when the body of Christ, which was poured out for the forgiveness of sins, is presented through the gospel to the human being in despair—when God's counsel to everlasting reconciliation is revealed to her, when the merits of the works and suffering of Christ are revealed to the exhausted soul, who is now in despair of all her own works, both her will and abilities, in her own prayers, her remorse, and everything that is in her—then she is summoned before him, just as she is, so lame, incomplete and so unworthy of God's grace, that she wants to collapse out of shame. When she collapses into the embrace of the bridegroom, the second man, then she belongs "to another, namely him, who has been raised from the dead" (Rom 7:4). And behold, then she will receive the entire fulfillment of the law in him, who was "the end of the law, righteousness for each and every person who believes." [. . .]

Certainly the old misconception of our own strength continues to grow back a thousand times. This is usually in the finer form, that through prayer and God's strength I can and ought to be and do so much. This betrays itself as being the delusion of Adam, in that I, I, I and not Christ, become the focal point of all my thoughts. [. . .] From this you can determine which people are *not* under grace, but instead under the law, namely those who are not killed by the law, as we now have seen, but instead still keep hold of their hope, their confidence in the law, in their own work and their prayers. They have not become sufficiently lost and despondent in their work, that they have needed to concede that they are lost, and surrender to grace. [. . .] Such people might be able to profess a rather accurate confession, but yet lack the reality of the inner condition, which can only be demonstrated through various signs, and which they ought to take into serious consideration if they are to be awakened at last. In particular, these signs are the following: first, that they do not recognize what the apostle is saying about the true function of the law, that he has been found "abundantly sinful by its message," that he has "become dead." By contrast, they think that they have become rather good and upright. For this reason, their song is not about the Lamb who was slain, but instead our piety, our holiness, or how we ought to be, we ought to live—in short, something about us. [. . .]

The second sign is that they cannot understand that we must be liberated from the law, in order to be saved and holy. [. . .] "It has to be the opposite," they think, "that if one is to bear fruit for God, our conscience must certainly be bound by the law; for our conscience to be liberated from the law, this would be the same as opening wide the gates for all manner of ungodliness." This is the sign, which betrays those people, who otherwise would highly resemble Christians. We ask: "Isn't this an all too common occurrence, which appears throughout the human race, that *each human being is always inclined to judge everything according to her own experience?*" Now when a human being has this mindset, that she regards a free evangelical [*fri evangelisk*] sermon (for example on the Christian's freedom from the law) as *harmful*, doesn't this demonstrate that her own experience has been such that she thinks it is only through the law and its threats that she is kept from sin? But this again demonstrates, of course, that she only responds to the law, that *she* has not been "killed off from the law," that she has not yet had the blessed experience that the more free grace is allowed to enliven her heart, the more desire she will have for everything holy and good. For if she herself had had this experience, then she would certainly be inclined to think that the same gospel, which so powerfully enlivens her to do what is good, would also have the same effect on others. For every human being is certainly inclined to judge everything according to her own experience.

The third sign is that they can never tell the difference between a *pious person* and a *Christian*. [. . .] To this can be attributed that they certainly understand the hazard that souls might be careless and corrupt the grace of God into a life of loose living. But they think that it is only through a legalistic sermon, through warnings and admonitions, that a person will be kept upright. Thus, they lack the distinguishing trait of a Christian, that he is *driven by love for Christ* and, as Paul says, "lives for God," precisely because he has been liberated from the law. [. . .] When a human being does not have the ability to realize this, but instead always only sees things according to the law and works, this certainly demonstrates that she has not herself experienced this and therefore does not know the difference between a *pious man* and a *Christian*. This difference is something one would certainly understand, if one had indeed, *through the law, been killed off from the law*.

Indeed, since *God* has taken upon himself this great, heavy burden, the accomplishment of my salvation, then I will gladly bear some of these lesser burdens: to take leave of the world and sin; to discipline my flesh and serve my neighbor in love, with deeds, with words, and with patience; to give the hungry bread, the homeless a home, to visit the sick and the prisoner; to forgive enemies and have patience with difficult people or a difficult calling in my life. Since my Lord has been gracious enough to allow himself to be delighted by small things like these, then it is as though I were halfway to paradise when I realize that I can already, here and now, do some service that will delight our faithful, precious Lord. I cherish all of these things dearly, because he was so abundantly good in establishing this kingdom of grace, that no sin would be held against me, that I would never need to be condemned under the law.

Such is the true motivation to do good. This is indicated by the words of the apostle: "Christ's love compels us, as we are convinced that one has died for all, and therefore all have died" (2 Cor 5:14). And this is what the apostle meant, when he said: "So you have been killed from the law, *so that we might bear fruit for God.*" [. . .] You can only do good *to the degree* that you have been so undeservedly pardoned and become *freed from the law*, only have so much of true sanctification and good deeds. Take note of this, and remember it well, and write it on your mind: you will only have sanctification to the degree that it proceeds from grace, from faith and love, from your freedom from the law.

PERMISSIBLE AND BENEFICIAL

P.P. Waldenström, 1891

(Guds eviga frälsningsråd)

"*Do not drink yourselves drunk on wine, which leads to debauchery, but fill yourselves up with the Spirit*" (Eph 5:18). The apostle challenges the believers in 1 Cor 6:20, saying: "Praise God in your body and your spirit," which belong to God. And this challenge is based in that the believers do not belong to themselves, but are the possession of Christ, dearly purchased by him. [. . .] But in the same regard as this notion of belonging to Christ was important for him, in the same regard it was also important for him that it was not merely the soul that needed to be sanctified to Christ, but the body, as well. About this he writes in 1 Thess 5:23: "May the God of peace himself sanctify you *in your whole being*, and may your whole spirit, soul, and *body* be kept blameless at the return of our Lord Jesus Christ." On this same matter, he challenges in Rom 6:12, saying: "For this reason, do not let sin reign *in your mortal body*, such that you obey its desires." It is God's will to not only have your soul and your heart in his service, but also your body. His will is to dwell in you, such that your body shall become his temple (1 Cor 6:19). It does not merely say the "spirit" or "heart" of the believer, but that also his body is God's temple. And this is meant first and foremost to teach us to correctly value and care for our body. It happens often, that believers in ignorance speak contemptuously of the body, calling it "worm-ridden," and similar things. But such speech is not right. Think, how differently the Spirit of God speaks, when he calls the body the temple of God! [. . .]

Drunkenness gives rise to all manner of other vices and crimes, such as sexual indecency, brawling, assault, murder, robbery, theft, and so on. Most of the inmates in our prisons have drunkenness to thank for what they have become. Had they not been led astray by drunkenness, then many of them might now be honorable, respected, and productive citizens, in whose home a brood of children might have been raised up to be healthy, good, and happy people under the loving care of their father. Instead, these children are left to the wind, and are growing up in sin and vice, following the same trail their father had blazed before them. [. . .]

But it is not actually the drinker we are focusing on here, but instead on the believer's relationship with the question of temperance, and that primarily from the viewpoint that he has a duty to set apart not only his soul and spirit, but also his body to God. It is clear, that the believer cannot be a "drinker" in the proper meaning of the term. Yet, there are many believers who have not taken this matter as seriously as they ought to have done. We began this reflection with the language used by the apostle, in which he tells the believers: "*Do not drink yourselves drunk on wine.*" We note here first, that he does not say: "*Do not consume wine,*" but instead, "*Do not intoxicate yourselves with wine.*" Wine can be of two varieties, some intoxicating, some not-intoxicating. [. . .]

An additional reason for the believers to altogether refrain from intoxicating drinks is the significance of example. The believers are called to be the salt of the earth (Mt 5:13). A quality of salt is that it counteracts spoilage. As the salt of the earth in the spiritual meaning, they have the task to counteract the spiritual spoilage of the world. And as part of this spoilage, drunkenness is a leading reason for many people's decline into misery and wretchedness in all manner of ways. But how shall the believer be able to be a salt, then, if he himself consumes intoxicating drinks? Certainly not in the same degree, as if he were to completely abstain. [. . .]

"All things are permissible for me, but not all things are beneficial. All things are permissible, but I shall not allow myself to be mastered by anything" (1 Cor 6:12). This is a remarkable saying. Many people really like the one part, but have neither the ears nor the heart for the other. The one who, for example, loves wine and strong drinks, he certainly knows no more delightful gospel than the words: "All things are permissible for me"—provided that he can place a period there and thus avoid these words: "But not everything is beneficial," and "I shall not allow myself to me mastered by anything."

There is a desire for pleasure that is deeply rooted in human nature. This desire is placed there by God, and therefore is no sin. The human being is created for a life of pleasure and blessedness beyond description. And that she yearns for this, this is good, as long as it takes place in the right ways. Nothing can be more pleasing to God than that you might search for that blessedness and pleasure, which is to be won through everything that is pure, noble, healthy, good, holy, and so on. But if in its place, your desire for pleasure seeks to satisfy itself through things that are impure, degrading, unhealthy, then this becomes sin.

It is very common that one hears it preached that a God-fearing person ought to suppress and kill all desire after pleasure. This speech is probably well-intentioned. But it is not truly correct. The desire after pleasure can neither be, nor ought to be, killed, since it is from God and is necessary for human development. It ought to, on the other hand, be satisfied, but with such things that are holy, good, and pleasing to God. This is also the one sure means of preventing the desire after pleasure from going astray into things that are impure and sinful. When Christ and the apostles challenged the believers to forsake the desires of the world, they simultaneously held up the heavenly blessedness, which is intended for the people of God. *It is toward this end* that their desire after pleasure should be directed. Then the desire after pleasure can become *uplifting* and *sanctifying*. When, on the other hand, it is directed toward that, which is impure and unholy, then it becomes *degrading* and *destructive*. [. . .]

The desire for tobacco is among those desires, which have a particular ability to take control over the human being, although it is often regarded as rather innocent. And in this reflection, we should share a few gentle, but serious words about this. There can be found even among believers many people who use tobacco. The ones who do, like to find their support for this in the words of the apostle: "All things are permissible for me." That the apostle adds: "But not all things are beneficial," to this they close their eyes. For they don't dare to speculate as to whether using tobacco for their recreation could have any spiritual or bodily benefit. Furthermore, it can be seen from the whole context that Paul is not speaking here of satisfying un-natural desires for pleasure. Even the most simple reflection on this should make this clear to us. And the desire for tobacco is unnatural. It does not lie in human nature, but has to *be implanted* in it. It would hardly be possible to imagine Christ or Paul with a cigar or a pipe in his mouth, or with a nose full of snus!

It is a sad situation to hear how those who are enslaved to tobacco try to convince themselves and others that they are not in fact slaves. "You know, we could quit whenever we wanted," they say. But if one answers them: "Then yes, quit, before you become slaves," to this they turn a deaf ear. And they ought to know that it is easier to quit before one becomes a slave than after. The person writing these words had himself for many years used tobacco. Back then, I could not read the above words by Paul without them leading my thoughts to the snus box. I did not like these words of Paul. I liked my snus much more. And each time Paul's words confronted me, I had a difficult time convincing myself that I was not in fact a slave to tobacco. The slave of tobacco feels listless when he is without his tobacco; and he will not be restored to good spirits until he gets his snus again or a cigar or a pipe or wad of tobacco. I experienced all of this myself, but nevertheless I tried to convince myself that I had not become a slave. Over time, I tried desperately to find anything I might use to defend the use of tobacco. Then one time I heard, for example, how the old priest [Peter Lorenz] Sellergren, who in his time was a great man of the Spirit, had been a big smoker. When a simple Christian one time reproached him for allowing himself such an indulgence of pleasure, he answered: "Well, it is an indulgence of pleasure, but I believe that God does not begrudge me this indulgence." This was a remarkable gospel. "God does not begrudge me this indulgence," I thought, and so I continued to snus and forgot for the moment Paul's words: "I shall not allow myself to be mastered by anything." On the other hand, this solace did not last long.

Another time there was an old, tried and true colporteur who said to me: "God has certainly created tobacco, so that people can use it." At this a light was lit for me, and in its glow I continued to snus and smoke yet a little while longer. But then, an acquaintance brought my attention to an issue of a German periodical, which I had not seen before. This issue featured an article on tobacco. And there I read something to this effect: "You say: God has certainly created tobacco so that people can use it. We ask, though: Is it really *for the Lord's sake*, to glorify him through the use of his gifts, that you are smoking?" And this question blew out that new light at once. For it was clear that I wasn't smoking and snusing for the Lord's sake, that was for sure.

CIVIL RIGHTS AND RESPONSIBILITIES

P.P. Waldenström, 1891

(Guds eviga frälsningsråd)

"May each and every person be subservient to the governing authorities. . ."
(Rom 13:1–7). The apostle speaks in these verses about the believer's relationship to civil authorities, and that this too is an important chapter in
the believer's life of sanctification. True Christianity encompasses and creates anew every aspect of a human being's life. It wants to manifest itself in
every thought, every feeling, every word, every action which moves within
or proceeds from her. Just as the sin from Adam has forced its way into and
poisoned every corner of our being, so will Christ through his Spirit force
his way into every corner in order to sanctify and purify us and restore us
to perfect righteousness. "If we walk in the light, as he is in the light, then
we have fellowship with one another, and the blood of Jesus Christ, his Son,
will cleanse us from all sin," says John (1 Jn 1:7). Christ himself has demonstrated perfect holiness and righteousness in all circumstances, and this is
his saving work to sanctify us in spirit, soul, and body so that we might be
perfect.

Now the apostle says here: *"Each and every person,"* or closer to the
original language, *"May every soul be subservient to the governing authorities."* The apostle takes it as a precondition that there shall be an authority,
which has power over the people. He has seen this situation to be ordained
by God, which he states immediately following. He explains now that every
soul, that is to say, every person without exception, without regard to age
or religion, shall submit to this authority. With this, the apostle has most
decidedly denounced the involvement of Christians in every way in con-
spiracies to overthrow this authority, in whatever form they might take.
The spirit of grumbling, defiance, and lawlessness, which moves through
the world, *is of the evil one.* The believer ought therefore to be *afraid* of
being contaminated by this, and should pray to God for the grace to be able
to flee from every association with it. It is a terrible occurrence when the
children of God become ensnared by this spirit. It undermines their peace
and joy in God, it cools off their love, it exhausts and embitters their spirit,
it makes them worldly, and destroys their spiritual life. Experience attests to
this regrettable development. But over time they think that they are correct,
and this causes them to not fear any danger in this. "Is there any risk in their
becoming involved in this?" they ask. And so they shut their eyes and do not
see how their childlike relationship to God all the more recedes, how their

brotherly love grows cold, how a bitter mindset all the more fills that place in their hearts, where before peace, contentment, and happiness dwelled.

In the letter to Titus (3:1), Paul says: "*Remind the believers to submit to the princes and authorities, to be obedient, to be ready to do every good work.*" Paul understood well enough that the believers would be tempted to disobedience over and over. It was particularly difficult for them, who lived under a tyrannical, heathen authority. But for precisely this reason he tells Titus to *remind* them about being obedient, so that they will not forget this. [. . .] As Paul speaks of this, so too does Peter, when he says, "*May you be submissive to all human order for the Lord's sake, whether it be the king, as sovereign, or the governors, who are sent by him to punish those who do wrong, and commend those who do right*" (1 Pet 2:13). [. . .] He does not leave it up to the believers' free choice to be subservient to the one, but to have contempt for the other, to the degree that they might determine that the one was worthy of honor and the other worthy of contempt. No, they are to be subservient to *every* human authority and order. And this is for the Lord's sake. If the person in authority is not worthy of honor, nevertheless *the Lord* is still worthy of you obeying him. [. . .]

Peter also demonstrates *why* it is so urgent to be subservient, when he immediately adds: "For it is God's will that you with good works shall be able to silence the ignorance of foolish people. May you be as free people, but not as though you had your freedom as a cloak for evil, but as God's servants" (1 Pet 2:15). It is apparent from these words that the ungodly have defamed the believers precisely because of their talk about freedom. They have interpreted this freedom as involving self-rule and disobedience to the authorities. Now it was up to the believers to silence this defamation of their ignorant accusers, through their humility and subservience. To be subservient is therefore not at all in conflict with freedom. Quite the opposite, God's children shall demonstrate that they are truly free precisely in that they in all things strive after what is good and pleasing to God and brings honor to his name. And to this also belongs their obedience and subservience to authorities, to *every* human authority, higher or lower. [. . .]

The deepest foundation for the believers' duty to be subservient to the authorities is given by Paul in our text, when he says: "*For there is no authority which is not of God; the authority that is in place has been ordained by God.*" Here we see first and foremost that authority is not a human invention, but is instituted by God. Thus it is an error and a source of much ruin to human life, when one believes that *authority is of the people*, and that it is dependent upon the people, such that the people can topple her whenever they will. The authority is *God's* representative and proxy before the people and exists to watch over law and justice in the best interests of the people. If it is instituted by God, then is it necessary for people, for God has not instituted anything that is superfluous. To remove authority would be a terrible misfortune. No authority can be so bad that it would not be sevenfold worse to have no authority at all. Therefore Luther says: *"The worldly government is a marvelous, divine ordinance and an excellent gift of God, which he has instituted and set in place, and will also sustain it as something, which we cannot do without. For if it were not so, then no human being would be before any other, the one would devour the other as irrational animals do with one another."*

But it is not only this, the apostle says, but instead even more, namely *that no authority exists without being of God.* O, what remarkable words! The authority under whom the believers in Rome suffered, was a heathen authority, the cruel emperor Nero. This emperor raged against the Christians in the most terrible way. This was the one who had Paul beheaded and Peter crucified. But despite the fact that he was this way, Paul said: *"the authority that is in place has been ordained by God."* [. . .]

"But," someone says, "this would certainly mean that we altogether abandon freedom, which is one of the most important rights of a people. And would it be Christian to excuse a wretched authority, and in doing so abandon the people into slavery?" [. . .] Above all it is God who directs the destiny of the nations; and only the people who has learned to obey him, has correctly learned how to use civil freedoms. The freedom that, through obedience to God, the people receive as a gift of grace from him, this alone is a freedom that can properly be expected to be a lasting blessing. The freedom that the people, in defiance of God's commands, struggle to obtain through violence and revolt, this will sooner or later turn into a curse to the people themselves. [. . .]

The apostle, as we have seen, has understood the difference between authority as an office, on the one hand, and the person in the office of authority, on the other hand. And this too we ought to distinguish. The office is always holy and divine and shall be respected by us, though the people holding this office may themselves be good or bad, worthy of respect or despicable. Now then, this is easy enough to say and comprehend, but to put this into practice in life is more difficult. In order to do this, it requires the great grace of God. [. . .] The spirit of the times is now such that people even mock subservience and respect for authority, as though it were some kind of old-fashioned nonsense. But you, people of God, do not let yourselves be contaminated by this, but instead obey God's word! [. . .]

In those cases where the authorities begin to look through their fingers at evil, as well as let these evils go unchecked, in these cases society is on its way to decline. Punishment is an expression of God's righteousness toward what is evil. As such, its purposes are on the one side, to deter people from evil, and on the other side, to awaken those who have sinned to reflect on this, so that they might rise from their sin and make improvement. The purposes of punishment are not, as many believe, to repay evil with evil, which would be unrighteous, but instead, as we have said, to awaken and deter from what is evil. When parents punish their children, then it is certainly not the intention to do them any harm, but instead exactly the opposite. [...]

"But," someone says, "it is yet impossible to unquestioningly obey the commands and prohibitions of the authorities. Neither Christ nor his apostles have done so. It does happen, of course, that the commands of the authorities conflict with the commands of God." Yes, this unfortunately happens often. And then the believer must obey God more than human beings. It is apparent that Paul's speech concerning subservience was not intended to mean that we, in *these* cases, should obey the authorities. This is clear from his own example and that of the rest of the apostles, and even more so by the example of Christ. But even in these cases, one can conduct oneself in a different manner. One can behave in humility and godliness with all respect, which is due to the authority as God's servant. But one might also behave in a proud and defiant manner, such that it is apparent that one has contempt for the authorities. And this latter option would be a sin.

Look at Christ! When he could not *obey* the authorities, he yet accepted their judgment as a lamb, which does not open its mouth when it is sheered. Neither was Paul able to obey the authorities in everything, but submitted to the burden of its judgment, first in a long prison sentence, and ultimately at the scaffold. Never does one see in his letters or in the accounts in the Acts of the Apostles about his time in prison any expression of defiance or discontentment. Peter and John explained before the council in Jerusalem that they had to obey God more than human beings (Acts 5:29). As a consequence of this, they had to face flogging and imprisonment. But rather than allowing this to lead them into defiance and rebelliousness, their hearts were instead filled with thankfulness because God had counted them worthy of suffering for the sake of Jesus' name. O, what a mindset! May God grant this to us as well! [...]

But it is an entirely different situation, when the authorities *intend* to institute laws that are in agreement with God's word, but in doing this, arrive at a different interpretation of this word than I have. What shall I do in this case? It is possible that *the authorities* have made a mistake and that *I* am right. It is also possible that *I* have made a mistake, and that the authorities are right. [...] We can take a few examples here. The authorities might request that all men of a certain age shall be trained for the defense of the nation in the event of war. Now suppose there are some believers, who regard it as wrong and sinful to fight in a war. They are not even able to pretend to support this, and therefore cannot submit themselves to participate in weapons training. For if they did this, then they would be seen to condone war. Over time there are other believers, who regard it as altogether proper, that a nation is prepared to defend its freedom, indeed even in the event that it is necessary to defend themselves with life and blood against an encroaching enemy. Now the former says: "God's commandments forbid us to kill." Upon which the latter say: "But the same God, who gave that command, also commanded Israel to carry out bloody war." [. . .] And thus they arrive at a point where neither side can convince the other. Then the authorities come and order them to train for war. And who will now be able to decide whether this is correct or not? [. . .]

Now say there is another believer who is called up for military service or to swear an oath or something of that sort, and he is bound by his conscience that such a thing would be against the commands of Christ. What shall he do? Shall he act against his conscience? We answer: He shall weigh the matter before God in prayer. If he finds that his opinion was incorrect, then he ought to let go of it, and submit to the commands of the authorities. If, on the other hand, he is not able to understand anything other than that he is right, then he shall do what he believes to be God's will, as well as peacefully and patiently suffer the civil punishment, which he has brought on himself, all the while thinking: "My God, you know that my will is to do what is right. And since I cannot understand the matter in any other way than I do, then I will gladly suffer. God, if I am making a mistake, which is well possible, then enlighten me about what is right." See, this would be a genuine Christian mindset, but where does one find this? [. . .]

"But," someone says again, "shall a believer unquestioningly submit to everything that a bad authority does and decides?" Answer: This he does not need to do. He can and ought to do much to improve whatever is bad. But he may not in the process do anything bad himself. For bad never cures bad, but will only make matters worse. [. . .] Citizens also have the right to, before God and with all legal and righteous means, work to replace a bad authority with a good authority. [. . .] It is a regrettable situation that so many believers do not realize that civil rights also correspond to civil responsibilities. They believe, that it makes no difference for them if they make use of their civil rights or not. They do not think about how if they engaged in the decisions regarding civil affairs, they would be able to bring about much good to the blessing of society, as well as avoid much bad, which now is taking place to the detriment of society. Through their reluctance to participate and their apathy they thus become responsible for the fact that the good which could be done, does not happen, and the bad which could be avoided, is not hindered.

YOU ARE THE SALT AND LIGHT OF THE WORLD

P.P. Waldenström, 1902

(Samlade Predikningar II)

Translator's note: this sermon was given on All Saints Day in Immanuel Church, Stockholm.

Text: Mt 5:13–16. The Savior says here to his apostles: "You are the salt of the earth." And what he says to them, applies to some degree to all Christians and in particular to all preachers of the gospel. He says this in regard to their work, their profession in this world. He had previously said to them: "Blessed are you, when human beings defame you and persecute you, saying all evil against you for my sake. Be glad and rejoice, for your reward is great in heaven. For in the same way they persecuted the prophets, who came before you." The reason why they must be prepared to suffer such persecution is precisely because they are the salt of the world and the light of the world. If the prophets had simply remained silent and let everything they saw pass by without further comment, then they could have been left in peace. [. . .]

If John the Baptist had contented himself with preaching for the people, and telling them that they should be well-behaved and god-fearing and pay their taxes and so on, then he would certainly have been praised. Perhaps he would have even become court preacher for Herod, and Herod might have exclaimed: "This is the best preacher in all my kingdom!" But when John did not stop with such sermons, but instead turned toward Herod himself and said: "Herod, you are living in sin, and this is no more permissible for you than for anyone else," then that was the end of any friendship between them. Then Herod said: "It will not be any good to allow John to continue, for this will incite rebellion among the people. We must throw him in prison." And so John sat there for a while. But then there came a day, when Herod had a feast, and had become drunk along with the rest of the company at his table. His unlawful wife's daughter came in and danced before them, and it pleased him so greatly that he, in his intoxication, granted her the head of John the Baptist. This is how things went for John, because he was the salt of the world. What if John had instead thought along these lines: "If I try to scold Herod, then I will probably irritate him and will risk being thrown in prison, and then it would be impossible for me to continue to preach for the people; it would therefore be better if I leave Herod in peace, and stick to preaching for the people; in doing so, many will be rescued, but who knows if Herod will be rescued by me speaking to him? My ministry will be brought to an end." Surely John was tempted to take this course, but he did not give in to this temptation. His work was to serve as the salt of the world, and so he scattered salt all around him. This stung when it entered into people's wounds, and it stung Herod too, since he was human like everyone else, though it was no more acceptable for him to live in sin than for anyone else to do so.

If Christ wouldn't have troubled himself with scolding the high priests and the scribes for their hypocrisy and false righteousness, then he would certainly have been celebrated by them, perhaps even acclaimed as Messiah. Who knows? If he had been content to simply scold publicans and prosti- tutes, and instead bowed deeply for the scribes and Pharisees, then people would have said: "Our people have never seen a greater prophet than this Jesus of Nazareth." Then he might have earned the acclaim of even Caia- phas. But when he turned to these men—who fasted twice a week and gave a tenth of all their property, and what is more, observed the three regulatory prayer times each day and other such duties that belonged to the divine service—when he turned to these men and said: "You brood of vipers, who has warned you to flee from the coming wrath," then they sang another tune. Then they said: "This Jesus of Nazareth is misleading the people, we need to be rid of him, one way or another. We must be rid of him." They tried several times to have him stoned, though they did not succeed. At last, they had him sentenced to death and executed. Why? Because he was a salt in the world, and the salt burned in their wounds.

The apostles acted similarly, and met with similar results. The one was beheaded, the other crucified. Similar examples can be seen in the lives of Wycliff, Hus, Peter Waldo, Luther and others. They were either burned, drowned, hanged or in some other way executed, or had to endure bitter persecutions, to the glory of God and to the service of humanity, as well as to the particular delight of the Pharisees and scribes and high priests. Why? Because they were the salt of the earth, and this salt burned in their wounds. And instead of seeking a cure for their wounds, these people instead tried to get rid of the salt. Therefore the Savior now says to his disciples: "You are the salt of the earth. Be prepared that your work will sting in the wounds of the world, and that you will receive the wages which will follow." [. . .]

Our Savior says further: "You are the light of the world." He calls himself the light of the world, when he says: "I am the light of the world: the one who follows me, he shall not wander in the darkness, but instead he shall have the light of life." Here he is now calling the believers the light of the world. But this is in another and lower meaning. One can say that the sun is the light of the earth, but also that the moon is a light of the earth. But the light the moon has, it receives from the sun and reflects onto the earth. In the same way, the disciples of Jesus receive their light from Christ, who is the sun, and this light is reflected through them out into the world. In this way, they too became the light of the world. [. . .]

This is how the Lord intends for the believers to be light in the world. They may be greater or lesser lights, they might stand in the market square, in the streets or inside a room, they may shine by the beds of the sick and the poor, or in some other place—each and every one of them is to shine with the light one has, until that point when their light has burned down or the master of the house has blown it out. You, who think that you are gifted with little, that your light is seen so poorly, do not be ashamed of your little light. Neither should you be jealous of those who have greater lights. And you who have a greater light, do not be proud over those with lesser lights. [. . .]

Now the Savior says to his disciples: "Let your lights shine before human beings, that they might see your good deeds and praise your Father, who is in heaven." [. . .] Good deeds are those, which proceed from a love of God, and which serve to magnify his name and to bless your neighbor. It is not said, therefore, that every good thing that is done is a good deed. For I can do something, which comes to the benefit of another, and my deed can nevertheless, when one looks closer at it, be anything other than a good deed. It may have been done with a bad intention, for example, so that I might win my own glory, or something of that sort. That a deed is great and shines is not at all to say that it is a good deed. We have an example of this in the text for the 23rd Sunday after Trinity. There were many rich people, who laid great gifts in the offering chest, which was good of course, but this was not therefore a good deed, and the Savior did not praise them for this either. For it is the characteristic of good deeds that not only the deed in and of itself is good, but also that the source, from which it proceeds, is good. Besides the deed can be good, even though it does not shine much, which is illustrated in the same story. For the Savior praised the widow, who laid two pieces in the offering chest, coins so small, that according to the regulations of the forefathers, it was forbidden to lay such coins in the offering chest. But the widow's deed was yet good, for it proceeded from a spirit of reverence for God. [. . .]

Let us pray to God to be able to shine in the world with our good deeds, each and every person, wherever we have been placed. Take pains to shine where you are standing, that through your light, some glory might be harvested for God and Christ. Take pains, that you might be a light before the Lord, whatever your position in this world. It is he, who will judge your light. And of a light, one expects nothing less than that it would shine with all the strength and ability that it has, and in the place where the master of the house has placed it. [. . .] Indeed, may God in heaven help us to this end, that we with all of our deeds might magnify God. This will not merely be through our preaching and mission and offerings, but also as each and every one of us faithfully does that which we know is the will of God, and that we do this in the place where we are standing. This is the whole point. Let us pray to God for the grace to be able to do it. Amen.

Waldenström on the grounds of the Mission School at Lidingö

6

Appendix: Historic Addresses

IT IS NOW LAWFUL TO CONGREGATE IN JESUS' NAME!

C.O. Rosenius, 1858

("Det är nu lofligt att församlas i Jesu namn!")

Without a doubt it is already generally known for most Christians in our country, that the king has now, in accordance with the law, accepted and sanctioned the new conventicle ordinance of this past Riksdag. In doing so, the old conventicle edict of 1726 has at long last been slain, after having for more than 130 years tormented and troubled so many pious souls in our country. With this, there will no longer be any talk of "unlawful gatherings" when we have congregated in Jesus' name. The unlawful has now become lawful. Indeed, before God and truly enlightened consciences it has always been lawful to do what the law of love demands, this law which is the regent and measure of all laws; but it has now also become lawful before the civil law and for those consciences, which are dependent upon that.

What we otherwise might be able to add here, we have already said before. And this can also be read in the wording of the new conventicle ordinance. May everyone with humility and reverence for God make use of this freedom of ours, which is now even acknowledged by law! Otherwise this freedom will only become harmful and give occasion for the indolent and insecure nature to despise what is good, whereupon even greater occasions will follow. Indeed, may the Lord Jesus, the great, Good Shepherd himself, preserve and care for his feeble flock according to their needs! In him we take our assurance. May he remain near us and gracious to us all! Amen.

SERMON FOR THE SECOND DAY OF EASTER

In The Church of the Holy Trinity in Upsala

The 28th of March 1864

"The resurrection that occurred in Jerusalem, when it became known that Jesus was resurrected."[1]

Ps 102:1 ; 107 ; 21:4 ; 102:4,8 ; 109:8

I. J. N.

Introduction: "Who has believed what we have heard? And to whom has the arm of the Lord been revealed?" (Isa 53:1)—With these words Isaiah begins his prophecy of Christ's death and resurrection [*uppståndelse*], and with good reason, for there is nothing more difficult than this belief. The prophecy is full of improbabilities. "He was despised and rejected. . ." and "He had no form or majesty that we should look at him" [Isa 53:2–3]. . . . But when one holds this to be true and begins to put this into practice, the obstacles to faith remain both difficult and numerous. The self-righteous heart is resistant to faith, and constantly wants to confuse grace with works. . . . Nevertheless, everything depends on this belief and prophecy. What is required here is for "the arm of the Lord to be revealed."

---

1. Translator's note: At some point during this ordination sermon, Waldenström apparently extemporaneously added the phrase "in terms of sin and grace there was no distinction between 'Judas and John, Cain and the Virgin Mary.'" It was partially this phrase that displeased the archbishop, but it does not appear in this draft of the sermon. The title was also not included in the draft. Waldenström recounts both these details in his memoirs.

The Gospel: Mt 28:9–15

Everything in Jerusalem was in a great commotion [*uppståndelse*]. The people had seen the most important event in world history. The question was: *what shall one believe about Jesus of Nazareth?*, this question which has upset the world more than any other question, and which in particular continues to upset our own time. One cannot deny that there is something odd, something unusual in the story of this man and his kingdom. But who is he? Indeed, this is the question.

His enemies today are just as unconcerned as then. They had taken his life, but—" the false prophet had said while he was alive that he would be resurrected."—Could one be certain that this was a lie? No, therefore, send word to the governor for guards! The stone must be sealed.

The same commotion occurred among the disciples concerning this question, although for different reasons. They had placed their hope in Jesus . . . "We hoped that He would be . . ." Now he was dead—they had witnessed it—and buried. What should they believe? That He had said he would be raised, this they had forgotten. There were no signs that this would happen, and furthermore it was against the laws of nature. Therefore they were in doubt.

It was the two women who were the first to come to their senses, one might say. They had resigned themselves to their fate. He was dead, and now their last service was to preserve his body with perfumes and oils, and then to say farewell to hope! What a telling picture of the soul, who in her misery has nursed a stubborn hope of salvation, finally reaches this point: "say farewell to God and die." This was the atmosphere—on that most marvelous and joyful day that earth has ever seen!

But now grace breaks through in its full splendor, now the connections begin to be made between what had been said and what had occurred. Now the disciples tremble with joy, and the council trembles with terror. The high priests now must meet together with the elders in order to *decide* on an answer to the urgent question, *what shall one believe about Jesus?*

But what does Jesus do during this time? Like a mother, he immediately races after the confused children, in order to comfort them in their grief. Meanwhile, he allows the pretended righteousness of the stiff-necked priests and Pharisees to go on. This is the general outline of the events in our gospel text. Now we will look closer at the details in order to learn *how*

Jesus behaves toward his friends and his enemies, as well as how they behave towards him.

1) *How Jesus and his friends behave among themselves.* The women had seen the vision of the angel at the grave in verse 8. When they meet Jesus, his first word is "Greetings!" "He does not chastise them for their sins," but instead greets them in peace and adds "Do not be afraid." Here is half of the lesson, for here we see what is meant by "the redemption that is called the forgiveness of sins" [Col 1:14]. A rational understanding of the law would hold that good would proceed from good and evil from evil. But the poor disciples had had enough judgment. No, instead it was "Do not be afraid," "Be glad," and "my brothers and Peter. . ." [Mt 28:9–10]. By this he teaches them about the *forgiveness of sins* and his *protection.*

Their consciences had been shaken, for they had lost not just a friend but a savior, which is what they needed. Had they merely lost a friend, they would not have had cause to tremble. And had they *only* feared the wrath of the Jews, then they could have avoided that by joining in the defamation—which Jesus would have deserved if He had been a deceiver. But here there was a greater interest at stake. The question was, "How could they now find peace in their consciences?" Here it was, Χαίρετε—Peace! and also "Be of good cheer, your sins are forgiven."

Why was their response of fear not enough? It was not enough for faith, as this story illustrates. If the conscience is to be at peace, Jesus must speak to it. No other sermons will work here. Therefore *he meets* them here and preaches to them in the manner of Isaiah 40:1. From this we learn first of all, a.) *that the Lord Jesus* with attentive eyes follows his sheep in all their ways. "Zion laments: the Lord has forsaken me, my Lord has forgotten me. . ." (Isa 49:14–15). It is not just how He behaves with the righteous, nor only in the light times, but most of all in the darkest valley. Therefore, when you are at your most miserable and weakest point, most oppressed by sin and think that you are destined to be handed over to your rebellious nature. . . remember that the Lord's eyes will follow you so that he may do good to you. "I know well, what my thoughts are about you," "It will be my desire (not displeasure, not trouble), that I might be good to you," "Therefore, the Lord waits to be gracious to you" (Isa 30:18).

Further on we learn b.) that *the Lord meets* his sheep, that is to say, will reveal himself to them, when they are in need, before they can even call out to him. . . . Mysterious are the ways of the Lord, but He always proves himself to be a deliverer. He cannot do anything other than what is good, His mercy is an overflowing well. . . . Therefore, when he hides himself from you, know this, that there is grace and after the rain the sun will shine (Ps 112:4; 97:11). But such times of grace and darkness are necessary, in order for us to begin to rely on God's faithfulness and to respect His Word, just as it was only after Christ's death and resurrection that the disciples really understood these things for the first time. It is just as essential as it is difficult, that each miserable soul experiences this posture, to wait in preparation, in order to decide what he shall believe about Jesus, namely that He overflows with grace, despite moving and acting in strange ways (Jer 3). He is called an "eternal grace," and does not waver, as our own feelings do.

"But what if I sin?" Answer: then you have a defender, who offers deliverance not only for the sins of the heart, but also for the sins of the hand and tongue . . . "If Christ is resurrected, then we are no longer in our sins." Think about this: what had the disciples gained with their unbelief? What did they receive? "Do not be afraid!" What? Yes, because "as *I* live, so shall you also live." Just as Christ is alive, the disciples will live. Their life shall not be dependent on their deeds. No, if Christ is resurrected, and he lives, and they are no longer in their sins. Thus: "In the world you have compulsion. . ." Compare Isa 41:14, 17; 43:1, 2 ; Ps 91; 57:2. "I am leading. . ." Ps 32:8; 23:3; 73:24; 37:24; 145:14; Isa 54:10. This is the nature of Jesus.

Once again, *the nature of the disciples* is such:

a) *that they cannot thrive* (cannot be happy) without Jesus, while their consciences are on guard, and they have no peace except in Him;

b) *that even in distress* they stay with Him, and even though he appears dead, they come to the grave, but they must *come*, because they are driven by their hearts;

c) *that they rejoice* when He reveals himself;

d) *that they pray to Him;*

e) *that they obey with joy* and go forth to proclaim His grace to others. For every Christian is called to proclaim His works. The obedience that comes from the law is a compulsory obedience, which does not bring pleasure to God.

2) *Jesus and his enemies.* During this time, the council needed to come together to decide, what they should believe. Perhaps they were driven by a certain zeal for the truth and the enlightenment of the people!! Rationality

cannot tolerate Christ. He has to be driven away, and it is necessary for lies to be told about Christ, His words, and His friends. Compare how [the newspaper] *Aftonbladet* translated ἐξ ἧς to "by him" in Mt 1:16,[2] and *Dagliga Allehanda* "The word of Christ": "each and every person will be saved by their faith"—"Jesus' true death." . . . They are not so careful with the truth, and try to escape Jesus' words. Why? Answer: they hate the light, because they know that their deeds are evil and would be judged as such if they came to the light. Instead, they would rather try to escape "unjudged" and by doing so risk damnation, rather than allow themselves to be judged into life. Nowadays there are no more popular books than those that boldly defame Christ. But "by their fruit shall you know them." Therefore, where Christ is allowed to enter, there will be humble, obedient. . . . joyful and loving souls. But where he is denied, there will be proud defamers, drinkers, and speakers of profanity. . .

But how does Jesus respond to this? The answer is that he lets them go their own way—a grave judgment! Indeed, he sends them off into their confusion, such that they will believe their lies. It is natural for Christians to want their Lord to "more powerfully" come to the defense of his church. But He knows what He is doing, and the Christian ought to be satisfied to know that the one who hopes in the Lord will not be put to eternal shame.

Amen.

(Note: The day after I held this sermon, I was summoned before Archbishop Reuterdahl to receive a serious reprimand for this, after which I had to submit an apology to an extra session of the archdiocese, if I wished to be ordained.)

---

2. Translator's note: Instead of "of whom"—". . .Joseph the husband of Mary, of whom Jesus was born. . ."—the other translation makes Joseph the father and challenges the divine conception of Jesus.

APOLOGY IN RESPONSE TO ARCHBISHOP REUTERDAHL'S REFUSAL OF ORDINATION TO WALDENSTRÖM, SUBMITTED TO THE ARCHDIOCESE OF UPSALA, THE 29TH MARCH 1864.

The relationship between the state of grace [nådeståndet] and sanctification with particular regard to 1 John 2:1–6, including the dangers that teachers of this subject face when preaching them to the congregation. Presented by P.W.

The second chapter of 1 John must be understood in connection to verses 5–10 in the previous chapter, which ταῦτα in chapter 2 refers to. There the apostle presented A.) *God as a light without darkness* (verse 5), B.) *human beings and particularly* the believer as having sin (verse 8), C.) *the relationship between God and the believer* as a relationship of i.) the *confession of sins* and the *forgiveness of sins* (verse 9) and ii.) of *mutual fellowship* through walking in the light (verse 7), which point is further clarified by contrast to verse 6. The apostle then explains the purpose of this presentation in chapter 2:1–2 and complements this in verse 3 with a closer explanation and greater emphasis of what he said in chapter 1 about walking in the light as being a necessary outcome and thereby a sign of being a child of God [*barnaskapet*], according to Christ's words: "By their fruit shall you know them."

From this we learn first: *that reconciliation*, which in the objective sense is made complete for "all the sins of the world" through Jesus' death and resurrection alone, prior to and without our repentance or conversion (Jn 1:29; 2 Cor 5:18,19; Rom 5:6,8; etc.), nevertheless only benefits a sinner when he has first received such a conviction of his sins that he is compelled to a sincere confession of sins and to embrace the undeserved grace of Christ.

But the second thing we learn from this is: *that the state of grace* [*nådeståndet*] is not conditioned by any action or accomplishment of the individual, but instead only by the individual becoming aware of his sins and confessing them, as well as by continually *renouncing* all works and by faith embracing grace as free grace. This is true in both the person's continued existence in grace as well as its initial manifestation. For however much walking in the light is an essential sign of the state of grace, it is never to be considered as a requirement or condition, in either the beginning or in its continuation, but instead always as an outcome. *The origin* is, from the beginning to the end, the deliverance that we have in Christ's blood, namely the forgiveness of sins (Eph 1:7), *the requirement* on the part of the individual, is only the heartfelt acknowledgement of sin, which is prompted by the Law. The agent is exclusively the grace in Christ embraced through faith, which is brought about through the gospel. These last two things, which Scripture calls Repentance and Faith, can be summed up under a common name, partly as *conversion*, with regard to the inception of the state of grace, and partly as *daily repentance*, with regard to its continuation.

But thirdly we learn from our text: *that a sinner* through the state of grace not only comes and remains (manet) in a right relationship to God but also what Paul in 2 Cor 5:17 calls καινὴ κτίσις, or in other words "a completely new person in heart, mind and spirit." He is brought out of the darkness, his entire state of being and his ways become different than before. This transformation is due to the fact that the sinner begins to *love* God, whom he previously hated (Rom 8:7). But this love expresses itself in that he a.) *no longer* can go without Jesus, since his conscience is now awakened and can only have peace in Him, because his heart's foremost desire here is to "comprehend Jesus" more and more completely, which again b.) *increasingly releases him* from earthly desires and fixes his hope on the perfect freedom from sin, "the glory that God shall give." His aim becomes first and foremost "Jesus sitting on His throne of glory" and the full, eternal union with Him in heaven through blessed death and resurrection. "Where your treasure is, there your heart will be also." But while he still lives on earth in the love of Jesus, his second aim, or more accurately, his aim for this life becomes: the glorification of Jesus on earth, through the proclamation of His name and the furthering of His kingdom. Therefore, this love also reveals itself as the pardoned sinner c.) *walks in the light* according to the words of Christ: Let your light [shine . . . Mt 5:16]. This walking is what our text describes as walking as Jesus walked. Here Jesus becomes the example for human beings, and the proper guide for life becomes the will of God revealed in the word (verses 4–5). This is not at all to mean that the complete freedom from sin should be considered as a sign of the state of grace, since this would contradict its definition as being a state of *grace* [*nådens* tillstånd]. Quite the opposite, John and Scripture in general teach that here is a battle between the spirit and the flesh, which often results in the Christian not being able to do what he wants to do (Gal 5:17). The mind, the spirit is certainly holy and righteous, and cannot be reconciled with sin. But "the law of the flesh" causes the Christian to fall and sin now and then, while yet continuing to fight against everything sinful. But while he has a "defender near the father" [*försvarare när fadrenom*] who is righteousness for the unrighteous, his state of grace is not disturbed, as long as he does not remain lying in sin or seek to make Christ a servant to sin. Instead, he always has access to the same eternal, immovable grace, exclusive of all merit or condemnation, as well as the same restoration and the same strength for daily renewal and continued growth in sanctification as he walks toward the great aim: the perfect following of God's will in thought, word, and deed, through God's love having been made perfect in him. Christ also says this about the disciples in Jn 17:6: "they have kept your word," rather than indicating that the disciples were of such character that they never sinned after they had become disciples.

Now concerning the dangers of a one-sided presentation of this truth, they include A.) *in general,* those that result from all falsification of God's Word, namely i.) *the misleading of people* through false presentation, ii.) *the negation* of all of the power of the Word and its effects, iii.) *a grave judgment* on the one who deceives in this manner. But B.) *in specie,* this can occur i.) *through the one-sided emphasis of a subjective life of faith,* which is a legalistic and sickly existence, without true peace in God and without true sanctification. For if the objective reconciliation, which was made complete for all human beings by the death and resurrection of Christ without qualification, is not allowed to be preached in its fullness as the A and Ω, then the subjective life of faith can neither come into existence or be maintained, but instead becomes self-righteousness, hypocrisy, and so on, or in a word: slavery to the law. It certainly is clear that it is only through free grace, separate from everything human, that any peace or strength is possible.—But on the other side the danger is just as great that ii.) *the one-sided emphasis of the objective reconciliation,* without regard to the subjective life of faith and sanctification, will both a.) *result in* the complete lack of guidance for simple [*enfaldiga*] souls, which will result in a life that is just as sickly as that mentioned above, and b.) *will bring* such souls into danger by "allowing the freedom that they have in Christ to give occasion to the flesh" (Gal. 5:1). Warning and self-examination and admonition are therefore of the utmost importance. Furthermore, by neglecting or keeping silent about the effects and fruits of grace, one is in danger of c.) causing these souls to *fall asleep in their false security,* while boasting of their status as children of God [*barnaskapet*], when they have not had the experience of grace, but only an intellectual faith [*kunskapstro*].

Therefore, the state of grace and sanctification belong together in a true life of grace, as the foundation and result, and therefore ought not to be confused or separated, which should always be clearly and distinctly preached and emphasized.

Amen, amen, amen!

In the margin is written:

"The presentation of this subject was written by me as requested by archbishop Reuterdahl as an apology to the accusation that the same bishop charged me with in regard to my sermon for the second day of Easter, 28 March 1864, for which he denied my ordination, unless I could submit a satisfactory answer to the subject in question at an extra session of the archdiocese at 4 o'clock in the afternoon on 29 March. For this reason, the presentation was written and submitted at the place and time in question. As a result the archdiocese did not find me to be a heretic, and on the following day 30 March 1864, I was ordained in Uppsala Cathedral. P. Waldenström."

"WAS THE APOSTLE PETER LEGALLY MARRIED?"

Speech to the Swedish Parliament, December 2, 1885

P.P. Waldenström

Civil marriage is considered by many people to be an unfortunate thing, and I have myself at times shared that opinion. The current ecclesiastic minister [ecklesiastikministern] explained at the 1878 church assembly [kyrkomöte] that he regarded civil marriage to be an unfortunate situation, which he accepted, despite the fact that he would rather have seen this avoided. More than twenty years ago, I had a lively debate about civil marriage with the now deceased professor [Klas Adolf] Hultkrantz. He defended civil marriage, and I fought against it. I regarded it namely to be a glorified form of concubinage. But when we had debated for a while, he asked me: "What kind of marriage do you believe the apostle Peter entered, civil or churchly?" In response, I had to admit, that it naturally had to be civil; and then I had nothing more to say. And I want to now, in regard to the idea that civil marriage would be unfortunate, at least point out, that the form of marriage, in which the Lord's apostles lived, cannot from a Christian perspective be considered a misfortune.

There are members of the Swedish state church, who do not believe in Christ, indeed, not even in God. They are atheists or materialists, and as such they despise and scorn both the church, her faith, and her clergy. Such is not at all an isolated occurrence. Now, say they want to get married. They must then send for a priest and then let him read over them those prayers and that blessing, which is contained in the churchly wedding ceremony, which they in their hearts and souls despise. As a Swedish priest, I have married people with such a disposition, and it has always been so repulsive to me that I have wished that I was a thousand miles away. For whom can it well be a blessing to force on such people the churchly blessing? Can it be for the party in question themselves? No, for them it must be in the first place offensive. By this they would be galvanized in their hatred. Can it be for the church or the state? To answer "yes" to this question were the same as saying, that a lie can be a blessing to the state or the church.

For example, imagine I am someone who wishes to enter civil marriage and for that purpose seek out the priest. He answers: "It is not possible, because you are both baptized and confirmed." So, I request to formally leave the state church, with the declaration that I intend to convert to the Baptist movement. Such an entry is now made in the church books. After waiting for the legally-mandated length of time, I return again and renew my application. Then I am recorded as someone who has truly exited the state church, and civil marriage is granted to me. After all this has been duly concluded, I find myself again before the pastor and say: "Herr Pastor, the Baptists do not want to accept me." What options now remain, when I request to re-enter the Swedish state church? I wonder, if this can be denied to me, or if my marriage can be dissolved because I entered into it in a civil form?

Bibliography

PRIMARY SOURCES

Rosenius, Carl Olof. *Samlade Skrifter af C.O. Rosenius.* Volume I. Rock Island, Illinois: Lutheran Augustana Book Concern, 1896.
("Alla trognas saliga hopp," 689–93, 695–96)
("De trognas frihet från lagen," 253–62, 274–75, 282–88, 291, 295–97)
("Guds folks borgerskap och umgängelse i himmelen," 668–69, 673–74, 676–78)
("Något att betänka wid Herrens nattward," 643–49)
("Något om helgelsen," 444–45, 450–55)
("Några ord om barndopet," 598–603)
("Om andligt presterskap," 483–84, 489–93)
("Om det heliga dopet," 576–79, 581–82, 584, 592, 594, 596)
("Skapelsen och människan," 1–3, 5–7, 11–13)
("'Stötestenen,' den stora hemligheten," 434–38)
("Syndafallet och dess följder," 32–35, 37, 42, 44)
("Upprättelsen och det första evangelium," 64–67)
———. *Samlade Skrifter af C.O. Rosenius.* Volume II. Rock Island, Illinois: Lutheran Augustana Book Concern, 1896.
("Kristi rike ett förlåtelserike," 207–9, 213–14)
("Låten Kristi ord rikligen bo ibland eder," 497–500)
("Om de hemska twiflen på allt heligt," 422–23, 425–30)
("Om den oföränderliga rättfärdighet, som de trogna hafwa i Kristus," 169–71)
("Om likheten och olikheten Guds barn emellan," 672–73, 676–79)
———. *Samlade Skrifter af C.O. Rosenius.* Volume III. Rock Island, Illinois: Lutheran Augustana Book Concern, 1896.
("Den gode herden," 52–54, 56–58, 60–63, 72–73, 79–80, 87)
("Den sanna kyrkan," 304–7, 316)
("Den tid, då du war sökt," 88–95, 97)
("Det är nu lofligt att församlas i Jesu namn!" 334–35)
("De skärande motsägelserna emot wårt barnaskap hos Gud," 188–98)
("Fjärde bönen. Wårt dagliga bröd gif oss i dag!" 598–607)
———. *Samlade Skrifter af C.O. Rosenius.* Volume IV. Stockholm: Fosterlands-Stiftelsens Förlags-Expedition, 1897.
("Andra Söndagen efter Trettondagen," 175–84)
("Guds eviga nådeval," 263–66)

("Några de wiktigaste förswaringsmedel emot förförelsen af falska läror," 236–39, 244, 246–48)

("Pietism," 215–20)

("En pietist," 220–27)

Waldenström, Paul Peter. "Apologi m. anledn. av ärkebiskop Reuterdahls vägran att prästviga W., inlämnad till Upsala Domkapitel d. 29. 3. 1864." In *Paul Peter Waldenströms minnesanteckningar 1838–1875*, edited by Bernhard Nyrén, 346–50. Stockholm: Svenska Missionsförbundets Förlag, 1928.

———. "Beqväm kristendom." In *Pietisten*. May 1893. Stockholm: A.L. Normans Boktryckeri-Aktiebolag. Inside front cover.

———. *Brukspatron Adamsson: Eller, Hvar bor du?* Stockholm: Svenska Missionsförbundets Förlag, 1937. 148–72.

———. *Davids Psalmer med utläggning.* Volume II. Stockholm: Aktiebolaget Normans förlag, 1904. 592–93.

———. *Den kristna församlingen.* Stockholm: Svenska Missionsförbundets Förlag, 1931. 3–18, 83–86.

———. *Dop och barndop: Samtal mellan Natanael och Timoteus.* Stockholm: Svenska Missionsförbundets Förlag, 1923. 20–25, 111–123, 132–135, 191–192.

———. *Dop-Predikan, hållen i Omaha, Nebr., den 28 juli 1889 af Lektor P. Waldenström.* Rock Island, IL: Lutheran Augustana Book Concern, 1889.

———. *Guds eviga frälsningsråd till uppbyggelse i tron och gudaktigheten.* Volumes I–VI. Stockholm: Svenska Missionsförbundets Förlag, 1938.

("Christ Sanctifies and Renews the Sinner," Volume II, 249–61)

("Christ's Office and Work on Earth," Volume I , 7–18)

("Civil Rights and Responsibilities," Volume VI, 54–59, 67–68, 70–76, 82–83)

("Communion," Volume III, 244–62)

("God's Love," Volume I, 19–34)

("Knowing God as Our True Father," Volume I, 336–37)

("Lord Jesus, Make Us Merciful Like You!" Volume V, 353–57)

("Permissible and Beneficial," Volume VI, 5–7, 10–12, 17, 22–25)

("What is Faith?" Volume II, 31–38)

———. *Gud är min tröst.* Stockholm: Svenska Missionsförbundets Förlag, 1938. 8–12, 18–19, 128–29, 260–61, 266–67.

———. *Herren är from: Betraktelser öfver Davids 25:te psalm.* Stockholm: Tidskriften Pietistens Expedition, 1901. 50–51, 79–85.

———. *I ingen annan är frälsning.* Stockholm: Svenska Missionsförbundet, 1938. 70–76, 79–80, 96–98, 106–7, 129, 157.

———. *Om Guds rike och församlingen: Bidrag till läran om de yttersta tingen och den tillkommande värlsåldern.* Turlock, California: California Publishing House, no date (but after 1912). 29–34, 37, 45–46, 51.

———. "Predikan på Annandag Påsk i Hel. Trefaldighetskyrkan i Upsala den 28 mars 1864." In *Paul Peter Waldenströms minnesanteckningar 1838–1875*, edited by Bernhard Nyrén, 341–45. Stockholm: Svenska Missionsförbundets Förlag, 1928.

———. *Samlade Predikningar.* Del I. Stockholm: Svenska Missionsförbundets Förlag, 1918. 171–76, 183–85, 187.

———. *Samlade Predikningar.* Del II. Stockholm: Svenska Missionsförbundets Förlag, 1919. 429–32, 435–36, 440–45.

————. *Smärtornas Man: Betraktelser över Jesajas 53:dje kapitel.* Stockholm: Svenska Missionsförbundets Förlag, 1938. 66–67, 176–77.

————. "Tjugonde Söndagen efter Trinitatis." In *Predikningar öfver Swenska kyrkans nya högmässotexter; Första Årgången, Andra delen,* 352–66. Stockholm: A.L. Normans Boktryckeri-Aktiebolag, 1875.

————. *Tänkvärda ord.* Brochure. Köping, Sweden: Bärgslagsbladets Tryckeri, 1919.

————. "Var aposteln Petrus lagligt gift?" In *Jungfrutalare i Riksdagen: Berömda riksdagstal från Engelbrekt till Per Albin,* edited by Aug. Borgström, 221–23. Stockholm: Natur och Kultur, 1947.

SECONDARY SOURCES

Anderson, Philip J. "Paul Peter Waldenström and America: Influence and Presence in Historical Perspective." *The Covenant Quarterly* 52:4 (1994) 2–21.

Bexell, Oloph. *Sveriges kyrkohistoria vol. 7; Folkväckelsens och kyrkoförnyelsens tid.* Stockholm, Sweden: Verbum, 2003.

Bredberg, William. *P.P. Waldenströms verksamhet till 1878; Till frågan om Svenska Missionsförbundets uppkomst.* Stockholm: Missionsförbundets Förlag, 1948.

Bröders gemenskap. Introduction by Torsten Nilsson. Stockholm: BV-Förlag, 2010.

Clifton-Soderstrom, Michelle A. "'Happily Ever After?' Paul Peter Waldenström: Be Ye Reconciled to God" *Ex Auditu* 26 (2010) 91–106.

Dahlén, Rune W. "Waldenström's View of the Bible." *The Covenant Quarterly* 52:4 (1994) 37–52.

En har dött för alla. Introduction by Torsten Nilsson. Stockholm: BV-Förlag, 2009.

Frisk, Donald C. "The Work of Jesus Christ." In *Covenant Affirmations: This We Believe,* 89–106. Chicago: Covenant Press, 1981.

Fritzson, Arne. "En Gud som är god och rättfärdig." In *Liv och rörelse: Svenska missionskyrkans historia och identitet.* Hans Andreasson, et al. Stockholm: Verbum, 2007.

Gud den underbare. Introduction by Ivan Hellström. Stockholm: BV-Förlag, 2008.

Guds Ande och Ord. Introduction by Torsten Nilsson. Stockholm: BV-Förlag, 2010.

Hallingberg, Gunnar. *Läsarna: 1800-talets folkväckelse och det moderna genombrottet.* Stockholm: Atlantis, 2010.

Hjelm, Norman A. "Augustana and the Church of Sweden: Ties of History and Faith." In *The Heritage of Augustana: Essays on the Life and Legacy of the Augustana Lutheran Church,* edited by Harland H. Gifford and Arland J. Hultgren, 19–36. Minneapolis: Kirk House, 2004.

Jarlert, Anders. *Sveriges kyrkohistoria vol. 6; Romantiken och liberalismens tid.* Stockholm, Sweden: Verbum 2001.

Jesus, bli när oss! Introduction by Torsten Nilsson. Stockholm: BV-Förlag, 2010.

Kjellberg, Knut. *Folkväckelse i Sverige under 1800-talet; uppkomst och genombrott.* Stockholm: Carlssons, 1994.

Lindberg, Lars. "En strid i försoningens ljus: Waldenström omläst och omvärderad." In *En historia berättas—om missionsförbundare,* edited by Rune Dahlén & Valborg Lindgärde. Falköping, Sweden: Kimpese, 2004.

Lindström, Harry. *I Livsfrågornas spänningsfält; Om P. Waldenströms Brukspatron Adamsson—populär folkbok och allegorisk roman.* Stockholm: Verbum Förlag, 1997.

Linge, Karl. *Carl Olof Rosenius; Sveriges främste lekmannapredikant.* Uppsala, Sweden: J.A. Lindblads förlag, 1956.

Lodin, Sven. *Carl Olof Rosenius; Hans liv och förkunnelse.* Stockholm: Evangeliska Fosterlands-Stiftelsens Bokförlag, 1922.

Moberg, Amy, and Lina Sandell-Berg. *Teckning af Carl Olof Rosenii lif och werksamhet.* Stockholm: Evangeliska Fosterlands-Stiftelsens förlag, 1874.

Norborg, Sverre. *Den Levande Rosenius.* Hässleholm, Sweden: EFS-förlaget, 1966.

Olsson, Karl A. *By One Spirit.* Chicago: Covenant, 1962.

Phelan, John E. Jr. "Reading Like a Pietist." *The Swedish-American Historical Quarterly* 63:2–3 (2012) 202–24.

Rättfärdig i Jesus. Introduction by Torsten Nilsson. Stockholm: BV-Förlag, 2009.

Safstrom, Mark. "Defining Lutheranism from the Margins: Paul Peter Waldenström on Being a 'Good Lutheran' in America." *The Swedish-American Historical Quarterly* 63:2–3 (2012) 101–34.

———. "Making Room for the Lost: Congregational Inclusivity in Waldenström's *Squire Adamsson.*" *The Covenant Quarterly* 71:3–4 (2013) 52–72.

———. "The Religious Origins of Democratic Pluralism: Paul Peter Waldenström and the Politics of the Swedish Awakening 1868–1917." PhD diss., University of Washington, 2010.

Sjögren, Per-Olof. *Anfäktelsen enligt Rosenius.* Uppsala, Sweden: Svenska Kyrkans Diakonistyrelses Bokförlag, 1953.

Sundström, Erland, editor. *Arvet från Waldenström: Läsestycken från Waldenströms skrifter.* Second, expanded edition. Falköping, Sweden: Gummessons, 1978.

Syndens dagliga plåga. Introduction by Torsten Nilsson. Stockholm: BV-Förlag, 2009.

Tomson, Ragnar. *En Hövding; Minnesteckning över P. Waldenström till 100-årsdagen av hans födelse.* Stockholm: Svenska Missionsförbundets Förlag, 1937.

Tredway, Thomas. *Conrad Bergendoff's Faith and Work: A Swedish-American Lutheran, 1895–1997.* Rock Island, IL: Augustana Historical Society, 2014.

Wadström, Bernhard. *Ur Minnet och Dagboken; Anteckningar från åren 1848–1898.* Stockholm: Fosterlands-Stiftelsens Förlags-Expedition, 1900.

Waldenström, P. "Sjuttio år." *Pietisten,* 22 Dec. 1911.

Westin, Gunnar. *George Scott och hans verksamhet i Sverige.* Stockholm: Svenska kyrkans diakonisyrelsens bokförlag, 1929.

PRIMARY SOURCES IN ENGLISH, FOR FURTHER READING

Rosenius, Carl Olof. *A Faithful Guide to Peace with God: Excerpts from the Writings of Carl Olof Rosenius, Arranged as Daily Meditations to Cover a Period of Two Months, with the Assistance of Bishop N.J. Laache.* Translated by George T. Rygh. Minneapolis: Augsburg, 1946.

———. *Day by Day with God: Daily Devotions.* Translated by Maj-len Henriksson. Bombay: Gospel Literature, 1976.

———. *Romans: A Devotional Commentary.* Translated by J. Elmer Dahlgren and Royal F. Peterson. Chicago: Covenant, 1978.

———. *The Believer Free From the Law.* Translated by Adolf Hult. Rock Island, Illinois: Augustana Book Concern, 1923.

Waldenström, Paul Peter. "Sermon for the Twentieth Sunday after Trinity, 1872." In *Covenant Roots: Sources & Affirmations.* Edited by Glenn P. Anderson. Translated by Herbert E. Palmquist. Chicago: Covenant, 1980.

———. *Squire Adamsson, Or, Where Do You Live?* Translated with commentary and notes by Mark Safstrom. Seattle: Pietisten, 2013.

———. "The Biblical Teaching on Sin, 1915." In *Covenant Roots: Sources & Affirmations.* Edited by Glenn P. Anderson. Translated by Herbert E. Palmquist. Chicago: Covenant, 1980.

———. *The Blood of Jesus: What is the Significance?* Translated by J. G. Princell. Chicago: John Martenson, 1888.

———. *The Lord is Right: Meditations on the Twenty-Fifth Psalm in the Psalter of King David.* Translated by J. G. Princell. Chicago: John Martenson, 1889.

———. *The Reconciliation: Who Was to Be Reconciled? God or Man? Or God and Man? Some Chapters on the Biblical View of the Atonement.* Translated by J.G. Princell. Chicago: John Martenson, 1888.

Made in the USA
Middletown, DE
14 September 2023

38504482R00146